# Dreamweaver MX 2004
# Design Projects

Rachel Andrew
Craig Grannell
Allan Kent
Christopher Schmitt

friendsof

DESIGNER TO DESIGNER™

*an Apress® company*

# Dreamweaver MX 2004 Design Projects

## Credits

**Lead Editor**
Chris Mills

**Technical Reviewer**
Vibha Roy

**Editorial Board**
Steve Anglin, Dan Appleman,
Ewan Buckingham, Gary Cornell,
Tony Davis, Jason Gilmore,
Chris Mills, Steve Rycroft,
Dominic Shakeshaft, Jim Sumser,
Gavin Wray

**Project Manager**
Sofia Marchant

**Copy Edit Manager**
Nicole LeClerc

**Copy Editor**
Ami Knox

**Production Manager**
Kari Brooks

**Production Editor**
Ellie Fountain

**Compositor**
Dina Quan

**Proofreader**
Liz Welch

**Indexer**
Kevin Broccoli

**Artist**
Kinetic Publishing Services, LLC

**Cover Designer**
Kurt Krames

**Manufacturing Manager**
Tom Debolski

# CONTENTS AT A GLANCE

# CONTENTS

## 2 News Portal

## Chapter 3: Corporate Website Draft One

NATIONAL COLLEGE
OF IRELAND
LIBRARY

## Chapter 4: Intranet Design Project . . . . . . . . . . . . . . . . . . . . . 195

# ABOUT THE AUTHORS

**Rachel Andrew** is a director of edgeofmyseat.com, a UK-based web solutions company, and is an experienced web developer. Rachel is a member of the Web Standards Project on the Dreamweaver Task Force, and hopes to encourage best practices in the support and use of W3C Standards in Dreamweaver. In addition to co-authoring several books, Rachel writes for various magazines and resource sites, both online and off.

When not writing code or writing about writing code, Rachel spends time with her daughter, tries to encourage people to use Debian GNU/Linux, studies with the Open University, and enjoys a nice pint of beer.

**Craig Grannell** was trained in the fine arts, but soon became immersed in the world of digital media and showed work at several leading European media arts festivals. His art ranged from short video pieces to odd performances, sometimes with the aid of a computer, televisions, and a P.A. system, and sometimes with a small bag of water above his head.

Craig soon realized he'd actually have to make a proper living. Luckily, in the mid-1990s, the Web caught his attention, and he's been working with it ever since. Along with writing for several prominent design-related magazines, he finds time to create websites for the likes of 2000 AD, write the occasional book, work on his eclectic audio project, and sporadically delve back into the world of video. Much of his work (and dancing trees) can be found at his website, Snub Communications (www.snubcommunications.com).

**Allan Kent** lives, works, and plays in Cape Town, South Africa. In the last 4 years, he's been implicated in at least 10 books dealing with PHP and web-related topics. When not being harassed by persistent editors about deadlines, he works doing new media design at Lodestone, which he co-owns. When not writing or programming, he enjoys relaxing at home with Wendy and their cats.

**Christopher Schmitt** is the principal of Heatvision.com, Inc., a new media publishing and design firm, based in Tallahassee, FL. An award-winning web designer who has been working with the Web since 1993, Christopher interned for both David Siegel and Lynda Weinman in the mid-1990s while an undergraduate at Florida State University for a fine arts degree with emphasis on graphic design.

He is the author of the *CSS Cookbook* (O'Reilly) and *Designing CSS Web Pages* (New Riders). He is also the co-author of *Adobe Photoshop CS in 10 Steps or Less* (Wiley) and contributed four chapters to *XML, HTML, & XHTML Magic* by Molly Holzschlag (New Riders). Christopher has also written for *New Architect Magazine*, *A List Apart*, *Digital Web*, and *Web Reference*.

In 2000, he led a team to victory in the Cool Site in a Day competition, where he and five other talented developers built a fully functional, well-designed website for a nonprofit organization in 8 hours.

Speaking at conferences like The Other Dreamweaver Conference and SXSW, Christopher has given talks demonstrating the use and benefits of practical CSS-enabled designs. In his continuing efforts to help spread the word about web design, he is the list mom for Babble (www.babblelist.com), a mailing list community devoted to advanced web design and development topics.

On his personal website, Christopher shows his true colors and most recent activities at www.christopher.org. Although he is 6'7", he does not play professional basketball, but wouldn't mind a good game of chess.

# ABOUT THE TECHNICAL REVIEWER

Success is putting your mind to an ambition and achieving that aim. **Vibha Roy** fully believes this, and with this belief she entered into the area of graphics, multimedia, and web designing 8 years back.

In her childhood, Vibha was fascinated by puppet shows, and she always dreamt of creating puppets. With the advent of computer graphics and multimedia her dream turned into reality—she could create as many puppets as she wanted and make them do whatever she wanted. She started her career as a graphic designer and then moved into 3D modeling and animations. Later, impressed by the reach and versatility of the Internet, she became interested in web concepts and now has to her credit many websites and portals in diverse sectors.

Vibha likes to stay abreast of the latest developments and technologies within this sector and always loves to read more and more about them and experiment with new concepts. She has reviewed more than a dozen books on web design and development and also has provided additional reading material to some of them.

She believes that her source of motivation is her one-time best friend, who now is her husband. Her creativity is also multiplied by the presence of her little son, Pranjal.

February 28, 2004

**U2LOG.COM MOBILE SERVICE**

Got WAP? Use your phone or PDA to
page can be reached at U2log.com/in

yanb | site | 05:59 PM | permalink

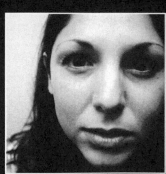

### The steps covered in this chapter to develop the site are

- Carrying out a site review of existing online resources
- Setting clear goals for a site
- Producing user profiles to define further the audience
- Planning a good, sensible site map
- Sketching out initial thoughts regarding the initial design
- Refining the design into wireframe diagrams and then producing them in Photoshop
- Working with Dreamweaver MX 2004 to easily construct an accessible, easy-to-maintain website

The four Irish men known collectively as U2 are recognized the world over as one of the best bands in the world for their best-selling and award-winning music that spans over two decades. U2 has more fans than they can keep count, especially with a reported "thousands of unofficial websites" (see www.findarticles.com/cf_0/m4PRN/2000_July_21/63597010/p1/article.jhtml).

In late 2000, the music group launched their own official web presence. Their site incorporates the usual trimmings often found on a music band site: a discography, news-related items, multimedia elements, an online forum, and, of course, the token e-commerce component. While this web destination helps U2 reach out to its fans, there *is* room for improvement that can come from an additional fan site in the crowded virtual space of U2 fan sites.

The new fan site primarily focuses on the latest the band is doing and provides material for new and old fans alike to use. A secondary focus of the site is to create an accessible website. Most, if not all, U2-related websites fail to adhere to accessibility guidelines set by Section 508 (see www.section508.gov) or the Web Access Initiative, or WAI (see www.w3.org/WAI/). By following these accessibility guidelines as best as possible, the website increases its overall reach as compared to other U2 fan sites.

# The origin of FAQs

To help people new to the Internet who were interested in learning about U2, a group of U2 fans put together a series of pages that answered common questions and posted them on the Internet. So even before the official U2 site existed, there were unofficial online resources for letting fans and potential fans know more about the music group. This resource was known as the U2 **F**requently **A**sked **Q**uestions, or U2 FAQ.

Writing and publishing FAQs has become a regular feature on the Internet, and the subject matter for FAQs isn't limited to just music groups. Since FAQs are often written by fans (or sometimes fanatics), the subject matter that FAQs cover is often as diverse as the Web itself. There are FAQs about Mentos (see www.mentosfaq.com), William Shakespeare's work (see www.shakespeare-online.com/faq/), and even kissing (see www.kissingbooth.com/kissfaq.htm). Figures 1-1 and 1-2 show the Mentos and kissing FAQs, respectively.

**Figure 1-1.** The FAQ for Mentos candy

**Figure 1-2.** The kissing FAQ

The practice of writing and distributing a FAQ seems to have come out of the days before the Web in USENET forums, where communication was based on writing virtual notes to others. To help people get up to date on discussions that had already transpired in certain forums, people would take it upon themselves to write FAQs.

# Planning

The first step in planning a website presence is to examine existing sites that cater to the same audience or deliver the same material. Typically, this would include several sites. For the sake of saving space, I focus only on three sites in the same market. And because this is only a fan site, there isn't that much urgency in cataloging every site related to U2. Since there are already thousands of them, that would take quite a while. What I want to do then is to take a look at the most successful U2-related sites and try to determine what makes them tick. The websites I review are U2.com, the official site of the band; U2log.com, a blog about the band; and @U2, one of the largest fan sites about U2.

When reviewing related websites for a proposed website project, I look to fill three items: a summary of the website, a table listing the features of the website, and screenshots of the website that day I reviewed it.

## U2.com (current incarnation)

The official online presence at www.u2.com comes in two flavors: lite and broadband. The content provided is rich and up-to-date regarding the band's activities and even spotlighting the lead singer's speaking engagements. The lite version, shown in Figure 1-3, is designed to be as "accessible as possible"; however, it fails accessibility tests for Section 508 as well as tests for valid HTML and CSS.

The following table presents more information about U2.com:

| Feature | Status/Description |
| --- | --- |
| Updates | At least once a week, a news item appears, even if the band is not on tour or releasing material. |
| Multimedia | Contains various multimedia items for download and presentation: screensavers, Flash-based e-cards, video clips, Apple QuickTime, Windows Media Player. |
| Accessibility | Fails Section 508 testing. |
| Production | HTML (unspecified version; Quirks mode), JavaScript. |
| Community | Community forum, Zootopia, is powered by Web Crossing software (www.webcrossing.com). |

*Continued*

**1**

| Feature | Status/Description |
|---|---|
| E-commerce | Operated through a third-party company, FanFire (www.fanfire.com). |
| Content | Rich in content, but poorly organized and hard to reach due to poor information architecture and production values. |
| Look and feel | Cluttered; white, gray, and dark blue colors. |
| Back-end | Apache/Lightning; Solaris 8. |

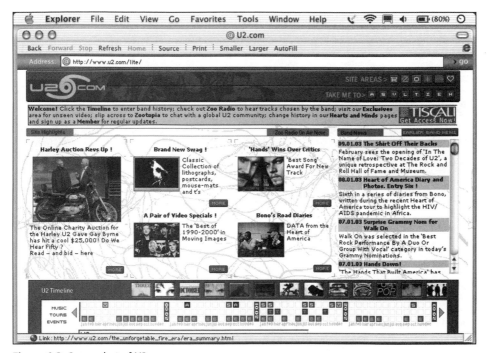

**Figure 1-3.** Screenshot of U2.com

# U2log.com

U2Log.com is a weblog or "blog." It started as a journal to log moments that were captured by an in-studio webcam that was on while the band finished their *All That You Can't Leave Behind* album in 2000.

After attracting a sizable audience, the site's creator decided to keep U2Log.com up and running. The audience is for the die-hard fans who want to get their U2 fix on an almost daily basis. Topics covered are news of the band or related band member's lives, reviews, and media, with a twist of humor thrown in. On a regular basis, this fan site, which you can see in Figure 1-4, appears to outscoop and better inform the fans about the band and their activities than the official U2 site.

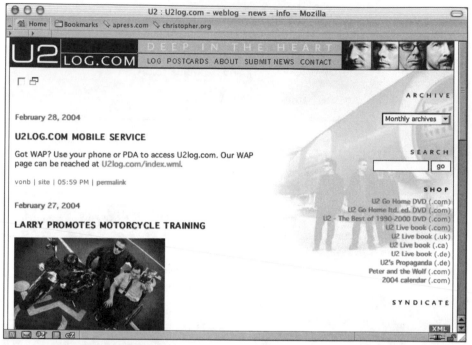

**Figure 1-4.** Screenshot of U2Log.com

The following table presents more information about U2log.com:

| Feature | Status/Description |
| --- | --- |
| Updates | Daily or once every other day. |
| Multimedia | None. |
| Accessibility | Fails Section 508 testing. |
| Production | HTML 4.01 Transitional; JavaScript. |
| Community | Mailing lists powered by Yahoo! Groups. See http://groups.yahoo.com/group/u2log_readers/join. |
| E-commerce | Affiliate links through Amazon.com, Amazon.co.uk, and CDNow. |
| Content | Updated daily, with easy access to archives; headlines of posts available for syndication in XML and RSS feeds. |

*Continued*

| Feature | Status/Description |
| --- | --- |
| Standards | HTML, CSS are not valid. |
| Look and feel | Clean and inviting; monochrome color scheme with gold as highlight, link color. |
| Server | Apache 1.3.26 (Unix); PHP 4.2; Linux. |

## @U2

Started in 1995, @U2, located at www.atu2.com, has grown to be the most extensive collection of U2-related content as well as the most respected fan site. In addition to common features like a discography, multimedia features, and lyrics, they also provide various unique services like a "this date in U2 history" feature, moderating mailing lists, and furnishing links to online stores that are offering deals on select U2 merchandise.

The downside to this site, shown in Figure 1-5, is that it is so vast, it falls underneath the weight of its own content. Without a clear and concise information architecture and label system, new and old fans will find this site difficult to maneuver at best.

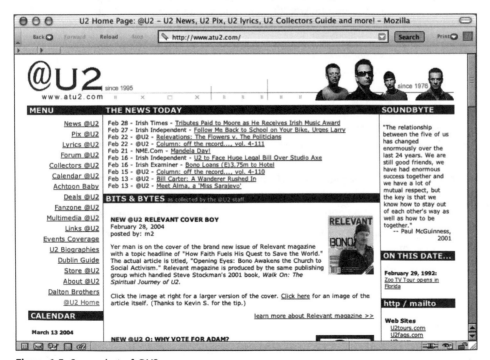

**Figure 1-5.** Screenshot of @U2

The following table presents more information about @U2:

| Feature | Status/Description |
| --- | --- |
| Updates | Daily or once every other day. |
| Multimedia | Midi sound snippets, wallpapers, screensavers. |
| Accessibility | Fails Section 508 testing. |
| Production | HTML (unspecified version; Quirks mode); JavaScript. |
| Community | Community mailing lists are powered by Yahoo! Groups. |
| E-commerce | Affiliate links through Amazon.com, Amazon.co.uk, CDNow, and others. |
| Content | Extensive collection of news postings are available via JavaScript links. |
| Standards | HTML, CSS are not valid. |
| Look and feel | Consistent color scheme set to a seasonal, Christmas theme. Without the picture of the band members in the upper-right corner, one wouldn't know it was a serious U2 fan site. Too many choices in the navigation create a cluttered look. |
| Server | Apache 1.3.22 (Unix; Red Hat, Linux); Linux. |

## Summary of related efforts

- Both official and unofficial websites that exist today provide valuable resources for both new and old fans to get up-to-date information about the band and their music.
- There is a lack of guides to help people who are fairly new to the band to learn more about the history of their music and backgrounds.
- Accessible online content is another aspect missing from these sites.
- Visitors trying to learn more about the band through most of these sites will likely get confused by inappropriate content or poor architecture.
- There is a need for a site that will act as an educational ramp for the musical group.

# Determining your audience

After reviewing the U2 sites, I want to take a look at who might be coming to these sites as well as my own fan site. U2's audience is a worldwide, multigenerational one. However, in terms of the website, the audience for this content can be defined as falling into these two categories:

- Existing fans
- New or potential fans

While U2FAQ.com can serve as a vehicle to market and sell the band to existing fans, the new U2FAQ.com can reach out and educate new fans about the history and music of the band as well. New music from artists is constantly being played on the radio, television, and Internet, while a band like U2 only produces and sells an album once every two to four years. In that time frame, people who are potential U2 fans may have never heard of the band before or realize their impact on music.

In terms of demographics of Internet usage and music purchases, the audience is fairly broad for U2's music and its web presence. According to Simmons data, both experienced Internet users *and* music listeners who use the Internet (with any degree of ability) fall primarily within the 18-to-54-year-old age range:

> *Simmons Market Research Bureau produces a software application called Choices 3. Choices 3 includes demographic and psychographic data from a nationwide survey called* National Consumer Study (NCS). *The purpose of the survey is to peer into the buying and media habits of the American public at large. It's used in part to help develop profiles of the audiences for companies. For more information, see* www.smrb.com.

## Age group 18–24

- Over 25% of this age group bought music from alternative rock and contemporary rock bands.
- 27% of people who used web-based bulletin/message boards are from the age group 18–24.

## Age group 25–34

- While this group predominantly doesn't buy alternative or contemporary rock music, they do make use of the Internet for purchasing and recreation.
- 27% of people who have used the Internet to make a purchase as well as gather product information are aged 25–34.
- 31% of people who have used the Internet technologies to gather product information are 25–34.
- More than 27% of people who have used chat forums and web-based bulletin/ message boards are 25–34.

## Age group 35–44

- More than 25% of those who bought alternative rock and contemporary rock bands were aged 35–44.

- Also, more than 25% of people who have used the Internet to make a purchase as well as gather product information were in between 35–44.
- And 27% of people using chat rooms were in between the ages of 35–44.

## Age group 45–54

- More than 25% of people buying music by contemporary rock bands and using the Internet to make a purchase online are between 45–54.

Based on overall Internet usage, Nielsen/NetRatings states that 31 million users ages 18 years old and up have downloaded music in the last 30 days. This represents 22% of the Internet population currently using the Internet. And 15% of the Internet population has purchased music in the last 3 months (see http://sanjose.bizjournals.com/sanjose/ stories/2003/05/05/daily51.html).

> **When a site serves a local audience:** *Due to the nature of the music group and the World Wide Web, the audience for a fan site encompasses people all over the world. But what happens if you are building a site for a business or a not-for-profit in a city?*
>
> *At MyBestSegments.com, you can type in a zip code and retrieve the information that helps define the habits of people in that area into six different groups. For example, you can see the data for the people in the zip code 94710, as shown in Figure 1-6, and determine the type of lifestyles for people living there.*

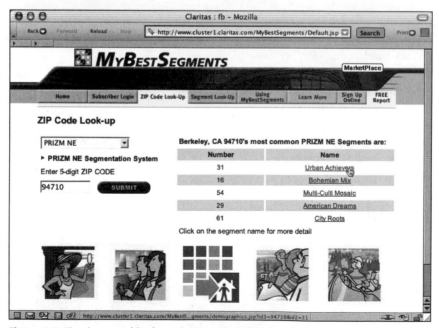

**Figure 1-6.** The demographics from the zip code 94710, home of Apress

> *This kind of information is mined and polished from public sources of information like the U.S. Census, death and marriage certificates, car registrations, etc. Other sources of information that we tend to give away freely when we fill out warranty information for a high-ticket item, answer a survey, or use frequent shopper cards can easily be bought from the companies that gather it.*
>
> *In one location, you can see six different profiles of the neighborhoods in each zip code. And with this knowledge, you can better build a custom site that appeals to those people in the community.*

So, from the preceding research, we can conclude that overall the target audience is a tech-savvy crowd willing to use the Internet in making purchasing decisions and/or buying online. Therefore the fan site for U2 has to be built with U2's longtime fans in mind, as well as have enough pizzazz to lure potential fans. It should have an easy-to-use front-end, informative content, and an intuitive e-commerce system to allow users to control their purchases of U2 music and related merchandise.

## Profiling the target audience

Now that I have a general understanding of who my audience is, the next step is to put more of a face on them. I want to create visitor personas—archetypal profiles of the target audience. What you want to do when you create your own sites is build up as realistic a profile of potential target audience members as possible, even though they are really only bits and pieces of description. Just having a mental image helps the design process. As a web builder putting a site design together and arranging the elements, it's good for me to have an idea in mind about my target audience, so I can build a site that serves them better.

### Stepping into virtual shoes

This helps me to step out of my shoes. No longer will I be building to my tastes. More times than I can recall I've been in meetings with project managers, programmers, and other Web team members discussing the plans for the website, and they will throw their two cents into the mix.

- "My daughter likes the color pink. So, let's add that in there."
- "I don't like Flash. It's *too* flashy."
- "It needs a drop shadow around the navigation links."
- "I don't like too much HTML text. Can we get rid of some of this copy or make it one image of GIF text?"

I've come to realize that this is a totally natural phenomenon. People who work on a project want to make it something they want to be proud of or at the very least can stomach to look at. However, what happens is that people—no matter how well intentioned—will bring their own feelings and thoughts on how to make the project work *for them*.

A way to combat this need of others surrounding the project is to do what I'm doing here in this project—do your research about who is the target audience and what is needed to attract them. And one of those tools is to build profiles of your target audience. By creating these profiles, you figuratively bring these people into the mix. It might not help you dissuade your boss from forcing the designer to include pink in the design project, but it will help disarm people who have the tendency to add unwarranted and ultimately unwanted additions to the site.

Since this is a personal fan site, it's very easy for my opinions to override research that's gone into the site or even not bother to do any research whatsoever. (It's my site after all and I'm doing this on my own time.) However, I want to make the best site possible, and to do that, I need to follow the process, and that entails doing the site reviews, performing audience analysis, and even creating user profiles.

## Creating the profiles

For this project, I've written up two profiles in order to represent the primary and secondary audience of this site. For the profiles, I first think about what features the site needs to have and then work backwards by asking basic questions like

- Why do visitors want to use the website? In other words, what's the motivation?
- How will visitors use the website? List features that already exist on the site as well as features that *should* exist!

I even add photos to help further the illusion that these are real people sampled from my audience as shown in Figures 1-7 and 1-8.

**Primary profile: "Never heard of them before now . . ."**

**Figure 1-7.**
Photos add believability to a user profile.

- **Age:** 18
- **Name:** Tara Banks
- **Gender:** Female
- **Marital status:** Single
- **Location:** Miami, but relocating to Tallahassee, FL
- **Profession:** Student

■ **Quote:** "My musical tastes are changing, I'm exploring new sounds—old and new."

■ **Personal background:** Leaving Miami to go to Florida State University to be one of the first students in its medical program. Tara wanted to stay in Florida while at college to be close to family, but not too close.

■ **Site goals:** While on the drive up to Tallahassee, the batteries in her portable CD player died on her. This left her no choice but to turn on the radio and scan for tunes. While scanning the frequencies, she happened upon a song she liked called "Electrical Storm." After the song, the DJ briefly mentioned the song was by U2. Wanting to know more about the song and the band, she makes a mental note to surf the Web when she gets her computer set up in her dorm room.

**Secondary profile: "I want to know what they've been up to ..."**

**Figure 1-8.**
Try to write as many user profiles as you can for your audiences.

■ **Age:** 31

■ **Name:** Tim McDonald

■ **Gender:** Male

■ **Marital status:** Married

■ **Location:** Raleigh, NC

■ **Personal background:** Tim McDonald is an accountant for a tech company. Tim's always been good with numbers, and when he proposed to his future wife, Sara, he compiled a financial summary of why it would be a good merger. Also included in the report was a string that at the end dangled a small ring with a huge diamond. In the background, U2's "All I Want Is You" was playing. That song was later played at their very festive, but fiscally responsible, wedding later that year. Currently, he and his wife are thinking about having children.

■ **Site goals:** While flipping channels on the television waiting for a football game to start, Tim noticed a bit about U2 on CNN's weekend music magazine show. Even though he caught only a little bit of the piece, Tim was interested in what the band had been up to. He had heard U2's experimental '90s albums, but didn't like them and definitely didn't know why everyone thought it was great stuff. "Whatever it was," he thought, "it was definitely not about the music." But the television made him see the "old U2" may have come back. He made his way to the computer to see if they had released a couple of albums the last few years.

### Extra credit: Taking people further

Once you've created profiles the next step is to drop them into scenarios. Scenarios are fictional situations where the people you created go about solving their problems and questions through your site. This method allows you to foresee solutions to the visual design and information architecture of the site.

### Defining the site goals

Now that I've reviewed the U2-related sites, determined the general nature of my audience, and created profiles of people from my audience, I can better define the goals for the fan site.

Of course, the goal of the site I've already mentioned:

- **Allow visitors to educate themselves about the band before jumping to other U2-related sites.**

But how? What will I do to help achieve that goal? These are the steps I've outlined to help make sure I'm on the right path:

- **Make the site accessible:** Of all the U2 websites, the three sites listed are the most popular among U2 fans. However, all the sites—both official and unofficial— fail to take into account basic accessibility guidelines like alt tags for all images. **By fulfilling this task**, I will have separated my site from those that are "harder to navigate" and opened the site up to more visitors potentially.

- **Use standards-compliant markup and CSS:** All the sites reviewed failed to be made with valid HTML and CSS. While browsers will display the content, there's no guarantee that future browsers will. I will take the time to build my site to standards so I won't have to update the structure of my pages every time the "latest and greatest" browser comes along. **By fulfilling this task**, I will build a site that will be easier to update and open to more web-enabled devices. I will simply have a larger reader base by simply not using propriety tags or technologies.

- **Create an enjoyable, polished look and feel:** Part of U2's appeal, to me at least, has been the design quality of their merchandise. However, their website in my opinion doesn't live up to the high standards that U2 have set for them. The goal I will try to achieve is to at least capture some of the energy from their music and display it in the designs. Well, it's a goal at least. **By fulfilling this goal**, I will create a visually stimulating environment for the readers.

## Taking stock of content

Now that I have the audience firmly in mind, let's take a look at the content. Already assembled by fans the world over, the U2 FAQ is another representation of what the Internet can do. However, with so many hands in the mix, it often leads to a hard-to-navigate document.

You can see by the naming convention of the HTML files (as shown in Figure 1-9) the problems that are inherent in the FAQ. What content is in file 4.html? How different is it from 7.html? If this type of organization makes it hard for fanatics to wade through the site (as shown in Figure 1-10), what hope do people with a passing interest possess? Reorganization is in order.

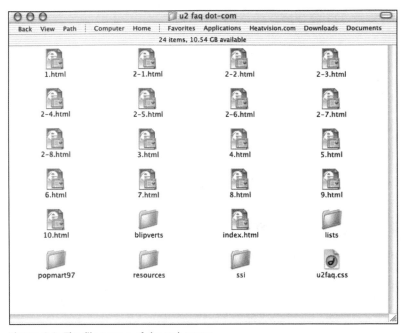

**Figure 1-9.** The file names of the web pages

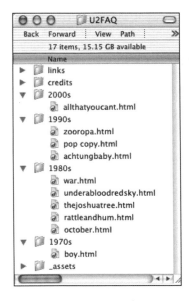

**Figure 1-10.**
Navigating the site map

To help the target audience to better navigate the content, I'm going to organize the FAQ in terms of the decades and U2's major album releases as shown in Figure 1-10. This method, I believe, will help site visitors find out more information about U2's music quickly and easily as well as forming a mental model of the progression of U2's career.

# Designing the site

With my planning wrapped up, I have enough ammunition to tackle the design. When I design for the Web, I don't think about the limitations of the medium. One might think that after I've earned my battle scars in web production on numerous projects both small and large I ought to know better. Actually, it's just the opposite.

I've worked with many talented designers who have pushed what I thought was possible with their designs. Instead of rejecting the designs outright, I took them as a challenge. Pretty soon, I began to realize that the envelope could be pushed and even torn in order to make a better website. With a handful of GIFs and JPEGs and a blank text file ready to be filled with HTML, it's amazing what one can pull off.

## Sketches from a brainstorm

One of the problems with working with computers is that people often start a web design project on them. Back in my high school journalism class, I would look at a blank canvas in an extremely early version of Photoshop waiting for inspiration to pick me up and point me to the right path. Instead, I ended up clicking a few buttons and trying a few filters, hoping for something magical when nothing happened.

So, from now on when I design a project, I take a piece of pen and paper and begin to lay out the design of the project as shown in Figure 1-11. This not only keeps me away from the computer, but also helps me focus on realizing the design concept before I work on the computer. Also, I find it's easier for me to hop from one layout idea to another than it is for me to open up a new file in Photoshop. Also, I can add shading and scribble notes off to the side. Of course, the drawback to this approach is no one understands what the heck I sketched. Based on an informal, very unscientific survey of holding it up to a co-worker, I've discovered that my sketches look like chicken scratch to the average human.

So in order to make my designs available for the consumption of others, I have to make a version available for others to digest. This entails using a vector-based illustration program like Adobe Illustrator in creating a wireframe model (as shown in Figure 1-12). A wireframe is a visual guide to the relationship of the web page's elements to their location on the page. With a wireframe model, my design sports crisp, clean layouts with legible text to denote content areas. This allows designers, production artists, clients, programmers, and anyone else involved in the project to readily determine the details of the page without trying to decipher my chicken scratch.

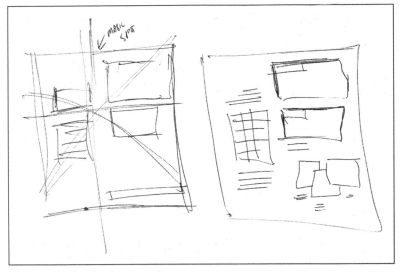

**Figure 1-11.** Sketches from my design pad

During the lifespan of a project, there might be moments when the site development is put on hold. There might be a lull in the span of the project that lasts for a few days to even a few months before the team returns to the project and resumes fleshing out the design. In case that happens, falling back on a sketch isn't a good idea. By converting a sketch to a wireframe model, the design is a reference to the team not only in the present, but also in the future, if the need arises to look back at the original concept.

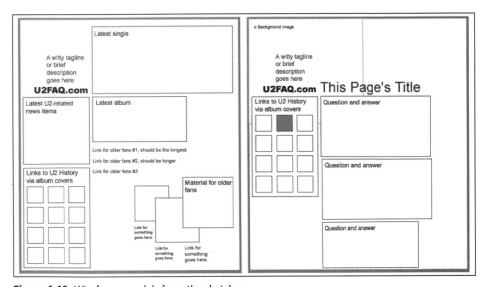

**Figure 1-12.** Wireframe models from the sketches

### Photographic content

Since the content is mostly text-based (as you can see by looking ahead to Figure 1-15), I need to spice up the design. Thankfully fellow U2 fan and site owner Matthias Muehlbradt has given me permission to use his photographs from the latest tour. You can check out his photos along with other fan photos at Elevation-Tour.com.

### Translating ideas into designs

With the wireframes in place, I move to my trusty friend, Adobe Photoshop. The illustrations in the following sections show the translation of the wireframes into finished designs. The development of the site is now at a stage where production can get under way and, of course, Dreamweaver MX 2004 can be employed. However, before I go into building web pages, I want to slice out the supporting images for the pages themselves.

> *Having skills in Adobe Photoshop is important to any level of designer. If you need to brush up on your skills or learn the program from top to bottom, check out* Adobe Photoshop CS in 10 Simple Steps or Less *by Mikah Laaker and Christopher Schmitt (Wiley & Sons, ISBN: 0-7645-4237-0).*

# Developing the website

With the planning and the designing all done, I turn my attention to putting the pieces together. First thing I do is set the site in Dreamweaver.

I place resources needed for production into an assets folder. I create a folder titled _assets in the root folder of the sites. Next, I create folders img and css in the _assets folder that keep images and Cascading Style Sheets (CSS) respectively in each folder. As needed, I create other folders for other type of assets. For this project, folders, CSS, and images are all that I need.

Dreamweaver MX 2004 comes along with a handy Assets panel. While this panel helps keeps items organized for you by having everything presorted, there isn't a substitute for having your resources sorted yourself instead across several directories. A clean work area not only keeps files from being misplaced, but also keeps your sanity during the development and further maintenance of the site.

My last step in the setup process is to complete the folder structure that I mapped out in the planning stages. I simply create new folders within the Files panel as you see in Figure 1-13.

### Complying with standards

When I open a new web document in Dreamweaver MX 2004, I can select the option of making it standards-compliant by checking the Make document XHTML compliant option at the bottom-right corner of the New Document dialog box (see Figure 1-14). By making this selection, I am ensuring my pages are built to web standards as set by the World Wide Web Consortium (see www.w3.org) instead of to whatever fresh, popular browser version has just been released.

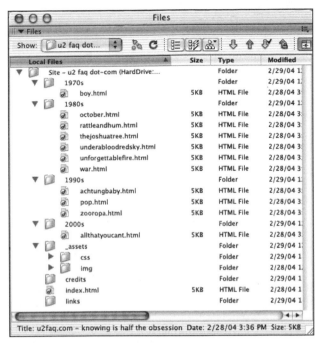

**Figure 1-13.** The folder structure

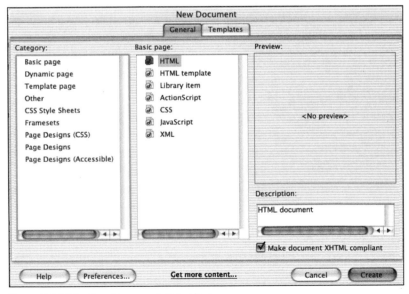

**Figure 1-14.** The New Document dialog box

The document Dreamweaver creates is built to the XHTML 1.0 Transitional doctype. This means that HTML files are now remapped as an XML document. There isn't much difference between an HTML document and an XHTML one as far as visitors to the site are concerned, if they are at all. Any modern browser is capable of rendering both. As far as how the page is assembled, however, it's a slightly different story. Here's the code Dreamweaver MX 2004 generates by default when an XHTML document is checked:

```
<!DOCTYPE html PUBLIC "-//W3C//DTD XHTML 1.0 Transitional//EN"
➥ "http://www.w3.org/TR/xhtml1/DTD/xhtml1-transitional.dtd">
<html xmlns="http://www.w3.org/1999/xhtml">
<head>
 <title>Untitled Document</title>
 <meta http-equiv="Content-Type" content="text/html;
➥charset=iso-8859-1" />
</head>
<body>
</body>
</html>
```

The first couple of lines consist of the <!DOCTYPE> tag and the opening <html> tag, which contains an xmlns attribute. These tell the browser how to render the page. In the '90s, while U2 was working and promoting their *POP* album, browsers did not support standards as well as they do now. The tendency on some projects was to build two different versions of each website: one for Netscape Navigator and one for Microsoft Internet Explorer. It wasn't that web builders really liked those two browsers; it was simply the case that most of the surfing population used either one or the other, and the two were substantially different enough that any attempt to put together one site for both browsers often failed aesthetically or was too much work.

By building to web standards, I am assuming visitors to my site will all use browsers capable of rendering standards-compliant code correctly. While this isn't a 100% guarantee for the future compatibility with browsers that haven't been invented yet, in principle, browsers built using standards should render my site correctly. Should a browser fail to do so, it will be because of poor support for the standards by the browser rather than the code put into building the site. Once all web builders have adopted standards, they will have earned themselves a free pass out of the development hell of revising their sites whenever a new browser comes out.

Is it harder to code to standards? Not much. Making a web page compliant with standards means I have to be more vigilant in how I code, and abandon some practices that were common in the late '90s. I also have to make sure my code validates using the W3C's validator (see http://validator.w3.org). However, the benefits far outweigh any added hassle.

## Setting the main stage

With blank files set up, I can start putting the pieces together. I start first with the main page of the site. First I assemble the column structure of the page, then work on setting the background image. Followed by the header graphic, I work on setting the type of the content of the page.

## Dividing the page into two columns

Since the page is basically a two-column layout, I want to separate the content into two sections using div elements. I set the id attribute to leftcol (for the small column placed on the left) and rightcol (for the column with the content) respectively.

```
<div id="leftcol">
[...header...newsfeed...album navigation...]
</div>
<div id="rightcol">
[...main content...]
</div>
```

For the most part I attempt to have the values for my CSS selectors symbolize the nature of the content. Since this site will be designed by CSS, I could easily switch the content placed in the left column div element from being on the left side of the page to the right and vice versa.

I want to make this content as semantically correct as possible because, down the road, with a different design, I might want to redesign the pages to have the column in a different location. By keeping the labels matched to the type of content it contains, I can easily mark up the content and avoid confusion down the road.

For example, if I label a paragraph like the following:

```
<p class="orangetext">Lorem ipsum dolor sit amet, consectetuer
adipiscing elit, sed diam nonummy nibh euismod tincidunt ut laoreet
dolore magna aliquam erat volutpat. Ut wisi enim ad minim veniam. <div>
```

And if I use CSS to stylize the text as orange like so:

```
.orangetext {
 color: #ffcc00;
}
```

the text would appear as orange, the desired effect. However, what would happen if I needed to change the color of the paragraph to red? Or puce? Or get rid of styling the color of the text altogether and need to apply other styles to the paragraph? The class selector has lost all meaning, probably even to the person maintaining the site. It's better to keep CSS selectors, id, and class attributes as reflections of the content they mark up.

For this site, however, I want you to do as I suggest and not as I do. For the production of the site I'm going to refer to the columns as left or right to keep things easier on myself as I build the site. This method will let you know what portion of the site I'm working on when I'm creating the CSS.

## Enter Cascading Style Sheets

When creating a style sheet from scratch, I place my rules in the document itself. By embedding the styles in the same document, I quickly add and edit the CSS rules. This method allows me to experiment and troubleshoot problems with one document instead of two (or more) files.

I place the CSS rules in the head of the document between the style container elements like so:

```
<head>
<style type="text/css">
/* CSS rules will go here*/
</style>
</head>
```

## Raising the columns

In order to get the two-column layout, the float property is the main tool. First, I tell the browser to place the content in the upper-left corner of the browser. By using the position property set to absolute, this takes the content out of the flow of the web page and overlaps the rest of the content of the page.

```
#leftcol {
 position: absolute;
 top: 0;
 left: 0;
 width: 240px;
}
```

Since the content is now jumbled with the content in the left column, I move the content out of the left column's way by adjusting the right margin to 270 pixels. This margin includes the width of the left column (and a little bit more for white space) and creates the illusion of a two-column layout.

```
#rightcol {
 margin: 0 20px 20px 270px;
}
```

Now, in order to center the two-column layout, I wrap a div element around the left and right column div elements:

```
<div id="frame">
 <div id="leftcol">
 [...header...newsfeed...album navigation...]
 </div>
 <div id="rightcol">
 [...main content...]
 </div>
</div>
```

Next I set the position of the "frame" div to be relative, the width to 774 pixels, and the margins for the left and right side to auto. By setting the value to auto, the browser automatically centers the contents of the web page.

```
#frame {
 position: relative;
 margin: 0 auto;
```

```
   width: 774px;
 }
```

To finalize the effect, I bring in a background image that spans the width of the web page. It's a simple background image—only 24 pixels tall, but tiles vertically—adding some slight depth to the page.

```
body {
  margin: 0;
  padding: 0;
  font-family: Verdana, Geneva, Arial, Helvetica, sans-serif;
  font-size: 1em;
  background-image: url("../img/layout_bkgd.gif");
  background-repeat: repeat-y;
  background-position: center;
  background-color: #999;
}
```

I also include a footer in the page, which contains the copyright and any other related information. To do this, I place a div element in between the frame.

```
<div id="frame">
<div id="leftcol">
[...header...newsfeed...album navigation...]
</div>
<div id="rightcol">
[…main content…]
</div>
<div id="footer">
</div>
</div>
```

Since the footer is going to be at the bottom of the page, I want to make sure that the content is aligned with the content of the right column. In order to do that, the margin on the right is set to 270 pixels.

```
#footer {
  clear: both;
  font-size: 0.68em;
  line-height: 1.5em;
  color: #666;
  margin: 10px 24px 10px 270px;
}
```

With the structure of the two-column layout set, I copy the CSS rules and place them into a separate file called layout.css and place it in the _assets/css folder.

Since the properties are separated from the page I was working on, I need to reassociate the style sheet to the web page. I do this by first creating a second style sheet with one rule:

```
@import url("layout.css");
```

Again, I put the style sheet in the css folder of the _assets directory. Then I go to the main page of the website and write the following line of code in the head of the document:

```
<link href="_assets/css/style.css" rel="stylesheet" type="text/css" />
```

By linking to a style sheet that then imports the layout rules, I stop 90s-era browsers like Netscape Navigator 4.x from picking up the styles and attempting to style the page. Why would I want to do this? Because browsers like Navigator 4 have very poor CSS support and, in my opinion, it's better to leave the site visitors with just the content of the web page than force them to decipher the poor CSS rendering. In a modern-era browser, the CSS rules in my layout.css are picked up without any troubles.

## The heading

With the layout rules now in a separate style sheet, I start adding rules to the top of the main page document between the style element containers. These new rules are only for the main page of the website, and the first thing worked on is the header.

```
<h1><a href="/">U2FAQ.com: Knowing is Half the Obsession</a></h1>
```

In order to increase the accessibility of the header graphic, I want to use CSS to slide in the graphic, leaving the HTML text for screen readers. In order to achieve this effect, I insert a span element between the text and the anchor element like so:

```
<h1><a href="/"><span class="no">U2FAQ.com: Knowing is Half the
Obsession</span></a></h1>
```

In my style sheet for layout.css, I'll add a new class selector and set the display property to none. This rule then hides the HTML text from CSS-enabled browsers while I add another CSS rule for the main page to include the image (as you see in Figure 1-15):

```
#leftcol h1 a {
  display: block;
  width: 240px;
  height: 84px;
  background-image: url("../img/home_logotagline.gif");
}
```

Since anchor elements are inline elements, like images, I convert the display property to a value of block. That enables me to set the width and height of the anchor link to match that of the header image. Then the background image property is set to the header image.

Next I want to position the header graphic a little lower than its current position. I do that by setting the style for the heading element itself (as shown in Figure 1-16):

```
#leftcol h1 {
  margin: 193px 0 0 0;
  padding: 0;
}
```

**Figure 1-15.** The heading graphic shows up.

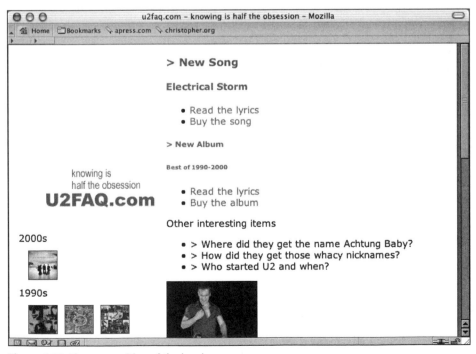

**Figure 1-16.** The new position of the header

## Adding the main teasers

To pull off the major visual impact on the main page that highlights the last song U2 has released, I wrap a div element around the content that specifically relates to it. div is a generic block-level element that represents a division in a document's structure. For the new song section of the main page, the HTML looks like this:

```
<div id="newsong">
 <h3><a href="">&gt; New Song</a></h3>
 <h4><a href="">Electrical Storm</a></h4>
 <ul>
  <li><a href="">Read the lyrics</a></li>
  <li><a href="http://www.amazon.com/">Buy the song</a></li>
 </ul>
</div>
```

The impact of the div element on the visual display of the web page is nil until I do a couple of things. First, I add the id attribute and its corresponding newsong value. Next, I apply the following CSS rules:

```
/* main teaser */
#rightcol #newsong {
 margin-top: 0px;
 width: 504px;
 height: 269px;
 background-image: url(../img/home_1stbonolites.jpg);
 background-repeat: no-repeat;
}
#rightcol #newsong h3 {
 margin: 0;
}
#rightcol #newsong h3 a {
 padding: 12px;
 background-color: white;
}
#rightcol #newsong h4 {
 color: white;
 font-size: 2.5em;
 font-weight: normal;
 margin: 0;
 padding: 12px 0 0 12px;
}
#rightcol #newsong h4 a {
 color: white;
}
#rightcol #newsong ul {
 margin: 0;
 padding: 0;
}
#rightcol #newsong ul li {
```

```
 color: white;
 margin: 0;
 padding: 0 0 0 12px;
}
#rightcol #newsong li a {
 color: #ccc;
}
```

In Figure 1-17 you can see the vivid effects accomplished by a well-placed div element and choice CSS rules. By setting a background image for the div element, the home_1stbonolites.jpg image is inserted into the mix much like a photograph used in a newspaper or magazine article.

**Figure 1-17.** The main teaser

## The same, once again, only smaller

I use the same method to modify the second-level teaser, but I reduce the size so that it won't compete head-to-head for attention from the reader.

```
<div id="newalbum">
 <h5><a href="">&gt; New Album</a></h5>
 <h6><a href="">Best of 1990-2000</a></h6>
 <ul>
  <li><a href="">Read the lyrics</a></li>
  <li><a href="">Buy the album</a></li>
 </ul>
</div>
```

Next, I include the CSS rules for the second teaser as shown in Figure 1-18:

```
/* Second teaser */
#rightcol #newalbum {
 margin-top: 12px;
 width: 328px;
 height: 180px;
 background-image: url(../img/home_2ndcrowd.jpg);
```

*Continued*

27

```
  background-repeat: no-repeat;
}
#rightcol #newalbum h5 {
  margin: 0;
}
#rightcol #newalbum h5 a {
  padding: 6px 6px 6px 12px;
  background-color: white;
}
#rightcol #newalbum h6 {
  color: white;
  font-size: 1.5em;
  font-weight: normal;
  margin: 0;
  padding: 6px 0 0 12px;
}
#rightcol #newalbum h6 a {
  color: white;
}
#rightcol #newalbum ul {
  margin: 0;
  padding: 0;
}
#rightcol #newalbum ul li {
  color: white;
  margin: 0;
  padding: 0 0 0 12px;
}
#rightcol #newalbum li a {
  color: #ccc;
}
```

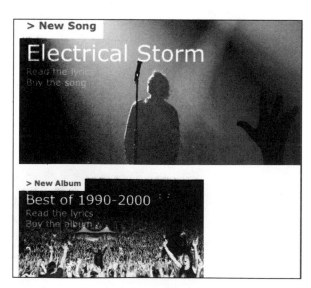

**Figure 1-18.**
The second teaser

Here is the rest of the CSS for the main page, which covers all the other styles in the page except for those that were covered in the `layout.css` and the navigation of the site, which I discuss in the "Navigating album covers" section of the chapter.

In Figure 1-19, you can notice the tiling effects of the band member photos. These are to highlight the other members of the band. Typically, these photos would be laid out from top to bottom like a set of blocks. With CSS rules, however, I move the position of the photos to overlap each other and place the bylines in alignment with the left edge of each photo.

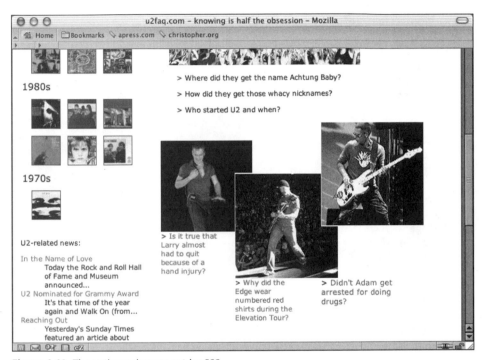

**Figure 1-19.** The entire main page set by CSS

```
/* Third level teaser */
#thirdteaser p {
 display: none;
}
#thirdteaser ul {
 margin: 0;
 padding: 0;
}
#thirdteaser ul li {
 margin: 0;
 padding: 12px 0 0 12px;
 list-style-type: none;
 font-size: 0.8em;
}
```

*Continued*

```
/* band member links */
#bandlinks {
 font-size: 0.8em;
 margin-top: 3.5em;
 float: right;
 width: 500px;
}
#larry {
 width: 155px;
 text-align: left;
}
#larry p {
 margin: 0;
 padding: 0;
 width: 100px;
}
#edge {
 position: relative;
 top: -175px;
 left: 125px;
 width: 155px;
 text-align: left;
}
#edge img {
 border-top: 2px solid white;
 border-left: 1px solid white;
}
#edge p {
 margin: 0;
 padding: 0;
 width: 100px;
}
#adam {
 position: relative;
 top: -515px;
 left: 275px;
 width: 155px;
 text-align: left;
}
#adam img {
 border-bottom: 2px solid white;
 border-left: 1px solid white;
}
#adam p {
 margin: 88px 0 0 0;
 padding: 0;
 font-size: 1.05em;
}
```

## 1

## Making the template before pouring the content

Before I put in the content in the blank pages, I need to create a template. The benefits of making a template are pretty basic, but very rewarding:

- With a template, all fresh content pages can have the template attached. This makes it easy to add the look of the site and simply focus on adding the new content.
- If the look of the site needs to be changed in terms of the HTML structure of the page, an automatic site-wide update can be started as soon as you save your changes to the template.

To start with the template, I select File ➤ New ➤ HTML Template. With the template page open, I start inserting the content areas that make up the page: the main heading, the navigation links, the newsfeed, the second column content, and the footer. While I create this page, I make sure to include the div elements carried over from the main page as well.

Just like the main page, I'll use the two-column layout structure for the other pages. Since the layout for the page is already available by link to the style.css, I create a link to the style sheet.

Since this is a template, I need to specify certain areas of the page as being editable. For this site, I'm going to have the title and content underneath it available for editing in two separate fields.

I highlight the title and hit my right mouse button to bring up the context menu. In this menu, I select Template ➤ New Editable Region. (Alternatively, from the menu, you could select Insert ➤ Template Objects ➤ Editable Region.) From here, I type the name of the editable region, which I will call contentTitle.

I do the same for the content region, naming it contentContent. Looking at the template page in Design mode, I see rectangles that surround the editable regions of the template. When I use this template in the content pages, this is where I can pour in my content or make changes to existing content.

The next step is to modify the style sheet for the content by hand. Following is the HTML template I made:

```
<!DOCTYPE html PUBLIC "-//W3C//DTD XHTML 1.0 Transitional//EN"
➥ "http://www.w3.org/TR/xhtml1/DTD/xhtml1-transitional.dtd">
<html xmlns="http://www.w3.org/1999/xhtml">
<head>
<!-- TemplateBeginEditable name="doctitle" -->
<title>u2faq.com - knowing is half the obsession</title>
<!-- TemplateEndEditable -->
<meta http-equiv="Content-Type" content="text/html;
➥charset=iso-8859-1" />
<link href="../_assets/css/style.css" rel="stylesheet"
➥type="text/css" />
```

*Continued*

```
<link href="../_assets/css/secondlvl.css" rel="stylesheet"
➥type="text/css" />
<!-- TemplateBeginEditable name="head" --><!-- TemplateEndEditable -->
</head>
<body>
<div id="frame">
  <div id="leftcol">
    <!-- Start of Left Column -->
    <h1><a href="/"><span class="no">U2FAQ.com: Knowing is Half
    ➥the Obsession</span></a></h1>
    <div id="navigation">
      <p>Read up on U2 History:</p>
      <ul>
        <li>2000s
          <ul>
            <li><a href="" id="albumall"><span class="no">All that You
            ➥Can't Leave Behind</span></a></li>
          </ul>
        </li>
        <li>1990s
          <ul>
            <li><a href="" id="albumpop"><span
            ➥class="no">Pop</span></a></li>
            <li><a href="" id="albumzoo"><span
            ➥class="no">Zooropa</span></a></li>
            <li><a href="" id="albumachtung"><span class="no">
            ➥ Achtung Baby</span></a></li>
          </ul>
        </li>
        <li>1980s
          <ul>
            <li><a href="" id="albumrh"><span class="no">Rattle and
            ➥ Hum</span></a></li>
            <li><a href="" id="albumjt"><span class="no">Joshua
            ➥ Tree</span></a></li>
            <li><a href="" id="albumuf"><span class="no">The
            ➥ Unforgettable Fire</span></a></li>
            <li><a href="" id="albumblood"><span class="no">Under a
            ➥Blood Red Sky</span></a></li>
            <li><a href="" id="albumwar"><span
            ➥class="no">War</span></a></li>
            <li><a href="" id="albumoct"><span
            ➥class="no">October</span></a></li>
          </ul>
        </li>
        <li>1970s
          <ul>
            <li><a href="" id="albumboy"><span
            ➥class="no">Boy</span></a></li>
```

```
        </ul>
      </li>
    </ul>
  </div>
  <div id="u2news">
    <p>U2-related news:</p>
    <dl>
      <dt><a href="">In the Name of Love</a></dt>
      <dd>Today the Rock and Roll Hall of Fame and Museum
      ➥announced...</dd>
      <dt><a href="">U2 Nominated for Grammy Award</a></dt>
      <dd>It's that time of the year again and Walk On (from...</dd>
      <dt><a href="">Reaching Out</a></dt>
      <dd>Yesterday's Sunday Times featured an article about how the
      Internet is...</dd>
    </dl>
    <p>Newsfeed from <a
    ➥href="http://www.u2log.com/">U2Log.com</a></p>
  </div>
</div>
<!-- End of Left Column -->
<!-- TemplateBeginEditable name="contentContent" -->
<div id="rightcol">
  <!-- Start of Right Column -->
  <!-- TemplateBeginEditable name="contentTitle" -->
  <h3>The Joshua Tree</h3>
  <!-- TemplateEndEditable -->
  <h4>Is The Joshua Tree the biggest U2 album ever?</h4>
  <p>{M2} Definitely. In the U.S., The Joshua Tree was #1 for nine
  weeks. In the UK it became the fastest selling album in history and
  went Platinum in only 28 hours! It stayed on the charts for 129
  weeks. It reentered the UK charts twice more, reaching #19 in 1992
  and #27 in 1993. It topped the charts in 22 different
  countries!</p>
  <h4>How many other bands have been on the cover of TIME
  ➥magazine?</h4>
  <p>{M2} The Beatles and The Who were the first two bands to be
  honored like that. U2 was the third, appearing on the cover of
  the April 29, 1987 issue with a headline of "Rock's Hottest
  Ticket."</p>
  <p>{JP} I think the only other band to be on the front of Time
  since has been Pearl Jam. </p>
  <p>{JT} Pearl Jam actually has never made the cover of Time, only
  Eddie Vedder.</p>
  <p>{PA} The Canadian music combo, The Band, appeared on the cover
  of Time magazine, (issue dated January 12, 1970). A photo of the
  cover can be seen here: http://theband.hiof.no/band_pictures/
```

*Continued*

```
        time_1.html1 . As far as Pearl Jam goes, it was Eddie Vedder only
        on the cover apparently, I am not familiar with the story, and not
        sure if you can really say that Pearl Jam was on the cover. Other
        individual performers have appeared on the cover, e.g.
        David Byrne. </p>
        <h4>Question First</h4>
        <p>Answer Next</p>
      </div>
      <!-- End of Right Column -->
      <!-- TemplateEndEditable -->
      <div id="footer">
        <p>All original material Copyright 2004 Christopher Schmitt. This
        is not an official site of the band. Their official site can be
        found here at <a href="http://www.u2.com/">u2.com</a>.</p>
      </div>
    </div>
    <!-- End of Frame -->
    </body>
    </html>
```

**Here is the CSS for** secondlvl.css:

```
#frame {
 background-image: url("../img/2nd_bkgd.jpg");
 background-repeat: no-repeat;
}
/* -------[ Left Column ]------- */
#leftcol h1 {
 margin: 210px 0 0 0;
 padding: 0;
}
#leftcol h1 a {
 display: block;
 width: 265px;
 height: 84px;
 background-image: url("../img/2nd_logotagline.gif");
}
/* -------[ Right Column ]------- */
#rightcol {
 padding-top: 235px;
 color: #333;
 margin-right: 55px;
}
#rightcol h4 {
 margin-bottom: .2em;
}
#rightcol p {
 margin-top: 0;
 margin-bottom: 1em;
}
```

I'm almost ready to attach the template to the content pages and start adding content to the site, but first I need to add some visual appeal to the navigation.

## Navigating album covers

As the site is now, the navigation consists of links, which isn't visually interesting. In order to spice things up, I transform the text links into album cover navigation. While the HTML—the unordered lists navigation—remains the same, the CSS creates the links out of album covers.

Since I'm making a separate style sheet for the content pages, I place the CSS rules for the album navigation into its own style sheet. Both the main pages and content pages can use the album navigation.

First, I create a library item that contains the markup of the links. I go to File ➤ New and then pick a basic page. One of the suboptions is Library Item. With the document open, I insert the navigation HTML.

For the next step, I create a new style sheet entitled albums.css and attach it to both the main page as well as the content template.

I open the blank content pages that were created at the beginning of the development process and attach the template. Attaching a template is done by selecting File ➤ New from the Template tag, and selecting U2 Site ➤ ContentTemplate. Then I can start populating the pages with content.

## Sweeping changes

Using templates in Dreamweaver isn't just about being able to pull up a copy of a file and start making a new page of a website. You can also carry out retrospective changes on a site-wide basis. Whenever I modify and save changes to the template for my content pages, Dreamweaver automatically prompts me if I want to carry these changes throughout all the pages that use my template.

Let me think about this: I can make all the changes manually, or I could let Dreamweaver do all the work? Sounds like I know which way to go!

## Checking for accessibility

With the site built, I want to make sure it meets accessibility guidelines. Dreamweaver does a good job of reporting back to me about any accessibility problems that may be present. By selecting Site ➤ Reports, a dialog box pops open, providing several reports Dreamweaver can run on the U2FAQ.com site—one of which is the Accessibility test (as shown in Figure 1-20).

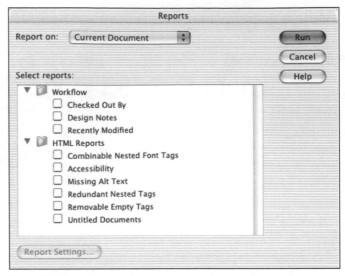

**Figure 1-20.** The Reports dialog box

I select the option for the Accessibility test and let it scan the entire site by choosing Entire Current Local Site. After it scans, a listing of any problems or questions is compiled for my review.

For further clarification of the problems reported by Dreamweaver, I select the information icon on the left of the report item (as shown in Figure 1-21). (The icon looks like the lowercase letter I trapped in a speech bubble.) Clicking the link opens the UsableNet Accessibility Guide, which provides background information regarding the problem.

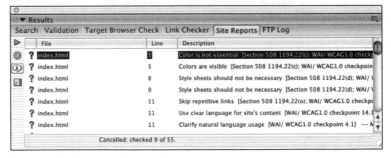

**Figure 1-21.** Generated items in the report

After I read the background information, I double-click the items on the list, one by one, to review each one and then address each one with modifications to the HTML.

## Reviewing the planning and construction

Now that I have the site built, I know that I'm not finished. Websites are grown, not launched, and they need to be nurtured. Over the course of the next couple of months, I'll be checking the site's log files from the server and determining how people are using the site. And, of course, as the band releases new music, the site needs to be updated and evolve.

Five die in collapse of Par
airport terminal

**In form:** Claudine Schaul of Luxembourg
holds the winner's trophy after defeating
American Lindsay Davenport during their fin

lhost/tvnews/news.php?story=1

**Entertainment**

**Slapfight stance revealed**
Thursday 3 June 2004

The art
clocking
arcade g
apparently
sources re
skill and
evidence i
it.

In this chapter we will be going through the process of building a news portal in Dreamweaver MX 2004.

This chapter will begin, as all well-planned web projects do, with the information architecture of the project. Here we will look at our goals, our audience, our requirements, and what the site will look like. Once we have this in place, our Information Architecture (IA) document will act as a blueprint for the actual building of the site. At this point we will get into Dreamweaver MX 2004 and start putting the code together. For this project there is no specific requirement that dictates we need to use a certain technology over another, so we can base our decision on issues like cost and convenience. We will be using PHP as the scripting language and MySQL as the back-end database, as both of these products are open source and can be hosted on practically any platform.

By the end of this chapter you will not only have a working news portal application, but you will have worked through the creation of an Information Architecture document, created a MySQL database, delved into PHP, and seen how we bring it all together within Dreamweaver MX 2004.

# Information architecture

The first step in any web project should always be the creation of the site's Information Architecture. The Information Architecture for a site encompasses setting out the goals for our website, creating mock-ups of the web pages themselves, and everything else in between. It may seem like a lot of unnecessary work to do, but by hammering out the details of the project right up front, you make sure that there is no miscommunication about the nature and functionality of the website and end up saving yourself time in the long run. Not only does this present a professional and efficient face to your client, but by setting out the architecture of the site before you begin coding it, you will find that you code with far more direction and spend less time reworking or redesigning sections of code. It's all down in black and white in the IA document.

The first thing we will want to do is define our goals for the site.

## Goals

Many sites exist simply because everyone else has one. This is not a good reason for putting up a website. By setting out our goals, we get down to the real reasons for creating this site, and once we know that, we will be better able to plan the rest of it.

In our case we are building a news portal. What are our reasons for building a news portal?

- Are we a traditional news agency (TV or newspaper) and have a vested interest in reporting news?
- Do we have a specific niche interest that we are providing news for?
- Are we simply providing news as a service that draws browsers to the site and we will then generate revenue from advertising on the site?
- Or do we want to take on the CNNs and BBCs of the world?

For the purpose of this chapter, we'll presume that our client is a national television station and they wish to extend their news programming to include up-to-the-minute news on their website. They do not wish to compete with CNN and report on every newsworthy item out there, but to report on local issues and ones that are important in the international arena. Their goal in this case is to not only add value to their station by providing an extra service, but also attract more viewers to their station.

Now that we have the goals firmly in our mind, we can begin looking at some background material that will help us in deciding what the functionality of our site will be.

# Background

In this section we will want to put together some relevant background information that we can use a basis for deciding on the content and functionality of our site. Areas that we will address here are the kinds of users we will be attracting to our site, what they will expect from the site, and investigating potential competitors.

## Audience

Invariably, the kind of site that you design will determine the kind of audience that you will attract. For this reason, you should decide up front the kind of person that you will want to attract to your site. Of course, you should design and plan your site for not only the kind of person that you wish to attract, but also the kind of person that will browse your site irrespective of your plans for whether they are the intended audience or not. Sure, if you are planning a site that provides news on the latest goings on in the hip hop music scene, you will want to attract fans of hip hop music. But that is not the only type of person who might browse your site. You may also find that music journalists read your site on the off-chance that you have scooped some news that they haven't. Executives from record labels may come to the site to see how the public is receiving their latest offering. When you're defining the goals for your site, you will have your **intended** audience clearly in mind, but you should not forget about your **incidental** audience as well.

So, let's now take a look at the audience from our perspective. Since we are working with a local news station, we do know that the majority of the viewers of the site will be people local to the area, interested in finding out about the local news. We didn't really define any goal that would single out a specific target audience, so we're looking at a more general audience here. In some ways, designing a site for a general audience may be a bit trickier, especially from a design point of view. For our hip hop site targeting a younger audience, we would have little debate on how we wanted our site to look, but in the case of general news, we have to be more careful.

Since we're extending our normal news service, we will find that the news that is reported on cannot be lumped into any specific category. We'll have top international stories, local content, financial news, sports, and weather. The local and international news content can further be broken down into categories such as politics, technology, science, nature, and the arts.

Our audience will be quite varied in terms of whom they are and what they will want to get out of the site. Our site therefore will have to be more functional in catering to a variety of possible interests, rather than having a specific look and feel to attract a specific kind of person.

A news company should already have demographics on the people that watch their news on the TV, but by moving onto the Internet, they are opening themselves up to a vast new audience.

To better understand the kinds of people that you will have coming to your site, it helps to construct scenarios for them. To do this, you need to imagine the type of people that will come to your site—this is sometimes called creating "personas." Then imagine why that person would come to the site, what they would want to see, and how they would try finding that information. By doing this you get a very good idea of how to eventually structure the site, and the kinds of things that you should include.

Let's look at a few scenarios:

### Scenario 1: The executive
This is an easy one. An executive sitting at their desk with nothing better to do decides to catch up on the news. In this case the person will have a fairly short attention span and will not want to have to wade through masses of information. But since they are looking for something to do with their time, if they see something that interests them, they will want to see more. This person will typically click at random, following links off the page until they find something that attracts their interest.

### Scenario 2: Sports fan
Again, not too difficult to conceptualize. A sports fan logs on to the site in the morning and wants to see the latest sports scores and reports. This person will hit the front page of the site and immediately want to browse to the area of the site that interests them.

### Scenario 3: Interested reader
By interested reader we mean someone who has a particular interest in a specific story for some reason or another. This person may be really interested in the Miss World beauty pageant, and will navigate to any story on the site that is related to this.

You could carry on like this forever, but as long as you have a few scenarios that cover the spectrum of your audience, you will be fine. Even if the entire spectrum of possible readers are not covered, by building personas you will be able to identify and relate to 80% of your audience. Already from just these three your mind may be ticking over with features and functionality that would attract each of these types of people back to our site. We'll start looking at these features in the next section when we deal with features and content. Before we get there though, we need to complete our background work and take a look at what our competitors are offering.

## The competition
When planning a site it's always a good thing to know what your (or your clients') competition is doing. By evaluating both what features the competition has as well as how successfully they implement them, you can plan your site to either fill a gap that they have left in the market or simply provide a superior service to the one that they have.

While features are a great thing to have on the site, also evaluate how successful they have been in presenting the information—is it laid out clearly, can you easily find your way around the site, and what sort of load times did you experience?

There are three sites that we will take a look at: the BBC News site, http://news.bbc.co.uk; CNN, www.cnn.com; and Independent Newspapers Online (IOL), www.iol.co.za.

## BBC

The BBC news site starts with a page that asks you to decide whether you wish to see local content—that which is relevant for people in the UK, or content for people in the rest of the world. We'll take a look at the World Edition.

The homepage is nicely laid out, as you can see in Figure 2-1. Down the left-hand side of the page is a navigation bar that remains there for all pages. It lists categories into which news stories are placed. Stories are categorized by broad geographical location, as well as subject. Links to each of these categories is provided in the navigation bar. In the middle of the page are the latest news stories—a précis of the story accompanied by an image and links to related stories. In a panel on the right-hand side, links to the current features on the site are provided.

**Figure 2-1.** The BBC World Edition homepage

After navigating into a subsection, that subsection is highlighted in the navigation bar so that you can quickly and easily see where in the site you are. Figure 2-2 shows the navigation bar after navigating to a story within the Science/Nature category.

**Figure 2-2.**
The Science/Nature category highlighted in the navigation bar

At all times a sidebar is provided that links to articles and sites of relevance for the current article, as shown in Figure 2-3.

**Figure 2-3.**
Related stories are shown in a sidebar.

Navigation within the current section is also provided in the same sidebar by providing links to the other top stories within this section (see Figure 2-4).

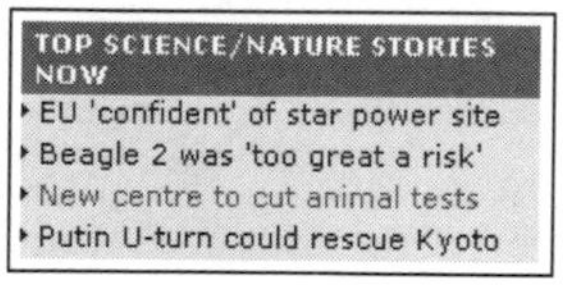

**Figure 2-4.**
Other stories within the same section

The navigation within the section is neatly split by providing only the top stories in the current section in the sidebar and at the bottom of the page providing a select box that lists all of the stories within the section, as you see in Figure 2-5. This approach also means that all of the past stories are available, and at the same time does not clutter up the sidebar with a large number of links.

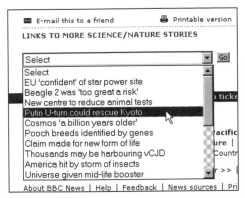

**Figure 2-5.** Older stories from the same news section

As far as features on the site go, there is not a lot to speak of. At the bottom of each article is a link to print or e-mail the URL of this story to a friend, as shown in Figure 2-6.

**Figure 2-6.** Links to e-mail the story to a friend and view a printable version

The BBC site does have a pseudo-interactive feature called Talking Point. In this section the editors provide a piece of editorial on a story, and readers are invited to send in their viewpoints (see Figure 2-7). Rather than providing an open forum that could easily be abused, the responses are all moderated and only some make it onto the website for inclusion.

**Figure 2-7.**
Users of the site can provide feedback on stories.

### CNN

CNN takes a different approach to the layout of their front page. On CNN.com's front page only one story is provided in great detail, as you can see in Figure 2-8.

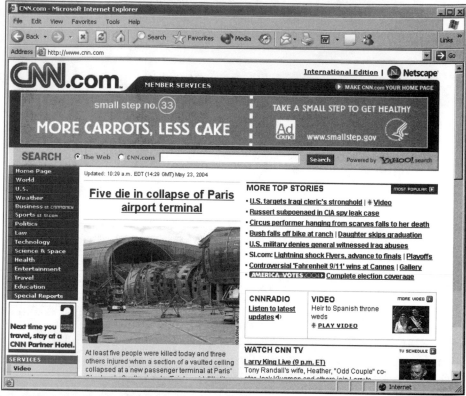

**Figure 2-8.** The CNN homepage

Along with this story are links to related news items. Other top stories are provided in an adjacent navigation area (see Figure 2-9).

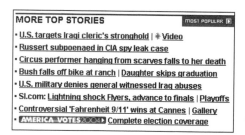

**Figure 2-9.**
Other top stories on the CNN website

Stories are also categorized within specified categories, and navigation to these sections is provided by way of a sidebar on the left, as shown in Figure 2-10.

**Figure 2-10.**
Navigation on the CNN website

A nice feature on the CNN site is that after the main story, an area is presented that lists the latest two or three stories for each section within the site (see Figure 2-11).

**Figure 2-11.** Latest stories within other sections on the site

Once you have navigated within the site to a specific story, you are presented with some story tools for the article, as shown in Figure 2-12.

**Figure 2-12.**
Story tools on the CNN website

CNN provides an area within the site where you can set various preferences for the site. On the preferences page you can select which edition of CNN you wish to use (Asia, Europe, or US), personalize the weather settings so that you get weather forecasts specific to your area, subscribe to receive e-mail news alerts, or set CNN as your homepage.

From a broadcasting point of view, CNN provides a link from their homepage to the CNN TV schedule.

### IOL

IOL is not related to a broadcaster in any way, but it is a news site and therefore warrants a look. The homepage is more like the BBC's than CNN—multiple stories are presented on the front page, as shown in Figure 2-13, along with the categorized navigation.

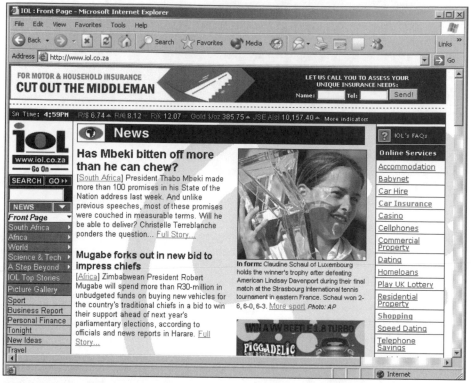

**Figure 2-13.** The IOL homepage

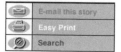

**Figure 2-14.**
Tools on the IOL page

When viewing a story, links to e-mail and print the story are provided as shown in Figure 2-14.

All of the sites included a facility to search for news stories.

## Summary

Of the three sites we've seen, the BBC site has the cleanest look. The CNN site gives the feeling of being cluttered. The IOL site can also have a clean look, but its use of a large watermark image in the background makes it seem too busy. It's all a matter of opinion, but you don't want to overwhelm the person browsing your site with masses of information. None of the sites were slow to load, and the categorized stories made browsing the sites straightforward. A slight drawback on the IOL site in this regard is that there is not a lot of cross-linking of news stories.

# Planning

We have our goals for the site, we know who our intended audience is, and we have seen how our competition and other sites in the industry have been implemented. We can now sit down and plan what we want to have on our site and how we intend to do it.

## 2

Let's start with the basic stuff that we'll need to include on the site. It's a news site, so we'll want to have news articles displayed. I much prefer the approach where a number of articles are presented, rather than a single headline story. For our news site, we want to be objective and not present editorial comment by putting one story ahead of another. That would be appropriate for a newspaper-type site, but not for a site that is simply reporting on news happenings.

Categorizing stories together allows the person browsing the site to quickly hone in on the articles that are of interest to them, and providing links to related news stories is a great way of supplying the history of a story.

Besides being able to browse for articles, the person must be able to search by keywords on the article, and it would be great if they could restrict that search to a specific category within the site.

That takes care of the basic news reporting, but what additional features can we add to the site to make the experience more pleasant and attract the person back to the site? The story tools that CNN provided are a good start—provide links to "printer-friendly" versions of the page and allow the user to e-mail the story to a friend.

CNN also allowed you to make CNN.com your homepage. If you cast your mind back to the audiences we defined earlier, one of them was a sports fan who wants to go straight to sports stories and scores. Let's extend the idea of setting the homepage and let the person mark the sports page (or any other section) as their "homepage" for this site. Whenever they load our site they will go straight to the section that interests them.

An offshoot of this idea and that of the linked articles is that a person may be interested in a specific news article. It would be a nice feature if they could mark the article as one of interest, and then all past and future news items related to this one would be highlighted on the site. As an example of this, let's go back to our sports fan. Say he reads an article about the 2010 World Cup soccer bid. He marks this as an interest, and every other article that is then added to the site and linked to this one is highlighted for him when he browses the site.

Since a television station backs the news site, we will also include a TV schedule and a "currently showing" highlight on the page.

An additional feature that is straightforward to implement is to provide our news as an RSS (**R**DF **S**ite **S**ummary—an XML file of our headlines that conform to a set specification) feed for people to use on their sites or in news ticker applications.

## Design

Right, so we know what we want to do, but how are we going to do it? This phase is where we look at what we are going to implement and decide how we intend to present it, and also how we are going to handle it in the background. It's all well and good saying that we are going to link articles together, but how exactly do we achieve that?

## Page layouts

First let's see what our site will look like. There are three possible pages/layouts that we can have: homepage, category page, and article page. Within each page we will want to retain our main navigation, as well as provide individual elements that are specific to that page.

The first then is the homepage, shown in Figure 2-15, where the person has not selected any specific section.

**Figure 2-15.** The homepage layout

As you can see, it's a fairly basic layout and nice and clean. The bar along the top provides the branding for the site and the search box where it's easily accessible.

Down the left-hand side of the page is category navigation that will take the person to the page for a particular category.

The area for listing the articles is divided into four sections: a heading, a thumbnail image on the left, the précis of the article on the right, and links to related articles underneath. This feature will repeat itself five times, displaying the five most recent news stories.

On the right is a box highlighting the TV program that is currently showing on the TV station, as well as a link to the full TV schedule. Below that is a list of other stories. These would be the latest ten stories, not including the five listed with the précis in the main story area.

The search results page would be similar to this page when the search is not limited to a specific category.

The second kind of page is when the person has browsed to a specific category. This is very similar to the main page, as you can see in Figure 2-16.

The main differences are that the current section is named in the bar along the top, the navigation is highlighted on the left, and the stories listed relate to this category. The other stories bar would also show stories within this category.

The search results page when limited to a category would be similar to this page.

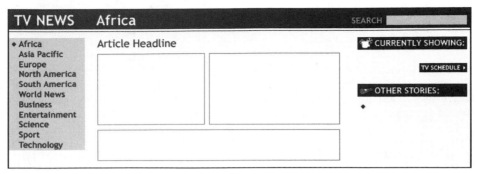

**Figure 2-16.** The layout within a section of the site

The third and last page appears when the person is viewing an article (see Figure 2-17).

**Figure 2-17.** The layout when viewing an article

This article is within the Africa category, so the category is still displayed in the top bar and in the navigation. The top bar now has the added Email and Print buttons for when people want to e-mail or print this story. An additional item on the right lists related stories to this one.

## Server setup

At this point we need to spend a bit of time setting up our development environment. The development of this application was done on a Windows XP machine, using the Apache web server and the MySQL database. For those of you who do not have this set up, this section will quickly explain the basics of getting it done.

### Apache and PHP

The Apache web server is available from www.apache.org and is open source software. For Windows users, a Windows installer is available for download that will step you through the installation process.

Once you have completed the installation, you will need to install and configure your Apache web server for PHP. Download the latest version of PHP from www.php.net. Here you will have the option of downloading either an archive file with the full PHP distribution or a Windows installer that contains the minimal files for PHP. While the Windows installer might seem like the preferred option, it does not include many of the modules that make PHP so powerful. The extra effort involved with installing the archive is well worth it.

Unzip the contents of the archive file to the C:\php directory. At the time of writing, the latest version of PHP was 4.3.6. It is worth noting that for the code in this chapter to work correctly you will need at least PHP version 4.1.0 or higher. This is because it makes use of a new set of predefined variables that offer increased security from hackers.

From the C:\php directory copy the php4ts.dll file into your Windows system32 directory. On Windows XP this will typically be C:\windows\system32 and on Windows NT or 2000 this will be C:\winnt\system32.

Some of the modules and functions within PHP require additional DLL files to function correctly. These can be found in the C:\php\dlls directory and should also be copied into the Windows system32 directory.

The last thing to do within the PHP directory is to copy the php.ini-dist file into your windows directory. Once you have copied it there, rename it to php.ini.

Now that all of the files are in place, we can configure PHP and Apache. The first thing we will configure is PHP, so open the C:\windows\php.ini (or C:\winnt\php.ini on Windows NT) file.

The php.ini file contains a number of directives that stipulate how PHP behaves and also where it should find certain things. We will just need to make two changes from the default settings—search for a section that begins

    [Session]

Make sure that the line that begins with session.save_path reads as follows:

    session.save_path = "c:\tmp"

When we need to maintain data from one page to another in PHP, we do it with something called a session variable. In order for PHP to save this data, it needs to know where it can keep it temporarily, and this is what we have just set up. You will now need to go and create the C:\tmp directory.

If you are running Windows and have an SMTP server on your machine, you can skip the next change, but if you do not, then you will have to tell PHP where your SMTP server is. An SMTP server is the server that your e-mail program uses to send e-mail on the Internet, and you should be able to find this setting from your e-mail program settings.

Find the line that starts

    SMTP =

And change it to point to the SMTP server that you normally use:

    SMTP = smtp.mydomain.com

If you do not have an SMTP server or do not know what it is, you should contact your ISP and ask them for the details of an SMTP server to use.

If you are using *nix, then you will need to alter the line that begins with

    sendmail_path =

to point to the location of your sendmail program.

Save and close this file and we can now open the Apache configuration file, httpd.conf. This file will live in the conf/ subdirectory off whatever location you installed Apache. If you chose the default installation path, then you will find it at C:\Program Files\Apache Group\Apache2\conf\httpd.conf—open it now in Dreamweaver.

All that we have to do here is tell the web server how to handle PHP pages. Search for the text LoadModule within the file and you will see a number of lines that all begin with LoadModule. At the end of these lines add the line

    LoadModule php4_module c:/php/sapi/php4apache.dll

This tells Apache to load the PHP module when it starts up.

The last piece we need to add to the configuration file is to tell Apache how to recognize a PHP file. Search for a line that begins with AddType, and add the following line after it:

    AddType application/x-httpd-php .php

And that's it. Save and close the file, and if Apache is already running, restart it so that your changes take effect. If Apache is not running, start it now.

### MySQL and phpMyAdmin
The MySQL website (www.mysql.com) provides binary installations for all of the popular computer platforms. Download the version that matches your platform and install.

By default MySQL will install to the C:\mysql folder. It will also install with no root password, so this is the first thing that we will have to change. The root user is the administrative username in MySQL, and as such it would be a large security hole to leave that username with no password.

In order to make the necessary changes to our settings and create the database, we will need to use a program to interface with the database server. MySQL comes with a command line program called the MySQL Monitor that allows you to do all of this, but in order to use it successfully you will need to understand and be able to use SQL to make all of the alterations. A much easier option, and a very popular one, is to use a web-based front-end called phpMyAdmin. This application is written entirely in PHP and is available for download from www.phpmyadmin.net/.

Download the latest version and extract the contents of the archive file to a directory within your web server structure. In my case my web server documents live in C:\htdocs, so I installed phpMyAdmin to the C:\htdocs\phpMyAdmin directory.

Open the C:\htdocs\phpMyAdmin\config.inc.php file in Dreamweaver and find the line that reads

```
$cfg['Servers'][$i]['auth_type']      = 'config';
```

This specifies that the username and password that we will be using in phpMyAdmin is coming from the config file. If you wish to put your root username and password in here, you can, but it is more secure to change the line to read

```
$cfg['Servers'][$i]['auth_type']      = 'http';
```

in which case you will be prompted for your username and password every time you open the phpMyAdmin program.

Another configuration parameter that you will need to set is to tell the phpMyAdmin program what its address is—look for the line

```
$cfg['PmaAbsoluteUri'] = '';
```

and change it so that it reads

```
$cfg['PmaAbsoluteUri'] = 'http://localhost/phpMyAdmin/';
```

Save the file now and open a web browser to the URL http://localhost/phpMyAdmin/.

The first thing that you will see is a dialog box prompting you to log in, as shown in Figure 2-18. Enter the root username with no password and click OK.

**Figure 2-18.**
phpMyAdmin is configured to prompt for the username and password.

Once you have logged in, you will be presented with the phpMyAdmin interface. At the bottom right-hand side of the window you will see a message alerting you to the fact that you have not yet set your root password (see Figure 2-19).

> Your configuration file contains settings (root with no password) that correspond to the default MySQL privileged account. Your MySQL server is running with this default, is open to intrusion, and you really should fix this security hole.

**Figure 2-19.** phpMyAdmin warns you when your root account has no password.

Our first step then should always be to secure our MySQL installation by giving the root account a password. On the right-hand side of the screen, there is a link to Privileges, as you can see in Figure 2-20.

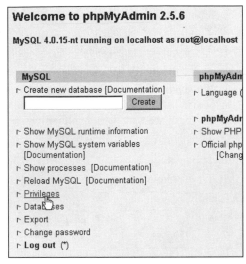

**Figure 2-20.** Click through to the Privileges page to set the root password.

Here you can add, edit, and delete user information. The page provides an overview of the users set up on your MySQL server as well as the privileges that have been assigned to them. Figure 2-21 shows a portion of the users table.

| | User | Host | Password | Global privileges |
|---|---|---|---|---|
| **User overview** | | | | |
| ☐ | Any | % | No | USAGE |
| ☐ | Any | localhost | No | SELECT, INSERT, UPDATE, DELETE, CREATE, DROP, RELOAD, SHUTDOWN, PROCESS, FILE, REFERENCES, INDEX, ALTER |
| ☐ | root | % | No | ALL PRIVILEGES |
| ☐ | root | localhost | No | ALL PRIVILEGES |
| | Note: MySQL privilege names are expressed in English | | | |

**Figure 2-21.** An overview of users of the database server

You will notice that there are two entries for the username root. One is for the localhost host—the local machine, the other for %, which is the wildcard. We will need to change the password for both of these entries. Click the Edit link next to either one of them. The following page (shown in Figure 2-22) contains information about the specific privileges for the root user. As you would expect, the super user root account has all privileges on all databases.

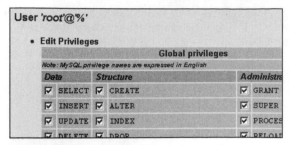

**Figure 2-22.** The privileges of the root account

We will look at what these privileges are a bit later when we create our own user; for now scroll down to the section of the page that lets you change the password (see Figure 2-23).

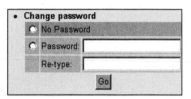

**Figure 2-23.**
Changing the password

Change the selected radio button from No Password to Password, and then enter the password into the boxes provided. Once you have entered your password, click Go. Do the same for both the root entries, and once you have done that, reload the MySQL server privileges using the link provided at the bottom of the Privileges page (see Figure 2-24).

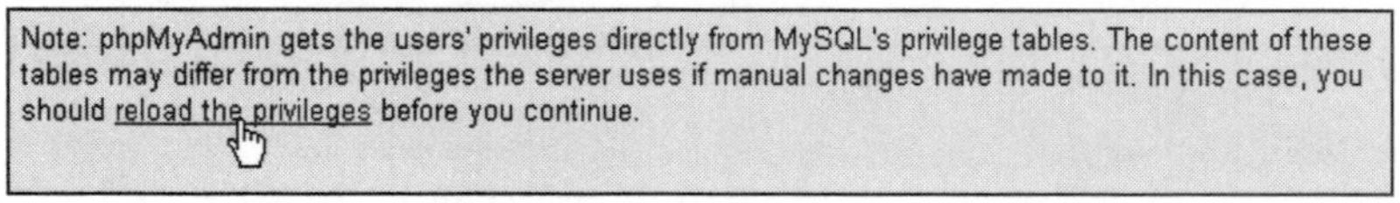

> Note: phpMyAdmin gets the users' privileges directly from MySQL's privilege tables. The content of these tables may differ from the privileges the server uses if manual changes have made to it. In this case, you should reload the privileges before you continue.

**Figure 2-24.** Reloading the MySQL privileges table

MySQL loads and caches all user information when it starts up, so any changes that you make to users will only be in effect once MySQL has been restarted.

## Database structure

Before we start developing, we need to design a database structure that will support the features that we wish to implement. Our requirements are fairly straightforward—we need categorized news items, a system to link articles together, and a TV schedule. The rationale behind each of the tables will be explained as we look at each one.

We will use phpMyAdmin for creating our database. If you still have your browser open at phpMyAdmin, close it and reopen it at that page. By doing this you will once again be prompted for your username and password, so enter root and the password you set up earlier.

The first thing to do is create the empty database, so on the main pages enter the name of the database to create (tvnews) and click Create (see Figure 2-25).

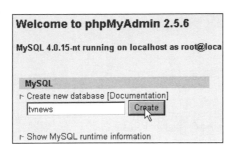

**Figure 2-25.**
Creating the tvnews database

This will immediately create this database and take you to the page where you can see the details of your new database, as shown in Figure 2-26.

**Figure 2-26.** The tvnews database

At the moment there are no tables in the database. You can either use the Create new table option, or enter the table creation SQL code. In order to make things quicker, the SQL code for creating the necessary tables is provided next.

Here is the SQL dump for the categories table:

```
#
# Table structure for table 'categories'
#

CREATE TABLE categories (
  cat_pk int(11) NOT NULL auto_increment,
  cat_code varchar(20) default NULL,
  cat_name varchar(30) default NULL,
```

*Continued*

```
    PRIMARY KEY  (cat_pk),
    KEY cat_code (cat_code)
);
```

Click the SQL tab at the top of the page and enter the SQL into the box provided, as shown in Figure 2-27.

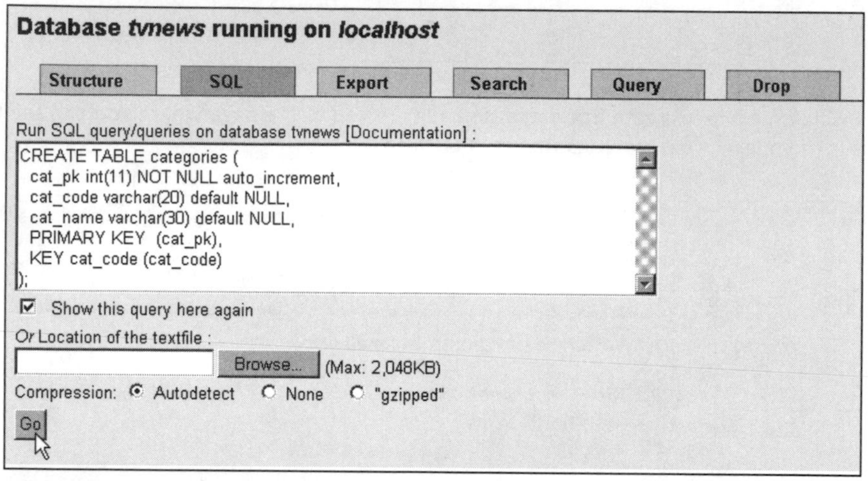

**Database *tvnews* running on *localhost***

| Structure | SQL | Export | Search | Query | Drop |
|---|---|---|---|---|---|

Run SQL query/queries on database tvnews [Documentation] :

```
CREATE TABLE categories (
 cat_pk int(11) NOT NULL auto_increment,
 cat_code varchar(20) default NULL,
 cat_name varchar(30) default NULL,
 PRIMARY KEY  (cat_pk),
 KEY cat_code (cat_code)
);
```

☑ Show this query here again

Or Location of the textfile :

[            ] [Browse...] (Max: 2,048KB)

Compression: ⦿ Autodetect ○ None ○ "gziped"

[Go]

**Figure 2-27.** Creating the categories table

The categories only require a primary key, an internal code, and a name. In order to provide easy linking to the category pages, we'll index the code field and allow people to specify it in the query string to the page. This way we won't need to use the primary key of the record all the time. Wherever possible we will use it as it will be more efficient, but for ease of use, the indexed code field will serve us well.

```
#
# Table structure for table 'news'
#

CREATE TABLE news (
  news_pk int(11) NOT NULL auto_increment,
  news_category_fk int(11) default NULL,
  news_date datetime default NULL,
  news_headline varchar(50) default NULL,
  news_precis varchar(255) default NULL,
  news_fulltext text,
  news_icon blob,
  news_icon_type varchar(20),
  news_icon_meta varchar(30),
  news_image mediumblob,
  news_image_type varchar(20),
  news_image_meta varchar(30),
  PRIMARY KEY  (news_pk)
);
```

*In the Relational Database Model, records in a table are identified by a value that is unique to that record. This unique identifier is known as the primary key. In order to link one or more tables together, we store the primary key of the table we wish to link to in our linking table—a concept known as a foreign key. Many Relational Database Management systems will maintain data integrity by using foreign key relationships when inserting and deleting records. The current version of MySQL does not support foreign key constraints, and we will therefore have to include this logic in our code when necessary. For more information on databases and database concepts, take a look at* Practical Web Database Design *by Chris Auld et al. (Apress, 2003).*

Each record in the news table will have its own primary key and a foreign key link to the categories table. The date is the date and time stamp that the article was entered. Another option for this column type would be the timestamp, which would automatically set the value of that field to the current date and time when a record is added. While this is a great feature, it does stop you from specifying your own date and time—a feature that editors might want to backdate articles. The headline field will provide the story headline for display above the article as well as in the story navigation on the right-hand side of the page. The précis is a short description or summary of the story that is provided on the main pages and in search results. Along with the précis a small image is displayed and this is stored in the icon field. This is a thumbnail image that is displayed next to the article précis. It's a blob field, which indicates that we will be storing the image data directly in the database rather than as individual files within the directory structure of the site. The blob field type is restricted to 64K in size, but if your thumbnail icon is larger than 64K, then you deserve to have your image truncated. The fulltext field provides the entire story text for the page that displays the story in full, and the image field stores the image that goes along with this story. This field is a mediumblob type, which means you can store more than 64K in it.

```
#
# Table structure for table 'links'
#

CREATE TABLE links (
   link_pk int(11) NOT NULL auto_increment,
   link_name varchar(20) default NULL,
   PRIMARY KEY  (link_pk)
);
```

We need to have some way of linking articles together. We could do it through a series of keywords attached to each news story—all you would do then is do a query on the database for stories that have keywords in common with the current story and you would get your related stories, but that could get messy in time and end up with articles linking to one another that are not meant to be linked. You'd also then be doing a textual search across your database, which is not efficient when you have a large number of stories in the database. A better option is to create a table of links—like categories, but more specific. The news editors can create as many of these as they need to and then when creating a new news story, just link that story to the link item. Any other story also linked to this item would then be linked. As an example, suppose we had a new news story on a sighting of the Loch Ness monster. The editor would create a link item with the name of "Loch Ness Monster". After creating the news article, they would link the story to the Loch Ness Monster link item. In two weeks time, another story comes through about an expedition to chart the bottom of Loch Ness to try and find the monster. This story is also linked to the Loch Ness Monster link item and because both stories are linked to the same link item, they become linked. When we build the page that displays the one story, we search the database for any other stories also linked to this and we'll have our list of related stories.

All we need now is some way of saving the links between news story and link item, and this is the linkmatrix table:

```
#
# Table structure for table 'linkmatrix'
#

CREATE TABLE linkmatrix (
  lm_links_fk int(11) default NULL,
  lm_news_fk int(11) default NULL,
  KEY lm_links_fk (lm_links_fk),
  KEY lm_news_fk (lm_news_fk)
);
```

Both fields are foreign keys to the links and news tables, and both are indexed to provide quicker searches when looking up related stories.

The last table holds usernames and passwords for the editors so that they can authenticate and add news stories:

```
#
# Table structure for table 'editors'
#

CREATE TABLE editors (
  editor_pk int(11) NOT NULL auto_increment,
  editor_username varchar(20) default NULL,
  editor_password varchar(20) default NULL,
  PRIMARY KEY  (editor_pk)
);
```

The username and password is used to authenticate the editor in the admin section of the site. Since our site is reporting on news stories, we do not need to record which editor entered a particular story—if we wanted to have a system where one editor could not make changes to another editor's story, then we would use the primary key of the editor as a foreign key in the news table to implement some basic security checks.

While we are on the subject of security, we should implement some further security measures on our MySQL server. We do not want to store our root username and password in our configuration files, nor do we want to use it as the username and password that connects to our database from the web application. What we will do now that we have finished creating our database and tables is create a MySQL user that only has rights to the tvnews database. We will then use this user to connect from our web application, and if our site is hacked, the hacker will only gain access to the tvnews database and not every database on our server.

Navigate back to the main phpMyAdmin page by clicking the Home link in the top left-hand side of the screen, as shown in Figure 2-28.

**Figure 2-28.**
Navigating back to the phpMyAdmin homepage

Browse to the Privileges page as we did earlier and then click the link to Add a new User (see Figure 2-29).

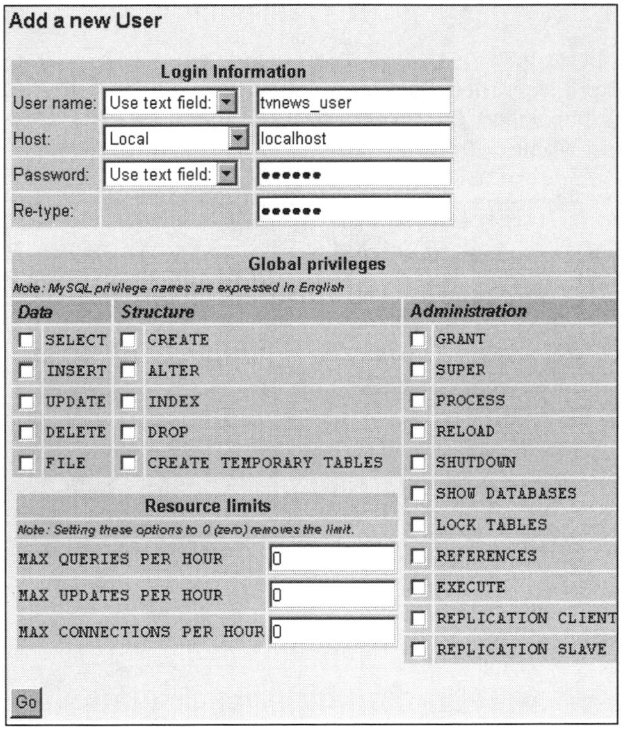

**Figure 2-29.** Adding a new user

Fill out the field for the username, select the host that this user can connect from as being the Local machine, and give the user a password by typing it into the two boxes provided. The privileges that you can assign on this page are global privileges for the database server as a whole, and if you assign the privileges here, this user will have the privileges you assign over all the databases in your server. We will instead want to assign privileges to only the tvnews database, so click the Go button.

The new user will be created and you will be taken to the page that you saw earlier when changing the root password. Scroll down to the section titled Database-specific privileges and select the tvnews database from the list provided (see Figure 2-30).

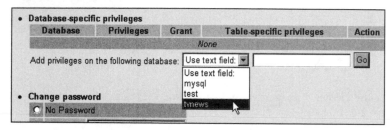

**Figure 2-30.** Assigning privileges on the tvnews database

Now check the boxes for Select, Insert, Update, and Delete privileges, as shown in Figure 2-31. The other privileges should only be assigned to an administrative user. Click Go and the privileges will be added. Once you have reloaded the MySQL server privileges again, this user will be available.

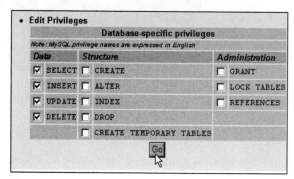

**Figure 2-31.** Assigning privileges on the tvnews database

# Development

Now that we know what we are aiming for, and what the underlying structure to support it is, we can start coding.

## Setting up

The first thing that we will have to do is set up our development environment. We'll be using the Apache web server, PHP as a scripting language, and MySQL as the database back-end. I am assuming that you have these set up and running.

In the document root folder for your website, create a folder called tvnews and a sub-folder called images. Then in Dreamweaver, create a new site, as shown in Figure 2-32.

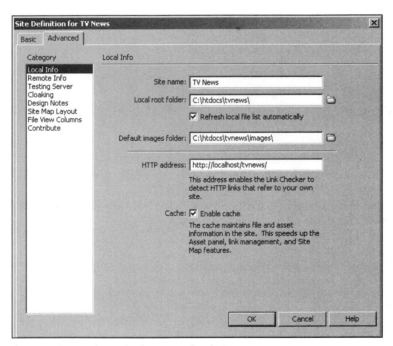

**Figure 2-32.** Creating a site for our project in Dreamweaver

The site is named TV News. The C:\htdocs folder on my machine is the Apache document root folder, so we set the local root folder of the site to C:\htdocs\tvnews. If you have installed Apache to the default location, then this will be C:\Program Files\Apache Group\ Apache2\htdocs\. We also set the images folder and the HTTP address of the site.

The next thing to do is specify the testing server. We're using the PHP MySQL server technology and accessing the files through our local machine (see Figure 2-33).

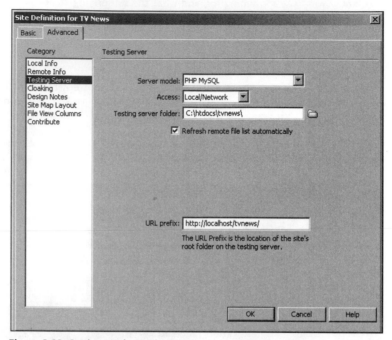

**Figure 2-33.** Setting up the testing server

Once we've set that up, we can click OK to add the site. Select the site and we should see our new site in the Files panel (see Figure 2-34).

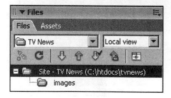

**Figure 2-34.**
The Files panel showing the contents of our site

Now that we have our site, we can go ahead and create our first page. Choose File ➤ New and select a Dynamic page, specifying PHP, as shown in Figure 2-35.

You can save this file as admin.php as the first page that we will be creating is the admin page for our site, so that we can create categories, links, and news articles.

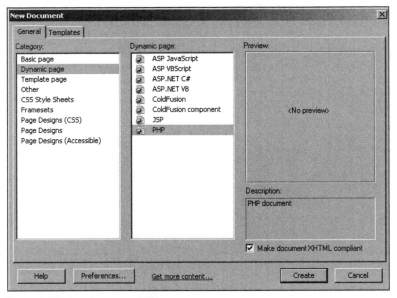

**Figure 2-35.** Creating a new PHP page

# admin.php

The first thing to do is add a connection to our database. From the Application panel, choose the Database tab, click the + button, and choose MySQL Connection. Then enter in the relevant information for your setup, as shown in Figure 2-36.

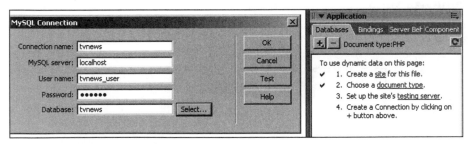

**Figure 2-36.** Adding a database connection

Now in your Application panel, Databases tab you will be able to browse through the hierarchy of your database (see Figure 2-37).

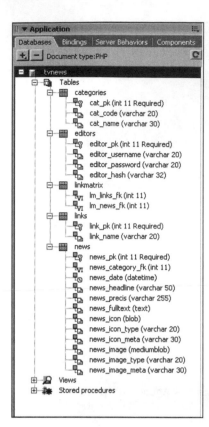

**Figure 2-37.**
The database structure can be viewed but not altered.

This may be an admin page, but we still want it to look decent, so let's create a style sheet for the page. We'll base the page layout and design on the look and feel for the main site. Our admin page will not have as complex a layout as our main pages in the site, so we can use a scaled-down version of the styles that we will need for the main pages.

## tvnews.css

In the Design panel, choose the CSS styles tab, and click the New CSS Style button, as shown in Figure 2-38.

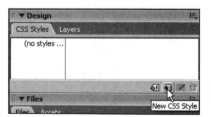

**Figure 2-38.**
Adding a new style

The New CSS Style dialog box is displayed. Select the option button that lets you redefine a tag and select the body tag from the list of HTML tags. We'll want to create this style in a new style sheet file (see Figure 2-39).

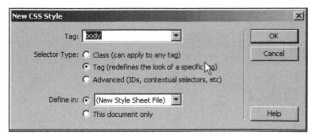

**Figure 2-39.** New CSS Style dialog box

Click OK and you will be prompted to save the new style sheet file (see Figure 2-40). Save this file as `admin.css`.

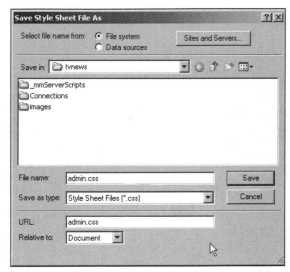

**Figure 2-40.** Saving the new style sheet

All that we will be defining in the <body> tag is the background color for the page, the margin offset for content in the page, and the font. Select a decent font like Verdana or Arial and set the font size to 12 pixels. Set the margin to 0 pixels and the background color to white. Click OK to add the body style to the `admin.css` style sheet.

The full style sheet is shown in the following code. You can either enter it by hand by opening the `admin.css` page in Dreamweaver, or use the Dreamweaver style sheet dialog boxes to add each individual style. The style elements that you see starting with a # symbol are style IDs and must be added by selecting the Advanced option as shown in Figure 2-41.

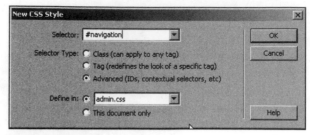

**Figure 2-41.** Creating a new style ID

Here then is the full listing for admin.css:

```css
body {
  font: 12px Verdana, Geneva, Arial, Helvetica, sans-serif;
  color: #000000;
  background: #ffffff;
  margin: 0px;
}
h1 {
  color: #ffffff;
  margin-bottom: 0px;
  margin-top: 0px;
  margin-right: 20px;
  font-size: 22px;
  font-weight: bold;
  float: left;
}
#head {
  background: #003366;
  margin-top: 0px;
  height: 35px;
  width: 680px;
  border-bottom: 3px solid #ffffff;
  float: left;
}
#header {
  height: 35px;
  padding: 0px;
  vertical-align: bottom;
}
#content {
  background: #FCFFE6;
  margin-top: 0px;
  padding: 10px;
  width: 660px;
  border-top: 1px solid #003366;
  float: left;
}
.text {
```

```
      font: 12px Verdana, Geneva, Arial, Helvetica, sans-serif;
      color: #000000;
      background-color: #F2E2A2;
      border: 1px solid #000000;
      width: 130px;
}
#button {
      font: 12px Verdana, Geneva, Arial, Helvetica, sans-serif;
      font-weight: bold;
      color: #FFFFFF;
      background-color: #990000;
      border: none;
}
```

As you can see, the CSS file is quite lengthy, but this is because we have moved all of the presentation of the page from the page itself and included it in the CSS file. Once this file is cached in the client browser, individual page downloads on the site will be a lot smaller, and any changes you want to make to the style can be changed in a single file. Let's take a look now at the code for admin.php. Simply by creating the new file and linking to the admin.css file you should already have the following code in your page:

```
<!DOCTYPE
html PUBLIC "-//W3C//DTD XHTML 1.0 Transitional//EN"
"http://www.w3.org/TR/xhtml1/DTD/xhtml1-transitional.dtd">
<html xmlns="http://www.w3.org/1999/xhtml">
<head>
<title>TV News Admin</title>
<meta http-equiv="Content-Type"
content="text/html; charset=iso-8859-1" />
<link href="admin.css" rel="stylesheet" type="text/css" />
</head>

<body>

</body>
</html>
```

To add the overall layout of the page, we add the following code within the body section of the page:

```
<div id="head">
 <table id="header">
  <tr>
   <td>
    <h1>TV NEWS Admin</h1></td>
   </tr>
 </table>
</div>
<div id="content">
</div>
```

If you take a look at this in Design view in Dreamweaver, it looks a bit strange because Dreamweaver isn't rendering the table in the header correctly, as you can see in Figure 2-42.

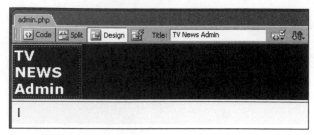

**Figure 2-42.** Our page in Dreamweaver

If you preview the page in a browser you will see that it looks just fine, as shown in Figure 2-43.

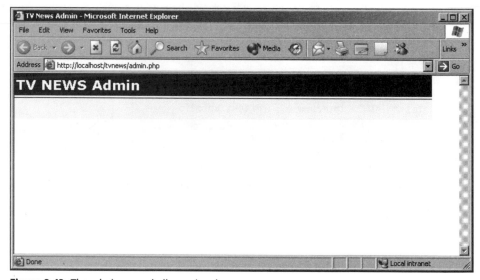

**Figure 2-43.** The admin page shell seen in a browser

As you can see from the HTML, our page is made up of two <div> tags—the first contains a table, for the simple reason that I wanted all of the elements in the header to align to the bottom of the header. Doing this in CSS would have involved setting top margins to push the text down—a fiddly solution that will break if we decide to change the font size in the future. Although tables are not supposed to be used for presentation purposes, it makes sense to use them when they are a neater and quicker option.

The styles applied to the two `<div>` tags take care of the rest. Now we can get on and build the actual admin section.

## Logging in

The first task that we have to take care of is handling user authentication. We don't want anyone who stumbles across this page to be able to change the contents of the site, so let's secure the page.

Dreamweaver MX 2004 ships with a set of Server Behaviors that allow you to handle user authentication and page security. With them you can restrict users who have not logged in from seeing the contents of your pages, and provide a quick and easy way for them to log in. Unfortunately, PHP has moved on since these Server Behaviors were first written and they use some code that has been deprecated in later versions of PHP. Let's go ahead and add the login code for the page and then we'll see how we can fix it so that it works with the latest versions of PHP.

The user authentication Server Behaviors work by checking if you have logged in or not—if you haven't, they redirect you to a page for unauthorized users. In our case we'll want that to be the login page, so before we do anything else, save the admin.php file if you haven't already, then save a copy of it as login.php. The login.php page is the page where users will be able to log themselves in. To this page, add some text and a simple form that asks for the user's login name and password (see Figure 2-44).

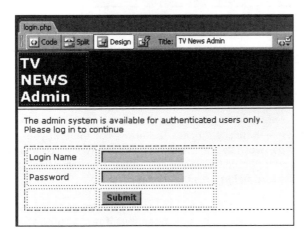

**Figure 2-44.** Our login form

Now comes the easy part. From the Server Behaviors **tab** select User Authentication ➤ Log In User Server Behavior. **The form that pops up looks a bit daunting but it's quite straight-forward.

Figure 2-45 shows the dialog box filled out for my form.

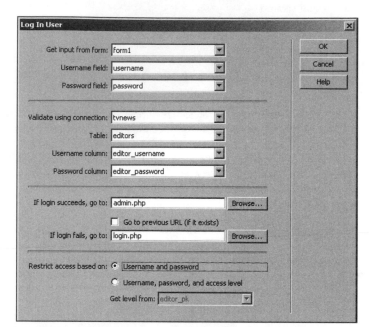

**Figure 2-45.** Filling in the Log In User dialog box

The first set of drop-down boxes let you specify which elements in your page are used to collect the information. We will be getting the username from a text field called username and the password from a text field called password in form1. These will relate to whatever you named your two text fields.

The second section of the dialog box is for you to set up how the Server Behavior must authenticate the user—basically it needs to know what table in your database to match the username and password against. We'll be using the tvnews connection, and our login details will be stored in the editors table. The editor_username field stores the username and the editor_password field stores the password.

The next section determines what must happen if you manage to log in successfully or not. If you do then you will continue to admin.php, but if not, you remain on the login.php page.

The last section of the dialog box specifies whether we are to use levels or not in the login—this provides a level of control where you can restrict pages to users who are of a certain category or level. We won't have this level of control in our pages, so leave this as only username and password.

Click OK to add the Server Behavior to the page.

Once the Server Behavior has been added, we need to make a small change in Code view so that we can actually log in on newer versions of PHP. Switch to Code view and look for the following block of code:

```
//declare two session variables and assign them
$GLOBALS['MM_Username'] = $loginUsername;
$GLOBALS['MM_UserGroup'] = $loginStrGroup;

//register the session variables
session_register("MM_Username");
session_register("MM_UserGroup");
```

What this code does first is set two global variables to the values of your user's login name and the login group they belong to. They then register two session variables called MM_Username and MM_UserGroup that the rest of the Macromedia User Authentication Server Behaviors will look for and use. There is a slight problem in that PHP version 4.2.0 session_register() has been deprecated because of security issues with automatically making variables global in scope, but this is easy to fix. All we need to do is remove the two lines that use the session_register() function and then change the $GLOBALS to use the new $_SESSION variable—the new preferred way of working with session variables. The block of code shown previously will change to be simply

```
//declare two session variables and assign them
$_SESSION['MM_Username'] = $loginUsername;
$_SESSION['MM_UserGroup'] = $loginStrGroup;
```

Save the file and open the admin.php page. This page needs to be restricted to users who have logged in, as shown in Figure 2-46—all that you need to do is select User Authentication ➤ Restrict Access To Page Server Behavior.

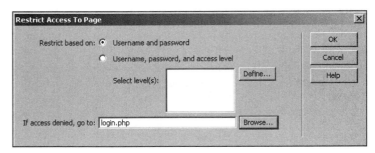

**Figure 2-46.** Restricting access to the admin.php page

The Restrict Access To Page dialog box is simple to fill in—simply select the type of access you want—in our case just a username and password and then enter the name of the page to redirect to if the user is not authenticated, login.php. Click OK to add the Server Behavior.

The Restrict Access To Page Server Behavior uses the $_SESSION variables correctly, so we won't need to make any changes to the page for this to work.

Before we can test this we need to add a record to the editors table, so that the Server Behavior has something to authenticate with. Open phpMyAdmin again, log in, and browse to the editors table in the tvnews database. Click the Insert tab and you can fill in the details for your user, as shown in Figure 2-47.

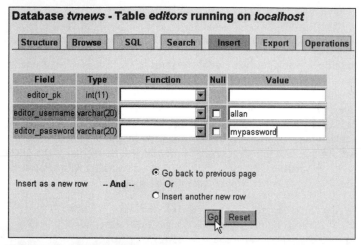

**Figure 2-47.** Creating an editor login

You don't have to enter a value for the editor_pk field as this will be automatically generated for you by MySQL. Click Go and the record will be added. Notice also that the password is not encrypted in the database. The User Authentication Server Behavior does not work with encrypted passwords in its default state. If you wanted to encrypt your passwords, you would be able to, but you would have to edit the code generated by the Server Behavior for logging in users.

Once you have added your editor, browse to the admin.php page. It should automatically redirect you to the login.php page. Enter the details for your editor and click Submit—you will be taken to the admin.php page. The contents for admin.php can contain functions to add new editor logins, manage the categories for news articles, and add new articles to the database. Let's look at how we can add news articles to the page.

## Adding news articles

In order to add news stories, we will build a form for entering the relevant news information. Part of that information will be drop-down boxes for the category of the news item and the link item, so we will need to create Recordsets for each of these: rstCategories and rstLinks (see Figures 2-48 and 2-49).

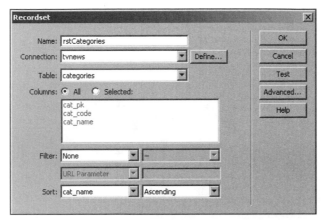

**Figure 2-48.** The rstCategories Recordset

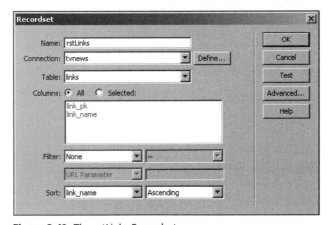

**Figure 2-49.** The rstLinks Recordset

Now, we build a form in the page to collect the information for the new news article (see Figure 2-50).

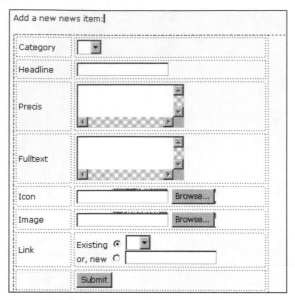

**Figure 2-50.** The form for capturing new articles

The form elements in the page are laid out in the following table:

| Label | Type | Name | Initial State | Value |
|-------|------|------|---------------|-------|
| Category | TextField | news_category_fk | -- | -- |
| Headline | TextField | news_headline | -- | -- |
| Precis | TextArea | news_precis | -- | -- |
| Fulltext | TextArea | news_fulltext | -- | -- |
| Icon | FileField | news_icon | -- | -- |
| Image | FileField | news_image | -- | -- |
| Link | RadioButton | radioLink | Checked | existing |
| -- | ListMenu | news_link | -- | -- |
| -- | RadioButton | radioLink | -- | new |
| -- | TextField | news_link_text | -- | -- |
| Submit | SubmitButton | Submit | -- | -- |
| -- | Hidden | MAX_FILE_SIZE | -- | 100000 |

The values for both of the ListMenu form elements are populated from the Recordsets we added to the page. Select the Category ListMenu and click the Dynamic button in the Properties inspector (see Figure 2-51).

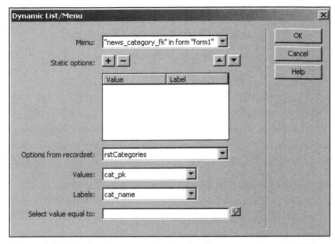

**Figure 2-51.** Setting the dynamic data for the news_category ListMenu

Select rstCategories as the Recordset to get the options from and make the values equal to the cat_pk field and the Labels cat_name.

Do the same for the Links ListMenu, but use the rstLinks Recordset, again making the value the ID field (link_id) and the label the link_name.

The purpose of having a drop-down list for the links, as well as a field to enter one, is that if the link item does not exist, the editor can enter it directly into this form and avoid having to go to a new form to create it first. The Hidden field with the name MAX_FILE_SIZE is for the file upload—it is a guide to the web browser of the maximum size file that we will allow to be uploaded. In this case it is 100K. In order to handle the file upload from the form, we will also need to make sure the form's Enctype is set to multipart/form-data. Select the form and in the Properties inspector set the Enctype and change the form name to frmNews.

The full code for the form should be

```
<form action="" method="post" enctype="multipart/form-data"
name="frmNews" id="frmNews">
  <table width="400" border="0" cellspacing="4" cellpadding="4">
    <tr>
      <td>Category</td>
      <td><select name="news_category_fk" id="news_category_fk">
        <?php
do {
?>
        <option value="<?php echo
```

*Continued*

```php
$row_rstCategories['cat_pk']?>"><?php echo
$row_rstCategories['cat_name']?></option>
          <?php
} while ($row_rstCategories = mysql_fetch_assoc($rstCategories));
  $rows = mysql_num_rows($rstCategories);
  if($rows > 0) {
      mysql_data_seek($rstCategories, 0);
          $row_rstCategories = mysql_fetch_assoc($rstCategories);
  }
?>
        </select></td>
      </tr>
      <tr>
        <td>Headline</td>
        <td><input name="news_headline" type="text"
        ➡id="news_headline" /></td>
      </tr>
      <tr>
        <td>Precis</td>
        <td><textarea name="news_precis"
        ➡id="news_precis"></textarea></td>
      </tr>
      <tr>
        <td>Fulltext</td>
        <td><textarea name="news_fulltext"
        ➡id="news_fulltext"></textarea></td>
      </tr>
      <tr>
        <td>Icon</td>
        <td><input name="news_icon" type="file" id="news_icon" /></td>
      </tr>
      <tr>
        <td>Image</td>
        <td><input name="news_image" type="file"
        ➡id="news_image" /></td>
      </tr>
      <tr>
        <td>Link</td>
        <td>Existing
          <input name="radioLink" type="radio" value="existing"
checked="checked" /> <select name="news_link" id="news_link">
          <?php
do {
?>
          <option value="<?php echo
$row_rstLinks['link_pk']?>"><?php echo
$row_rstLinks['link_name']?></option>
          <?php
} while ($row_rstLinks = mysql_fetch_assoc($rstLinks));
```

```
    $rows = mysql_num_rows($rstLinks);
    if($rows > 0) {
        mysql_data_seek($rstLinks, 0);
          $row_rstLinks = mysql_fetch_assoc($rstLinks);
    }
?>
            </select>
          <br />
or, new         <input name="radioLink" type="radio" value="new" />
<input name="news_link_text" type="text"
id="news_link_text" /></td>
      </tr>
      <tr>
        <td><input name="MAX_FILE_SIZE" type="hidden"
id="MAX_FILE_SIZE" value="1000000" /></td>
        <td><input type="submit" name="Submit" value="Submit" /></td>
      </tr>
    </table>
  </form>
```

We can now go ahead and add the Insert Record Server Behavior. Because we named our form fields the same as the field names in the news table, Dreamweaver will automatically match them up for us (see Figure 2-52).

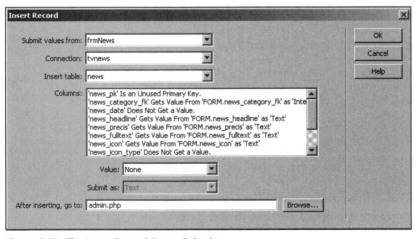

**Figure 2-52.** The Insert Record Server Behavior

If you scroll down through the Columns box in the dialog box you'll notice that some of the columns don't get values from our form. This is because these are values that we will have to calculate and determine manually. Switch to Code view and we'll take a look at that.

First, find the block of code that handles inserting the record into the database. The block of code is shown here:

```
if ((isset($_POST["MM_insert"])) && ($_POST["MM_insert"] == "frmNews"))
{
  $insertSQL = sprintf("INSERT INTO news
(news_category_fk, news_headline, news_precis, news_fulltext,
 news_icon, news_image) VALUES (%s, %s, %s, %s, %s, %s)",
             GetSQLValueString($_POST['news_category_fk'], "int"),
             GetSQLValueString($_POST['news_headline'], "text"),
             GetSQLValueString($_POST['news_precis'], "text"),
             GetSQLValueString($_POST['news_fulltext'], "text"),
             GetSQLValueString($_POST['news_icon'], "text"),
             GetSQLValueString($_POST['news_image'], "text"));

  mysql_select_db($database_tvnews, $tvnews);
  $Result1 = mysql_query($insertSQL, $tvnews) or die(mysql_error());

  $insertGoTo = "admin.php";
  if (isset($_SERVER['QUERY_STRING'])) {
    $insertGoTo .= (strpos($insertGoTo, '?')) ? "&" : "?";
    $insertGoTo .= $_SERVER['QUERY_STRING'];
  }
  header(sprintf("Location: %s", $insertGoTo));
}
```

Basically what this code is doing is grabbing the relevant form fields from the page and matching them with the columns in the database table and building an SQL query to insert the data. The GetSQLValueString() function you can find at the top of the page—this takes care of handling quotes in the string and returns the value in the correct format for adding to the database.

The changes that we are going to have to make are

1. Adding the current time that the record was added

2. Formatting the précis and the text of the article so that it displays correctly in HTML

3. Handling the images uploaded for the icon and the article by reading in their actual data and determining their width, height, and type

This sounds like a lot of work, but you'll see that it's not that bad. The changed code is shown here, after which we will go through it bit by bit and look at what it is actually doing.

```
if ((isset($_POST["MM_insert"])) && ($_POST["MM_insert"] == "frmNews"))
{
  if(is_uploaded_file($_FILES['news_icon']['tmp_name'])) {
    $news_icon = implode ('', file($_FILES['news_icon']['tmp_name']));
    $news_icon_type = $_FILES['news_icon']['type'];
```

```php
  $news_icon_meta = implode('',
array_slice(getimagesize($_FILES['news_icon']['tmp_name']),3,1));
  }
  if(is_uploaded_file($_FILES['news_image']['tmp_name'])) {
   $news_image = implode ('', file($_FILES['news_image']['tmp_name']));
   $news_image_type = $_FILES['news_image']['type'];
   $news_image_meta = implode('',
array_slice(getimagesize($_FILES['news_image']['tmp_name']),3,1));
  }


  $insertSQL = sprintf("INSERT INTO news
(news_category_fk, news_date, news_headline, news_precis,
news_fulltext, news_icon, news_icon_type, news_icon_meta,
news_image, news_image_type, news_image_meta)
VALUES (%s, NOW(), %s, %s, %s, %s, %s, %s, %s, %s, %s)",
            GetSQLValueString($_POST['news_category_fk'], "int"),
            GetSQLValueString($_POST['news_headline'], "text"),
            GetSQLValueString(nl2br($_POST['news_precis']), "text"),
            GetSQLValueString(nl2br($_POST['news_fulltext']), "text"),
            GetSQLValueString(addslashes($news_icon), "text"),
            GetSQLValueString($news_icon_type, "text"),
            GetSQLValueString($news_icon_meta, "text"),
            GetSQLValueString(addslashes($news_image), "text"),
            GetSQLValueString($news_image_type, "text"),
            GetSQLValueString($news_image_meta, "text"));

 mysql_select_db($database_tvnews, $tvnews);
 $Result1 = mysql_query($insertSQL, $tvnews) or die(mysql_error());

 $newsItem = mysql_insert_id();

 if($_POST['radioLink']=='new' &&
strlen(trim($_POST['news_link_text'])) > 0) {
   $insertSQL = sprintf("INSERT INTO links (link_name) VALUES (%s)",
GetSQLValueString($HTTP_POST_VARS['news_link_text'],"text"));
     mysql_select_db($database_tvnews, $tvnews);
     $Result2 = mysql_query($insertSQL, $tvnews) or
die(mysql_error());
     $linkItem = mysql_insert_id();
 } else {
   $linkItem = $_POST['news_link'];
 }
 if ($linkItem > 0 && $newsItem > 0) {
   $insertSQL = sprintf("INSERT INTO linkmatrix
(lm_links_fk, lm_news_fk) VALUES (%s, %s)",
       GETSQLValueString($linkItem,"int'),

       GETSQLValueString($newsItem,"int"));
```

*Continued*

```
        mysql_select_db($database_tvnews, $tvnews);
        $Result3 = mysql_query($insertSQL, $tvnews) or
    die($insertSQL.mysql_error());
      }

      $insertGoTo = "admin.php?stamp=".time();
      header(sprintf("Location: %s", $insertGoTo));
    }
```

OK, let's work through the code. The first line remains the same—we're just checking to make sure that the form has been POSTed.

```
    if ((isset($_POST["MM_insert"])) && ($_POST["MM_insert"]
    ➥== "frmNews")) {
```

This next section is new—in it we are going to check to see if the user has included a file in the news_icon field, and handle it accordingly. The function is_uploaded_file() tests to see whether the file name that has been passed to it is in fact a file that has just been uploaded.

```
    if(is_uploaded_file($_FILES['news_icon']['tmp_name'])) {
```

The $_FILES array provides you with any of the information that you need about the file:

| Key | Purpose |
| --- | --- |
| name | Original filename on the person's machine. |
| type | The MIME type of the image. |
| size | The size of the file that was uploaded in bytes. |
| tmp_name | The temporary filename where the uploaded file is being stored. |
| error | An error code for the upload. If an error occurred, you can use this to determine what went wrong. |

```
        $news_icon = implode ('', file($_FILES['news_icon']['tmp_name']));
        $news_icon_type = $_FILES['news_icon']['type'];
        $news_icon_meta = implode('',
    array_slice(getimagesize($_FILES['news_icon']['tmp_name']),3,1));
      }
```

First we grab the contents of the image file. The file() function returns an array of lines of data for the file specified, implode() joins those array elements together into a single variable, joining them with the character specified. Since we don't want to introduce any extra characters into our image data, we join the elements with a blank. This combination of implode() and file() is a neat way of pulling the contents of a file into a single variable.

> *If you are using PHP version 4.3.0 or later, you can do the same thing in a single step with the* `file_get_contents()` *function—this file reads the contents of a file from disk into memory and returns the contents to you in a string variable. The PHP can be simplified to*
>
> `implode ('', file($_FILES['news_icon']['tmp_name']))`
>
> `file_get_contents($_FILES['news_icon']['tmp_name']).`

We then need to know what type of file we are dealing with. This is not important for storing the data in the database, but we will need it later when we output our image data to the browser—we'll need to send a header to the browser, telling it what type of data to expect, and we'll get that from the `$_FILES['news_icon']['type']` variable.

The last piece of information that we need is the width and height of the image. We'll use this when displaying it in the page so that the browser renders the page correctly the first time and doesn't have to move data around as the images download into the page. It's also good practice to do this. The way that we will get the width and height is by using the function `getimagesize()`—this returns an array specifying the width, height, and type of the image, and more importantly, it also supplies a text string with the `height=""` and `width=""` strings that can be plugged directly into an `<image>` tag. Since the `getimagesize()` function returns an array, we'll need to extract just the element that we need (index 3). The `array_slice()` also returns an array, so we'll use our trusty `implode()` function on the returned array to convert it to a string.

We then go through the same process for the image data:

```
    if(is_uploaded_file($_FILES['news_image']['tmp_name'])) {
      $news_image = implode ('', file($_FILES['news_image']['tmp_name']));
      $news_image_type = $_FILES['news_image']['type'];
      $news_image_meta = implode('',
    array_slice(getimagesize($_FILES['news_image']['tmp_name']),3,1));
      }
```

And now we can build the SQL command to insert our news record. I've altered the original line quite substantially, adding in our additional fields. We're adding the news_date, which will simply be the MySQL NOW() function, and then the four additional fields with the extra image information in them.

```
    $insertSQL = sprintf("INSERT INTO news
    (news_category_fk, news_date, news_headline, news_precis,
     news_fulltext, news_icon, news_icon_type, news_icon_meta,
    news_image, news_image_type, news_image_meta)
    VALUES (%s, NOW(), %s, %s, %s, %s, %s, %s, %s, %s, %s)",
                GetSQLValueString($_POST['news_category_fk'], "int"),
                GetSQLValueString($_POST['news_headline'], "text"),
```

Our text is coming from a textarea input, so we will want to convert any newline characters to <br /> characters when we store it in the database so that the spacing is preserved:

```
GetSQLValueString(nl2br($_POST['news_precis']), "text"),
GetSQLValueString(nl2br($_POST['news_fulltext']), "text"),
```

In our altered SQL we need to include the image data in the query, as that is what is being stored in the database. Since our image data is binary, we don't know what sort of characters could appear in the data, so we must use the addslashes() function to escape any characters that could cause our SQL to break (such as quotes). We then add the values for the image type and metadata (width and height string). Both of these values are textual. Do the same for both the icon and the image.

```
GetSQLValueString(addslashes($news_icon), "text"),
GetSQLValueString($news_icon_type, "text"),
GetSQLValueString($news_icon_meta, "text"),
GetSQLValueString(addslashes($news_image), "text"),
GetSQLValueString($news_image_type, "text"),
GetSQLValueString($news_image_meta, "text"));
```

```
mysql_select_db($database_tvnews, $tvnews);
$Result1 = mysql_query($insertSQL, $tvnews) or die(mysql_error());
```

Once we have run the query, we need to get the primary key of the record that we just inserted. We'll use this in the linkmatrix table to create the links between news stories:

```
$newsItem = mysql_insert_id();
```

The next block of code has to do with the portion of the form where we had the radio buttons for selecting either an existing or a new link item value. We need to determine which the person has chosen and if necessary insert the link item into the database. We check to see if the person has selected the new radio button, and also that the value they have entered is not blank:

```
if($_POST['radioLink']=='new' &&
strlen(trim($_POST['ews_link_text'])) > 0) {
```

If they have selected new and entered a value, we build the SQL string and execute the query:

```
$insertSQL = sprintf("INSERT INTO links (link_name) VALUES (%s)",
GetSQLValueString($HTTP_POST_VARS['news_link_text'],"text"));
    mysql_select_db($database_tvnews, $tvnews);
    $Result2 = mysql_query($insertSQL, $tvnews) or
die(mysql_error());
```

We will need this new link items primary key to use in the linkmatrix table:

```
    $linkItem = mysql_insert_id();
} else {
```

if they have chosen an existing `linkItem`, then we grab the value they chose from the drop-down list:

```
$linkItem = $_POST['news_link'];
}
```

Our form does not have any error checking to see whether the person has chosen a valid link item, or that they have bothered filling any of the fields in. This is something that you could handle at the client side with a JavaScript Validate Form Behavior. To save space I've left that out here, as it's fairly straightforward to implement. We're also dealing with the editors of news stories here and not the general public, so we can assume a certain level of training in the use of the admin tool. This is not to say that they won't put some strange data in the form, but for now, let's assume they get it right.

To make sure we don't get strange results in our linkmatrix table, we check to see that both the link item primary key and the news story primary key are both greater than 0 before inserting the record in the linkmatrix table. If one of these is not greater than 0, then a previous insert failed or something went wrong in the page and we should not try and create the link.

```
if ($linkItem > 0 && $newsItem > 0) {
    $insertSQL = sprintf("INSERT INTO linkmatrix
(lm_links_fk, lm_news_fk) VALUES (%s, %s)",
        GETSQLValueString($linkItem,"int"),
        GETSQLValueString($newsItem,"int"));
    mysql_select_db($database_tvnews, $tvnews);
    $Result3 = mysql_query($insertSQL, $tvnews) or
    ➥die($insertSQL.mysql_error());
}
```

Once we have done inserting our records we can redirect back to the admin page. I've removed the Macromedia code that appends the existing query string to the page, as all we want to append is the current Unix timestamp—this will make sure that the page we redirect to is always refreshed by the browser:

```
$insertGoTo = "admin.php?stamp=".time();
header(sprintf("Location: %s", $insertGoTo));
}
```

Before we try and insert some records into the news table, we will need some categories to put them in. Here is the sample data that I have in my database for the categories, which you'll need to add to the database using your administration program:

```
INSERT INTO categories VALUES (1,'africa','Africa');
INSERT INTO categories VALUES (2,'asiapacific','Asia Pacific');
INSERT INTO categories VALUES (3,'europe','Europe');
INSERT INTO categories VALUES (4,'northamerica','North America');
INSERT INTO categories VALUES (5,'southamerica','South America');
INSERT INTO categories VALUES (6,'worldnews','World News');
INSERT INTO categories VALUES (7,'business','Business');
```

*Continued*

```
INSERT INTO categories VALUES (8,'entertainment','Entertainment');
INSERT INTO categories VALUES (9,'science','Science');
INSERT INTO categories VALUES (10,'sport','Sport');
INSERT INTO categories VALUES (11,'technology','Technology');
```

Now that we have some categories in our database we can go ahead and add our first news article, as shown in Figure 2-53.

You'll notice that I've enlarged the text areas somewhat to make it easier to put the text in. Our drop-down box of existing link items is empty, so I've selected to create a new one and entered it as Slapfight.

After clicking Submit I am redirected back to the admin page, and I can now go take a look at the data in the database to see what has been inserted. You'll notice in the admin page now that Slapfight is available as an existing link item in the Links ListMenu.

In phpMyAdmin choose the Browse option to view the data in the news table. Figure 2-54 provides a partial screenshot of the data.

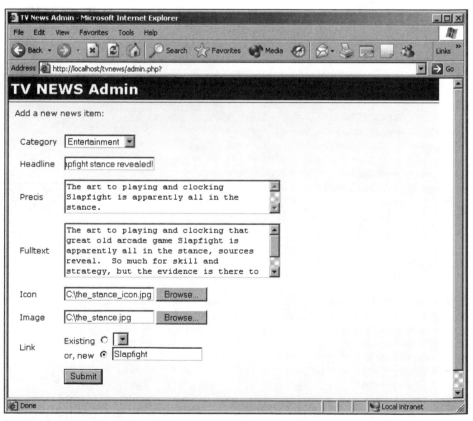

**Figure 2-53.** Adding our first news item

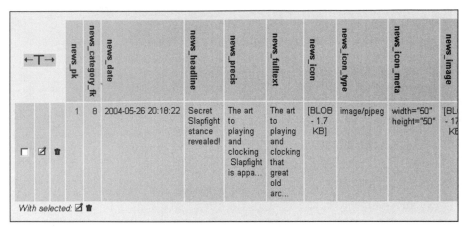

**Figure 2-54.** The data for our first news article in phpMyAdmin

All of the data is there in the news table. The primary key of this record is 1, so we will look out for that in the linkmatrix table. Take a look at Figures 2-55 and 2-56 to see what is in the links and linkmatrix tables.

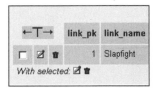

**Figure 2-55.** The data in the links table

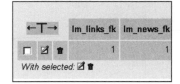

**Figure 2-56.** The linkmatrix table

The link item is the first one entered into the database, and so also has the primary key of 1—in the linkmatrix table you can see that the news item and the link item are correctly represented.

Now, to see how our article looks in the main page, we need to go and create it.

# index.php

The layout for your index.php page will be quite similar to that of the admin page. We can use both the admin.php page and the admin.css file as a basis for building the main page.

Here is the code for the tvnews.css file, which we will use for styling all of the pages within our public portion of the site:

```
body {
    font: 12px Verdana, Geneva, Arial, Helvetica, sans-serif;
    color: #000000;
    background: #ffffff;
```

*Continued*

```
    margin: 0px;
}
p {
    font: 12px Verdana, Geneva, Arial, Helvetica, sans-serif;
    margin-top: 0px;
    margin-bottom: 5px;
    margin-left: 5px;
    margin-right: 5px;
    text-align: justify;
    clear: both;
}
.HeadLine {
    font: 13px Verdana, Geneva, Arial, Helvetica, sans-serif;
    font-weight: bold;
    color: #336699;
}
.NewsDate {
    font: 10px Verdana, Geneva, Arial, Helvetica, sans-serif;
    color: #666666;
}
a:link {
    text-decoration: none;
    color: #003366;
}
a:visited {
    text-decoration: none;
    color: #003366;
}
a:hover, a:active {
    text-decoration: underline;
    color: #003366;
}
h1 {
    margin-bottom: 0px;
    font-size: 22px;
    font-weight: bold;
}
#head {
    color: White;
    background: #003366;
    margin-top: 0px;
    width: 680px;
    border-bottom: 3px solid #ffffff;
    float: left;
}
#head form {
    margin: 0px;
    padding: 0px;
    clear: none;
```

2

```
}
#header {
  height: 35px;
  padding: 0px;
  width: 100%;
}
#header td {
  vertical-align: bottom;
}
.toolbox {
  text-align: right;
}
#content {
  background: #FCFFE6;
  margin-top: 0px;
  width: 680px;
  border-top: 1px solid #003366;
float: left;
}
#navigation {
  width: 125px;
  color: #003366;
  background: #F1E1A1;
  float: left;
}
#navigation ul {
  margin: 0;
  padding: 0;
  list-style-type: none;
}
#navigation li {
  margin: 0;
}

#navigation a {
  font-weight: bold;
  display: block;
  padding: 0px 0px 0px 15px;
  width: 125px;
}
#navigation a:link, #navigation a:visited {
  text-decoration: none;
}
#navigation a:hover, #navigation a:active {
  text-decoration: none;
  color: #000033;
}
#navCurrent {
```

*Continued*

```
      background-image:  url(images/nav_current.png);
      background-repeat: no-repeat;
      background-position: 0% 50%;
    }
    #article {
      width: 350px;
      float: left;
    }
    #sidebar {
       width: 178px;
      float: right;
    }
    #sidebar ul {
      list-style-image: url(images/bullet.gif);
      margin: 0px;
      margin-left: 10px;
      padding: 0px;
      padding-left: 10px;
    }
    .imgLeft {
      float: left;
      padding: 3px;
    }
    .More {
      float: right;
    }
    .text {
      font: 12px Verdana, Geneva, Arial, Helvetica, sans-serif;
      color: #000000;
      background-color: #F2E2A2;
      border: 1px solid #000000;
      width: 130px;
    }
    .button {
      font: 12px Verdana, Geneva, Arial, Helvetica, sans-serif;
      font-weight: bold;
      color: #FFFFFF;
      background-color: #990000;
      border: none;
    }
```

As you can see, we have set up the overall styles for the body, paragraphs, links, and headings, and then all of the remainder CSS code uses IDs to refer to specific elements within the page. The IDs that we give to elements in our page will automatically retrieve the correct style from the style sheet.

The basic code for the layout of the page is shown here:

```
<!DOCTYPE html PUBLIC "-//W3C//DTD XHTML 1.0 Strict//EN"
  "http://www.w3.org/TR/xhtml1/DTD/xhtml1-strict.dtd">
<html>
<head>
  <title>TV News</title>
  <link href="tvnews.css" rel="stylesheet" type="text/css" />
</head>
<body>
<div id="head">
<table id="header">
  <tr>
   <td>
     <h1>TV NEWS <h1></td>
   <td class="toolbox">
     toolbox</td>
   </tr>
 </table></div>
<div id="content">
 <div id="navigation">
 <ul>
 <li><a href="#">Home</a></li>
 </ul>
 </div>
 <div id="article">
  </div>
 <div id="sidebar">
  </div>
 </div>
 </body>
 </html>
```

This very basic code combined with our style sheet provides us with a layout that is very similar to the admin page, except that we have a navigation bar on the left and an area of sidebars on the right. In Figure 2-57 you can see the page layout as well as the highlighted sidebar area on the right.

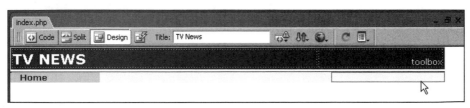

**Figure 2-57.** Our page layout in Dreamweaver

Because the navigation, content, and sidebar areas are simple <div> tags that are placed and styled with CSS, we can very easily alter the layout of the overall page, just by modifying the CSS file.

But let's start building the page dynamically. The first thing that we will want to do is build the navigation area on the left. I've added in a navigation item to the homepage as a placeholder; we'll replace this with the actual categories now. Create a Recordset called rstCategories, exactly as we did for the admin page. The screenshot of the Recordset dialog box can be seen in Figure 2-58 if you need to jog your memory. Now that we have the Recordset, we can use this dynamic data in the page. First, switch to Code view, delete the Home text, and insert a Dynamic Text Server Behavior in its place, displaying the cat_name column from the rstCategories Recordset.

Next, using the Tag Selector in the status bar, select the <a> tag and click the Browse for File button in the Properties inspector. This will bring up the Select File dialog box for you to choose a file to link to. We'll link to index.php, but we will pass the selected category code as a parameter to the page. Click the Parameters button and add a parameter called category that has the value of cat_code from the rstCategories Recordset. Click OK to add the parameter and OK to update the link. Now we need to make sure that this is repeated for every category, so select the entire <li> tag and apply a Repeat Region Server Behavior to it, repeating for every record in the rstCategories Recordset.

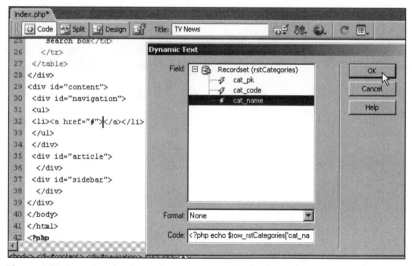

**Figure 2-58.** Inserting the Dynamic Text Server Behavior in Code view

The code for your navigation should read as follows:

```
<ul>
   <?php do { ?>
   <li><a href="index.php?category=<?php echo
 $row_rstCategories['cat_code']; ?>"><?php
echo $row_rstCategories['cat_name']; ?></a></li>
   <?php } while ($row_rstCategories =
mysql_fetch_assoc($rstCategories)); ?>
 </ul>
```

Save the page and view it in a browser. You can see in Figure 2-59 that the navigation has all been dynamically created from the database and the links point to the correct places. The beauty of creating the navigation in this way is that, if you create a new category, it is automatically added to all of your pages without your needing to go and edit any pages themselves.

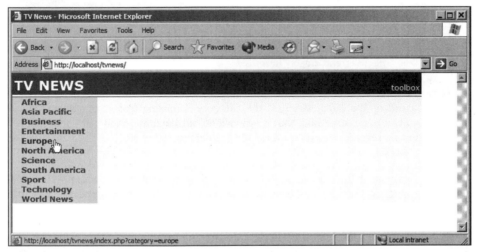

**Figure 2-59.** Navigation added dynamically

If you try and navigate to any of the sections, you'll notice that nothing happens. Let's now make the page display to you the section that you are currently in.

Create a new Recordset called rstCurrentCategory. Figure 2-60 shows the setup for the Recordset.

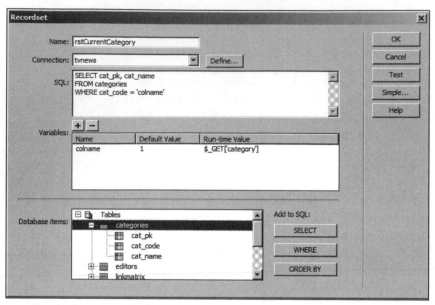

**Figure 2-60.** The rstCurrentCategory Recordset

We're simply selecting the record from the categories table where the category is equal to the one passed on the query string. If the category is missing from the query string or someone edits it to be something that is not valid in our database, then our Recordset will simply return no records. We can now include the data from our rstCurrentCategory in the page.

First, add a Dynamic Text Server Behavior displaying the cat_name column from the rstCurrentCategory after the TV News heading. This will only display if there is a record returned in rstCurrentCategory. If you remember our CSS for the page, we had an ID selector defined called #navCurrent, which set a small background image. What we need to do is test each of our link items in the navigation, and if the category for the current link item is the same as the current category, then we must set the ID of that item to navCurrent. The code that you have for the <li> tag is as follows:

```
<li><a href="index.php?category=<?php echo
$row_rstCategories['cat_code']; ?>">
<?php echo $row_rstCategories['cat_name']; ?></a></li>
```

Change it to read

```
<li><a href="index.php?category=<?php echo
$row_rstCategories['cat_code']; ?>"
<?php if ($row_rstCategories['cat_pk']==$row_rstCurrentCategory
['cat_pk']) echo " id=\"navCurrent\""; ?>><?php echo
$row_rstCategories['cat_name']
; ?></a></li>
```

The code that we have added is the following piece of PHP:

```
<?php if ($row_rstCategories['cat_pk']==$row_rstCurrentCategory
['cat_pk']) echo " id=\"navCurrent\""; ?>
```

What this does is test the value of $row_rstCategories['cat_pk'] (the category item we are currently writing out) with the value of $row_rstCurrentCategory['cat_pk'] (the category for this page). If the two match, then we add the ID of navCurrent to this item. Figure 2-61 shows this in action.

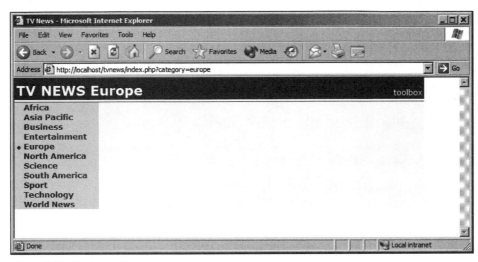

**Figure 2-61.** Displaying the current category

Right, this is looking good, so let's get some articles displayed in the page. Create a new Recordset and call it rstLatestNews. The SQL is

```
SELECT news.news_pk, news.news_category_fk, news.news_date,
 news.news_headline, news.news_precis, news.news_icon_meta,
 categories.cat_name
FROM news, categories
WHERE news.news_category_fk=categories.cat_pk AND
 categories.cat_code LIKE 'category'
ORDER BY news.news_date DESC LIMIT 5
```

We're grabbing all of the relevant news data, plus the category that the news story falls into where the category code is like the current category code for the page. Add a parameter for the query called category, set its default value to % (the SQL wildcard) and the runtime value to $row_rstCurrentCategory['cat_code'] (the current category). If you test that, it should return just the one record. The wildcard character makes sure that when we are on a page that doesn't have a category (like the homepage) we return records from all story categories. We're ordering by the date they were added and limiting the number of results to five, so we'll always get the latest five entries returned in this Recordset.

Switch to Code view and take a look in the body of the page for the <div> with the ID of article. In here we will display the articles that have been returned by our rstLatestNews Recordset. First add a Dynamic Text Server Behavior to display the value of the news_headline column, and below that add the news_precis column. On a third line add the text Full Story, select it, and link it to a file named news.php (which we will create later). We'll want to add a parameter to the page that passes the ID of the current news story, so add a parameter called story and give it a value of the news_pk column from the rstLatestNews Recordset.

The last thing we will need to do is include the icon for this story. Add a new image immediately before the Dynamic Text Server Behavior that adds the précis to the page. The src of the image will be showimage.php, another script we'll need to write. The full code for this <img> tag will be

```
<img src="showimage.php?show=icon&story=<?php echo
$row_rstLatestNews['news_pk'];
 ?>" class="imgLeft" <?php echo
➥$row_rstLatestNews['news_icon_meta']; ?> />
```

Assigning the image the class of imgLeft will make it float to the left-hand side of the page and have some space between it and the précis text flowing around it.

The code that you should have is as follows:

```
<div id="article">
<p>
<?php echo $row_rstLatestNews['news_headline']; ?><br />
<img src="showimage.php?show=icon&story=<?php echo
$row_rstLatestNews['news_pk']; ?>" class="imgLeft" <?php echo
$row_rstLatestNews['news_icon_meta']; ?> /><?php echo
$row_rstLatestNews['news_precis']; ?><br />
<a href="news.php?story=<?php echo
$row_rstLatestNews['news_pk']; ?>">Read More</a>
</p>
</div>
```

If you view the page your image will be broken, as you can see in Figure 2-62.

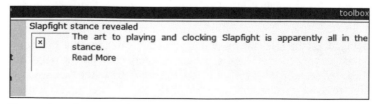

**Figure 2-62.** The page with a broken image

The code for the broken image is

```
<img src="showimage.php?show=icon&story=1"
class="imgLeft"  width="60" height="60" />
```

which is perfect—it has the correct width and height from the database and the correct parameters are being passed to the showimage.php script.

Before we take a look at the showimage.php script, let's just apply some formatting to the page. Select the headline Dynamic Text and apply the HeadLine style to it. Select the Read More link and apply the More style to it so that it floats to the right-hand side of the page. Then select the entire <p> .. </p> tag and apply a Show Region If Recordset Not Empty Server Behavior to it, checking against the rstLatestNews Recordset. This will stop a broken image and a broken Read More link appearing if there are no news articles in the database. With the same code still selected, apply a Repeat Region Server Behavior, repeating all of the records in the rstLatestNews Recordset.

# showimage.php

Create a new Dynamic PHP file and save it as showimage.php. This script won't be displaying anything except the image data, so we can switch to Code view, select everything, and delete it. Create a new Recordset called rstImage with the following SQL:

```
SELECT news.news_icon, news.news_icon_type, news.news_pk
FROM news
WHERE news.news_pk = story
```

story is a variable with a default value of 1 and a runtime value of $_GET['story'].

Switch to Code view and we can finish off the script.

The first thing we want to do is dynamically re-create the SQL script dependent on whether we want to show the icon or the full image. We could retrieve both in our query, but there's no point in retrieving data we are not going to use.

Following is the code block:

```
$story_rstImage = "1";
if (isset($_GET['story'])) {
  $story_rstImage = (get_magic_quotes_gpc()) ? $_GET['story'] :
 addslashes($_GET['story']);
}
```

Add these lines:

```
$show_rstImage = "icon";
if (isset($_GET['show'])) {
  $show_rstImage = (get_magic_quotes_gpc()) ? $_GET['show'] :
 addslashes($_GET['show']);
}
```

It's essentially a copy of the previous block, but this time we are grabbing the show variable out of the query string.

Then alter the line that builds the SQL query from

```
$query_rstImage = sprintf("SELECT news.news_icon,
news.news_icon_type, news.news_pk FROM news WHERE
news.news_pk = %s ", $story_rstImage);
```

to

```
$query_rstImage = sprintf("SELECT news.news_%s AS data,
 news.news_%s_type AS type, news.news_pk FROM news WHERE
 news.news_pk = %s", $show_rstImage, $show_rstImage,
 $story_rstImage);
```

We are replacing the relevant portion of the field name with the value of the variable show in the query string. When we say show=icon, we will be selecting the news_icon and news_icon_type fields, and when we say show=image, we will be selecting the news_image and news_image_type fields. Also, since we will want to retrieve these values later, we use the AS keyword to rename the fields in the query results so that we won't need to use any more logic later on when pulling the data from the Recordset.

After this line:

```
$totalRows_rstImage = mysql_num_rows($rstImage);
```

add the following lines:

```
header("Content-type: ".$row_rstImage['type']);
echo (get_magic_quotes_gpc()) ? $row_rstImage['data'] :
 stripslashes($row_rstImage['data']);
```

We're sending the correct header (as stored in the database) and then outputting the image data. We're also stripping out any slashes that PHP would have added to the image data when adding the image to the database originally. By testing to see if the magic quotes directive is on or off, we don't try and remove slashes from something that PHP may already have done for us automatically.

The full code for showimage.php is as follows:

```
<?php require_once('Connections/tvnews.php'); ?>
<?php
$story_rstImage = "1";
if (isset($_GET['story'])) {
  $story_rstImage = (get_magic_quotes_gpc()) ? $_GET['story'] :
 addslashes($_GET['story']);
}
```

```
$show_rstImage = "icon";
if (isset($_GET['show'])) {
  $show_rstImage = (get_magic_quotes_gpc()) ? $_GET['show'] :
addslashes($_GET['show']);
}
mysql_select_db($database_tvnews, $tvnews);
$query_rstImage = sprintf("SELECT news.news_%s AS data,
 news.news_%s_type AS type, news.news_pk FROM news WHERE
 news.news_pk = %s", $show_rstImage, $show_rstImage,
 $story_rstImage);
$rstImage = mysql_query($query_rstImage, $tvnews) or
die(mysql_error());
$row_rstImage = mysql_fetch_assoc($rstImage);
$totalRows_rstImage = mysql_num_rows($rstImage);
header("Content-type: ".$row_rstImage['type']);
echo (get_magic_quotes_gpc()) ? $row_rstImage['data'] :
 stripslashes($row_rstImage['data']);
mysql_free_result($rstImage);
?>
```

Refresh the index.php page and you should see the image displayed as shown in Figure 2-63.

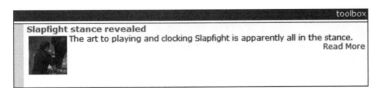

**Figure 2-63.** The showimage.php script is working.

## index.php, continued

The parts that we will be adding to the page to finish it off require additional articles in the database. Add some news items using the admin.php page, and make sure that some of them are linked to the same link items.

The code that we add now will be added to the sidebar <div>—the first element will be the next ten news stories. The latest five are displayed in the main page; this element simply provides an easy way to see some of the previous articles.

The Recordset to return these records is very similar to the rstLatestNews Recordset, so right-click rstLatestNews, select Copy, then click in a blank area and choose Paste as shown in Figure 2-64.

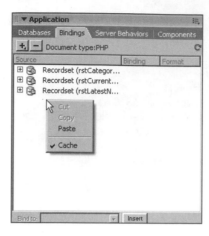

**Figure 2-64.**
Making a copy of the rstLatestNews Recordset

A new Recordset (Recordset1) is created—double-click it to edit it.

Rename it to rstOtherNews, and then alter the SQL to read

```
SELECT news.news_pk, news.news_category_fk, news.news_date,
 news.news_headline, news.news_precis, news.news_icon_meta,
 categories.cat_name
FROM news, categories
WHERE news.news_category_fk=categories.cat_pk AND
categories.cat_code LIKE 'category'
ORDER BY news.news_date DESC LIMIT 5,10
```

The only change is in the LIMIT section where we are changing it from LIMIT 5 to LIMIT 5,10—this limits it to ten records and offsets the records returned by five—the first five we have already displayed in the main portion of the page.

When you click OK you will be informed that the renaming of Recordsets is done by the Find/Replace dialog box, as shown in Figure 2-65.

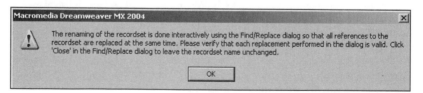

**Figure 2-65.** Dreamweaver informs you about renaming Recordsets.

Click OK and you are presented with the Find and Replace dialog box, as shown in Figure 2-66.

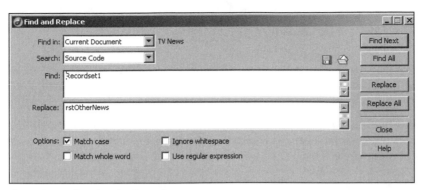

**Figure 2-66.** Changing the Recordset name

Add the image othernews.gif into the sidebar <div>. Under the image, add an unordered list. Because the list is in the sidebar <div>, it will pick up the style from the style sheet. Create a single <li> that contains a Dynamic Text Behavior displaying the news_headline column from the rstOtherNews Recordset. Select the Dynamic Text Behavior and in the Properties inspector click the Browse for file button to link the text. Link to the file news.php and add a parameter called story that has the value of the news_pk field from the rstOtherNews Recordset. Select the list item and apply a Repeat Region Server Behavior to it, repeating all of the records in the rstOtherNews Recordset. Then select the entire list and apply a Show Region If Recordset Is Not Empty Server Behavior to it, using the rstOtherNews Recordset. Save the page.

If you have either more than five news items and are viewing the main page index.php, or have more than five news items in a specific category, you will see the stories listed on the right, as shown in Figure 2-67.

**Figure 2-67.**
Other stories displayed in the sidebar

Let's now build the page to display the full news story.

## news.php

Our news page is going to have a lot in common with the index page. The main differences are that the category must be retrieved from the story record in the database; the Other Stories box will not be offset by five, but will display the first five stories; the related stories must be displayed; we'll need to include the Email and Print buttons; and, of course, the story list in the main area will be replaced with the full text of the news story.

Let's get to it then. Save index.php as news.php, and we can start off by cleaning up the Recordsets and Server Behaviors that we don't need.

In the Server Behaviors panel you can remove the Show Region and Repeat Region Server Behaviors that are associated with the rstLatestNews Recordset. You can also remove the rstLatestNews Recordset and all of the code inside the center <div> that was displaying the latest five news articles.

Instead of the latest news items, we will be retrieving only a single news item, identified by the variable story in the query string. Create a new Recordset called rstNewsItem with the settings shown in Figure 2-68.

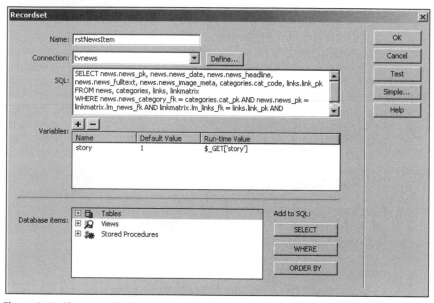

**Figure 2-68.** The Recordset for the current news item

```
SELECT news.news_pk, news.news_date, news.news_headline,
 news.news_fulltext, news.news_image_meta, categories.cat_pk,
categories.cat_code, categories.cat_name, links.link_pk
FROM news, categories, links, linkmatrix
WHERE news.news_category_fk = categories.cat_pk AND
news.news_pk = linkmatrix.lm_news_fk AND linkmatrix.lm_links_fk =
links.link_pk AND news.news_pk = story
```

What this query is doing is joining together the news, categories, and links tables together using the relationships between their primary and foreign keys. The categories table links to the news table through the categories.cat_pk and news.news_category_fk relationship; the links table is joined via the linkmatrix table to the news table (see Figure 2-69).

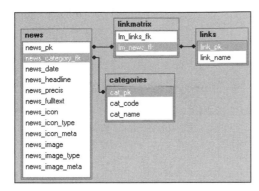

**Figure 2-69.**
The table relationships of the rstNewsItem Recordset

We then filter it all out by selecting the single news record that corresponds to the value passed to the script in the query string.

The new Recordset is entered into the code at the bottom of the existing Recordsets, so we will need to switch to Code view and move the code to the beginning of the Recordsets. The reason for moving the Recordset to earlier in the page is that we are retrieving the other stories in this category, and until we have retrieved the category code for this news item, we won't know which category it is in. Find the following code:

```
$story_rstNewsItem = "1";
if (isset($_GET['story'])) {
  $story_rstNewsItem = (get_magic_quotes_gpc()) ? $_GET['story'] :
addslashes($_GET['story']);
}
mysql_select_db($database_tvnews, $tvnews);
$query_rstNewsItem = sprintf("SELECT news.news_pk,
 news.news_date, news.news_headline, news.news_fulltext,
 news.news_image_meta, categories.cat_pk, categories.cat_code,
 categories.cat_name, links.link_pk FROM news, categories, links,
linkmatrix WHERE news.news_category_fk = categories.cat_pk
 AND news.news_pk = linkmatrix.lm_news_fk AND
 linkmatrix.lm_links_fk = links.link_pk AND news.news_pk = %s",
 $story_rstNewsItem);
$rstNewsItem = mysql_query($query_rstNewsItem, $tvnews) or
die(mysql_error());
$row_rstNewsItem = mysql_fetch_assoc($rstNewsItem);
$totalRows_rstNewsItem = mysql_num_rows($rstNewsItem);
```

And move it to before this line:

```
$colname_rstCurrentCategory = "1";
```

The first ten lines of your script should now look like the following:

```php
<?php require_once('Connections/tvnews.php'); ?>
<?php
mysql_select_db($database_tvnews, $tvnews);
$query_rstCategories = "SELECT * FROM categories ORDER BY cat_name
➥ASC";
$rstCategories = mysql_query($query_rstCategories, $tvnews)
or die(mysql_error());
$row_rstCategories = mysql_fetch_assoc($rstCategories);
$totalRows_rstCategories = mysql_num_rows($rstCategories);

$story_rstNewsItem = "1";
if (isset($_GET['story'])) {
```

We have now made the rstCurrentCategory Recordset obsolete, so we can go ahead and remove this Recordset. As you see in Figure 2-70, Dreamweaver will alert you to the fact that some of your Server Behaviors rely on the rstCurrentCategory Recordset.

**Figure 2-70.** Dreamweaver warns you when you remove elements that have dependent items.

Click OK and then open the Find and Replace dialog box, shown in Figure 2-71, from the Edit menu.

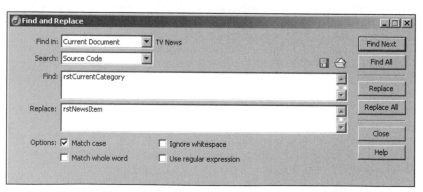

**Figure 2-71.** Find and Replace dialog box

Click Replace All and Dreamweaver will do the rest.

An easy change to make is to the rstOtherNews Recordset. We're currently employing an offset to the LIMIT clause—we need to remove this. Open the Recordset and alter the LIMIT SQL clause from

```
LIMIT 5,10
```

to

```
LIMIT 5
```

The next element of the page to add is a list of related news items to the current news story. Create a new Recordset called rstRelatedNews. The SQL is

```
SELECT news.news_pk, news.news_headline
FROM news, linkmatrix
WHERE linkmatrix.lm_news_fk = news.news_pk AND linkmatrix.lm_links_fk =
➥linkitem
ORDER BY news.news_date DESC LIMIT 5
```

where linkitem is a variable we need to create. Give it a default value of 0 and a runtime value of $row_rstNewsItem['link_pk']—this is the link item that our current news item is linked to. Here we are selecting all of the news records that are linked to the same link item.

Add the relatednews.gif heading image below the unordered list that displayed the other news items and then we'll add a new unordered list exactly as we did for displaying the contents of rstOtherNews. The individual link items will display the news_headline field and link to news.php, passing the value of the news_pk field as a parameter called story. Just as we did before, select the individual list item and apply a Repeat Region Server Behavior to it and coat the entire unordered list in a Show Region If Recordset Not Empty Server Behavior. The code for this section of the sidebar <div> is

```
<img src="images/relatednews.gif" width="178" height="21" />
<?php if ($totalRows_rstRelatedNews > 0) { // Show if recordset not
➥empty ?>
<ul>
  <?php do { ?>
  <li><a href="news.php?story=<?php echo
$row_rstRelatedNews['news_pk']; ?>"><?php echo
 $row_rstRelatedNews['news_headline']; ?></a></li>
  <?php } while ($row_rstRelatedNews =
  ➥mysql_fetch_assoc($rstRelatedNews)); ?>
</ul>
<?php } // Show if recordset not empty ?>
```

Now in the article <div> we can add the Dynamic Text Server Behaviors to display the actual article. We'll want to display the news_headline column, news_date, news_fulltext, and the image that goes with the article. If you don't feel like doing this manually, you can copy the code you used for displaying the article précis information on the main `index.php` page and just modify the Recordset and field names where appropriate. The code that you should end up with in your article `<div>` is

```
<div id="article">
  <p>
    <span class="HeadLine"><?php echo
$row_rstNewsItem['news_headline']; ?></span><br />
      <span class="NewsDate"><?php echo
$row_rstNewsItem['news_date']; ?></span><br />
        <img src="showimage.php?show=image&story=<?php echo
$row_rstNewsItem['news_pk']; ?>" class="imgLeft" <?php echo
$row_rstNewsItem['news_icon_meta']; ?> /><?php echo
$row_rstNewsItem['news_fulltext']; ?><br />
  </p>
</div>
```

As you can see it's fairly similar to the code we created in the `index.php` page, except we've added the date and formatted it with the `NewsDate` style. If you preview this in a browser, your page should be laid out as in Figure 2-72.

**Figure 2-72.**
The news article

The date doesn't look all that great though—you can see it's year-month-day and the time the article was added, but we won't want to display it like this on the actual web page. PHP itself comes with a function for formatting date and time strings called `strftime()` but it operates on a Unix timestamp, which is not how we have stored our dates in the database. The Unix timestamp is the number of seconds that have passed since the beginning of 1970 and is a standard way of presenting a date that doesn't worry about the order in which the month and day are stored. While you may be tempted to store your dates in this way and then simply use `strftime()` to format them for human consumption, using the MySQL internal date column type is more effective and will certainly in the long run provide you with more features.

There is a MySQL function called `DATE_FORMAT()`, which does the same thing as the `strftime()` function in PHP. You pass the function the date column that you want to format and then a string that defines how you want the date formatted. The formats are specified using a % character and then an identifier for what you want, so %W would give you the full name of the day, like Monday or Saturday. A full list of the characters you can use can be found in the MySQL manual entry that you can read in the URL given in the following sidebar.

*If you wanted to retrieve a list of all the articles that were published in December, you would have a difficult time doing that if you were storing your dates as Unix timestamps. You would first have to work out the Unix timestamp for the beginning of December and then another for the end of December, and your query would have to retrieve all the records where the stored timestamp fell between those two values. But then what if you wanted all the Decembers, not just for one year? Suddenly you'd have a far greater problem. By using a MySQL date column, you can use the MySQL date and time functions to easily* `SELECT * FROM news WHERE MONTH(news_date) = 12`.

*There are a large number of these functions, which are extremely helpful when building queries based on dates and date ranges. You can read all about them in the MySQL manual at* `http://dev.mysql.com/doc/mysql/en/Date_and_time_functions.html`.

We'll want the day name, date, month, and year, so the format string will be

```
%W %e %M %Y
```

The line in the `news.php` page that we need to change is

```
$query_rstNewsItem = sprintf("SELECT news.news_pk,
news.news_date, news.news_headline, news.news_fulltext,
news.news_image_meta, categories.cat_pk, categories.cat_code,
 categories.cat_name, links.link_pk FROM news, categories, links,
linkmatrix WHERE news.news_category_fk = categories.cat_pk
 AND news.news_pk = linkmatrix.lm_news_fk AND
linkmatrix.lm_links_fk = links.link_pk AND
news.news_pk = %s", $story_rstNewsItem);
```

The changes will be around the news.news_date column; the updated line looks like so:

```
$query_rstNewsItem = sprintf("SELECT news.news_pk,
 DATE_FORMAT(news.news_date,\"%%W %%e %%M %%Y\") AS
 news_date, news.news_headline, news.news_fulltext,
news.news_image_meta, categories.cat_pk, categories.cat_code,
categories.cat_name, links.link_pk FROM news, categories, links,
linkmatrix WHERE news.news_category_fk = categories.cat_pk
 AND news.news_pk = linkmatrix.lm_news_fk AND
linkmatrix.lm_links_fk = links.link_pk AND news.news_pk = %s",
$story_rstNewsItem);
```

Notice that we've escaped the " character with a backslash and had to specify the % characters as %%—this is because the % character is already an identifier for the `sprintf()` function, so to make sure that we don't break that we use a double %%.

The formatting in the page can be seen in Figure 2-73.

**Figure 2-73.** The full page

As you can see, the page we're viewing is news.php and we've passed the story ID in the query string. The story is displayed correctly with the full-size image, and the top bar has correctly displayed that this article belongs in the Entertainment category. Our navigation bar is also bulleted next to the Entertainment category, indicating that this is the category we are in. On the right-hand side of the page, we have a list of the latest stories in this category, and in the Related Stories area, we see only the stories that are related to this link item.

Some of you might have noticed that we haven't added our Print and Email buttons or search box to the page. This is pretty straightforward and we can add them in now quickly. Add a form that contains a text box and a Submit button. Inside the <form> tag add the email.gif and print.gif images. Give the text box the name of txtCriteria and set the action of the form to search.php. Once we have done that we can link the buttons to their respective pages: select the Email button and in the Link box of the Properties inspector link the image to javascript:;—this does nothing except create an <a> tag around the image to which we can now attach our Behavior. Select the <a> tag and from the Tag Inspector panel choose Behaviors and add a new Open Browser Window Behavior. Click the Browse for File button and enter the filename email.php. Add a parameter called story that has the value of the news_pk column from the rstNewsItem Recordset. Give the window a width of 400 pixels, a height of 300 pixels, and the name winEmail. Click OK to add the Behavior (see Figure 2-74).

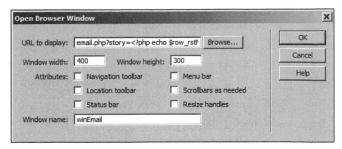

**Figure 2-74.** Adding the Open Browser Window Behavior

Look at the Behaviors panel and change the event from onLoad to onClick as shown in Figure 2-75.

**Figure 2-75.**
Changing the Behavior event

Now we need to do the same for the Print button—select the Print button and link it to javascript:; to create the <a> tag. Then from the Tag Inspector panel, Behaviors tab, select the Open Browser Window Behavior. Click Browse to find the file to link to—in the file name box enter print.php and add a parameter named story with a value of news_pk from rstNewsItem. Make the window 600 pixels wide by 500 pixels high and turn on the menu bar, scrollbars, and resize handles and name the window winPrint. Click OK, and change the Event to onClick.

We now need to create the email.php and the print.php pages. Create a new dynamic PHP page and save it as print.php.

## print.php

To begin with we want the page to look the same, style-wise, as the rest of the site. In the CSS Styles tab of the Design panel, right-click and choose Attach Style. Select the tvnews.css file. Then create a new Recordset called rstNewsItem, as shown in Figure 2-76.

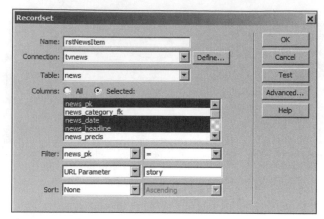

**Figure 2-76.** The rstNewsItem Recordset

Then open `news.php` and copy the contents of the article `<div>` into the body of the `print.php` page. That's the content of the page and since our Recordsets are named the same we don't have to change a thing (see Figure 2-77).

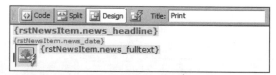

**Figure 2-77.** The print page in Design view

You can save `print.php` and test out the Print button, as shown in Figure 2-78.

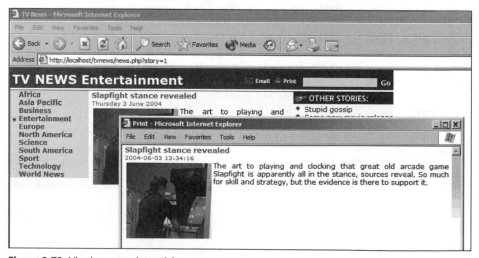

**Figure 2-78.** Viewing our print article

In the preceding image you can see the news page in the background with the Email and Print buttons, and in the foreground you can see the window with just the article for printing (no navigation or features).

The page to e-mail the article is a little bit more complex; let's take a look.

## email.php

On this page we will need to create a form for the person browsing the site to enter the e-mail address of the person they wish to e-mail the story to. We should also get the name and e-mail address of the person sending the message so that the person on the receiving end knows who it's from. Once we have that we can use PHP's built-in mail() function to send the mail.

Create a new Dynamic PHP page and save as email.php. Attach the tvnews.css style sheet to the page as we did for the Print page and then create a new form. Set the action of the form to sendemail.php, a page we will still need to create.

Inside the form, create a table with four rows and two columns. Insert three input boxes into the second column of the first three rows, and a button with the label of Send Email in the second column of the fourth row. Then label the input boxes in the first column as shown in Figure 2-79.

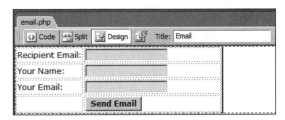

**Figure 2-79.**
The e-mail form

Name the input boxes txtRecipientEmail, txtSenderName, and txtSenderEmail, respectively.

From the Behaviors tab in the Tag Inspector panel choose Validate Form. Set txtRecipientEmail to Required Email Address, txtSenderName to Required, and txtSenderEmail to Required Email Address. Click OK and Dreamweaver will insert the relevant code to make sure that the fields are filled in correctly (see Figure 2-80).

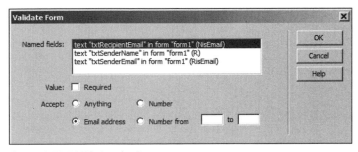

**Figure 2-80.** Validating the form

The last thing we have to do before we create our sendemail.php script is to insert a hidden input type that stores the value of the story that we are e-mailing. The sendemail.php script will use this value to build the e-mail message. Insert the hidden input, change its name to hidStory, and set its value to

```php
<?php echo $_GET['story']; ?>
```

We can now move on to creating the sendemail.php script.

## sendemail.php

This script will simply be building the e-mail message, sending the e-mail, and displaying a message to say that the message was sent. To do this we will first need to retrieve the news story information from the database. Create a new Dynamic PHP page, change its title to Email, and save it as sendemail.php. Attach the tvnews.css style sheet, and we can create the Recordset. Call the Recordset rstNewsItem and set it up as shown in Figure 2-81.

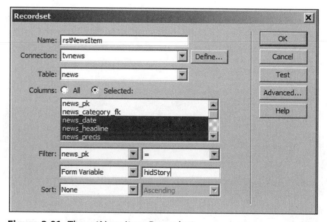

**Figure 2-81.** The rstNewsItem Recordset

All we're going to select is the news_headline, news_date, and news_précis fields. The story ID was passed through to the script via our hidden field hidStory.

Switch to the Code view and we can complete the page. All of the code that we will be writing goes between the <body> and </body> tags:

```php
<?php
$strTo = $_POST['txtRecipientEmail'];
$strSubject = $_POST['txtSenderName']." thought you might enjoy this
➥article";
$strMessage = "<html><body>\r\n";
$strMessage .=
"<p><strong>".$row_rstNewsItem['news_headline']."</strong></p>\r\n";
$strMessage .= "<p>".$row_rstNewsItem['news_precis']."</p>\r\n";
$strMessage .= "<p><a href='http://".$_SERVER['SERVER_NAME'].
```

```
"/tvnews/news.php?story=".$_POST['hidStory']."'>
Full Story</a></p>\r\n";
$strMessage .= "</body></html>";
$strHeaders = "MIME-Version: 1.0\r\n";
$strHeaders .= "Content-type: text/html; charset=iso-8859-1\r\n";
$strHeaders .= "From: ".$_POST['txtSenderName']."
 <".$_POST['txtSenderEmail'].">\r\n";
$success = @mail($strTo, $strSubject, $strMessage, $strHeaders);
if ($success) {
?>
<p>Your message was sent successfully</p>
<?php
} else {
?>
<p>Your message was not sent successfully</p>
<?php
}
?>
<p><a href="javascript:window.close();">Close</a></p>
```

Let's take it bit by bit and see what's happening.

```
<?php
$strTo = $_POST['txtRecipientEmail'];
$strSubject = $_POST['txtSenderName']." thought you might enjoy this
➥article";
```

The first block is setting up the recipient and the subject of the e-mail. The recipient e-mail is in the input box txtRecipientEmail. We then build a friendly subject line for the e-mail so that the recipient knows what it's about and who it is from.

```
$strMessage = "<html><body>\r\n";
$strMessage .=
"<p><strong>".$row_rstNewsItem['news_headline'].
"</strong></p>\r\n";
$strMessage .= "<p>".$row_rstNewsItem['news_precis']."</p>\r\n";
$strMessage .= "<p><a href='http://".$_SERVER['SERVER_NAME'].
"/tvnews/news.php?story=".$_POST['hidStory']."'>
Full Story</a></p>\r\n";
$strMessage .= "</body></html>";
```

Next we set up the message itself. Pretty much every e-mail program today can handle HTML mail, so we'll use this and build a variable called $strMessage that contains the HTML of the message. It's fairly straightforward—we've got the headline of the story at the top, and below that the précis. Below that we provide a link to the full story on our website. We build the URL from the server variable SERVER_NAME. SERVER_NAME is the Internet address of our web server and onto the end of that we append the full path to the news.php file. We also need to append the query string of the story ID so that the news.php page can display it.

```
$strHeaders = "MIME-Version: 1.0\r\n";
$strHeaders .= "Content-type: text/html; charset=iso-8859-1\r\n";
$strHeaders .= "From: ".$_POST['txtSenderName'].
" <".$_POST['txtSenderEmail'].">\r\n";
```

Because we are sending HTML mail, we need to create mail headers that specify it as such. We also create a mail header that defines who the e-mail is from, and set this to the name of the person who is sending the message.

Now that we have all the pieces we need to send e-mail, we can send it. The PHP mail() function has the following syntax:

```
bool mail(string to, string subject, string message
[, string headers] [, string parameters])
```

The to, subject, and message are self-explanatory. The optional headers, as we have seen, are for specifying any additional mail headers that we wish to send, and the optional parameters argument is used to pass parameters to the mail program that is sending the actual mail. The mail function returns a Boolean value of TRUE or FALSE, depending on whether the mail was successful or not.

```
$success = @mail($strTo, $strSubject, $strMessage, $strHeaders);
if ($success) {
?>
<p>Your message was sent successfully</p>
<?php
} else {
?>
<p>Your message was not sent successfully</p>
<?php
}
?>
```

We send the e-mail and store the result of the mail() function in the $success variable. We can then test to see whether the mail was sent successfully or not. The @ symbol on the front of the mail() function tells PHP to not display any error messages from the mail() function. This way if the mail() function fails, we can just display a message to the user and not have the error message displayed.

```
<p><a href="javascript:window.close();">Close</a></p>
```

The last part of the page is a link to some JavaScript that closes the Email window.

You can now test the Email button (see Figure 2-82).

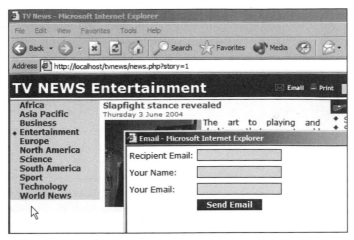

**Figure 2-82.** Sending e-mail from the site

What we need now is to let people search for news articles.

## search.php

The contents of search.php is closest to index.php (listing news items), so open index.php and save a copy of it as search.php.

What we want to do here is replace the main content area of the page with our search results, and replace the contents of the Other Stories box with the latest five stories across all categories. You will realize that we already have the Recordset to display in the Other Stories area—rstLatestNews. The parameter for the link on the headline, the headline text itself, and the Repeat Region and the Show Region Server Behaviors all need to be modified from using rstOtherNews to using rstLatestNews. rstOtherNews can be removed as can the contents of the article <div>, but leave the <div> itself in place.

Remove the rstOtherNews Recordset. Then select everything inside the article layer and delete it.

We'll now always want to display the Search Results heading, so in the title bar, remove the Dynamic Text Server Behavior that displays the category and replace it with the text "Search results".

We can also dispense with the rstCurrentCategory Recordset as it's not needed in this page. Once you've removed it, switch to Code view and find the line of code that is setting the highlight bullet on for the current category in the navigation:

```php
<?php if ($row_rstCategories['cat_pk']==
$row_rstCurrentCategory['cat_pk']) echo " id=\"navCurrent\""; ?>
```

Remove this code so that the sidebar is now built without it:

```
<ul>
  <?php do { ?>
  <li><a href="index.php?category=<?php echo
$row_rstCategories['cat_code']; ?>"><?php echo
$row_rstCategories['cat_name']; ?></a></li>
    <?php } while ($row_rstCategories =
mysql_fetch_assoc($rstCategories)); ?>
  </ul>
```

Now all we need to do is build the Recordset that returns our search results, display them in the page, and we're done.

Create a new Recordset called rstSearchResults. The setup is fairly straightforward—we're grabbing all the records from the database where the string that the user entered in the search box called txtCriteria is contained in the article text (see Figure 2-83).

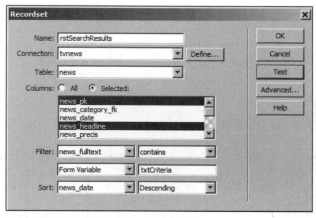

**Figure 2-83.** The rstSearchResults Recordset

Once you have inserted it, switch to Code view and find the line that sets the initial value of $colname_rstSearchResults and set it to a blank string. The Recordset dialog box won't let you set an initial value to nothing.

The line that you are looking for is

```
$colname_rstSearchResults = "1";
```

Change it to read

```
$colname_rstSearchResults = "";
```

You can now format your search results as you choose. For my page I simply listed the headlines one under the other and linked each one through to the news.php page, passing the news_pk column value through as the story parameter. Select the entire line and apply a Repeat Region Server Behavior to it, but only displaying ten records.

Place the cursor in the page immediately below the Repeat Region Server behavior and from the Insert menu choose Application Objects ➤ Recordset Paging ➤ Recordset Navigation Bar (see Figure 2-84).

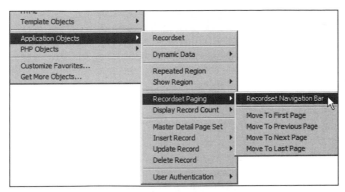

**Figure 2-84.** Adding Recordset paging

You can test the search function by entering a word found in one of your stories in the search box (see Figure 2-85).

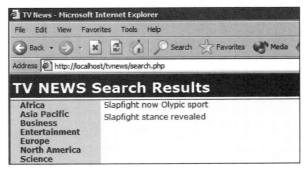

**Figure 2-85.** Search results

# Summary

Through the course of this chapter we have covered a fair amount of ground. The main purpose of the chapter was to take a project and work through the initial planning and design stages, all the way through to implementation.

The first part of the chapter dealt with the Information Architecture of the project—what things we need to do before we start coding. We looked at the goals for the site—what the client expects to achieve with this website. We also looked at background information about the site—what audience you would expect to see on the site and how we might expect these different types of people to affect the way in which the site was planned and designed. Once we had taken a look at what the competition had to offer, we decided which features we wanted to have on our site—features that furthered the goals we defined for the site. We then finished off by designing the site with some page layouts and the underlying database structure.

The second part of the chapter was where we looked at how we could use Dreamweaver MX 2004 to implement some of the features we decided on earlier. We built an admin tool to add new news items to the site and then built the front page that displayed the news items. This page also managed the navigation through the various categories on the site. We then built a page to display the full news story and one to display search results. We also looked at how we could build pages to print and e-mail from the site.

While we did not have enough time to show every feature that we initially spoke about, we have covered all of the techniques that you will need to implement any of the missing ones if you wish. The techniques that we covered included many Dreamweaver Server Behaviors: Show Region, Repeat Region, Dynamic Text, and Recordset Paging. As we worked through the chapter, we came across situations where we had to mix Dreamweaver Behaviors and hand-coding in PHP—the handling of file uploads, storing image data in a database, joining together multiple tables in a single SQL query, and the displaying of image data from the database.

# 3 CORPORATE WEBSITE DRAFT ONE

In this section of the book, we're going to create a corporate website, geared at the small-to-medium-sized enterprise (SME) marketplace. As with the other projects in this book, the source files are in the code download for the book. Feel free to experiment with these files and incorporate ideas from this section of the book into your own websites.

To work through this chapter, I'm going to make a few assumptions. The first is that you're comfortable working with a PC or Mac. What platform you choose is up to you: Dreamweaver is virtually identical on PC and Mac, and, apart from testing the final site, there's nothing that we'll be doing that requires a specific platform. I'm also going to assume you have some knowledge of Dreamweaver, HTML, CSS, and how to work with a graphics package. Should you need to brush up a little on HTML or CSS, a good site to visit is www.w3schools.com.

At the start of the chapter, I will lead you through processes step-by-step, but will gradually move towards just providing summaries of how to deal with areas of the website, by using knowledge you've already gained.

With browser technology continuing to evolve and most web standards now adhering to W3 recommendations, I will be placing a firm emphasis on **web standards**. Because of the way the site will be authored, the result will be **future-proof**.

Although large companies tend to employ advanced database solutions for their sites, such costs are often out of the range of smaller businesses. Therefore, many have someone in-house who deals with building and maintaining a site in an application such as Dreamweaver.

> *Should the situation arise where several people—including those without expertise in Dreamweaver—wish to make the occasional update to your website, it might be worth checking out Macromedia Contribute. This software enables nontechnical users to make basic changes to a website without affecting the underlying styles and design. More information is available at www.macromedia.com/software/contribute.*

However, just knowing how to use the application itself isn't enough, so I'll show you how to structure a corporate site, provide online branding and design tips, and demonstrate effective usability.

Although our site will be aimed at the corporate market, many things we'll be discussing are appropriate to all websites. For instance, within Dreamweaver, we'll be making use of templates and Cascading Style Sheets (CSS), the combination of which considerably speeds up creating and maintaining a website. In some cases, we'll work directly with code, because once you have a basic grasp of HTML and CSS, you'll be able to create superior, tightly honed sites. Also note that I'll be referring to you, "the reader," as a member of an SME company, working in-house. However, the vast majority of the advice within this chapter is suitable for a typical jobbing designer creating a site for a client SME.

By the end of this section, we'll have completed a website and will have worked through the following:

- **Planning:** Deciding on an aim for the site, knowing its audience and their requirements, collating content, and constructing a site map
- **Design:** Working with layout, and deciding on a basic page structure
- **Development:** Building pages in Dreamweaver, working with both Code and Design views; discovering CSS; creating templates; dealing with legacy web browsers and printing; and thinking of ideas for updating the site later
- **Testing and debugging**
- **Deployment and maintenance**

# Background

Corporate websites vary wildly in effectiveness and quality. Some become extremely successful, while others are a pale representation of their parent company's brand and ideals. The best employ simple rules: they are easy to use and navigate; information is ordered logically; the company brand is well represented; content is interesting, succinct, and up-to-date; and they encourage end users to contact the company, and make it easy to do so. Finally, "proof" of company expertise is a must, in the form of customer quotes or case studies.

Websites for SMEs should obey such rules, although the actual sites might be smaller in scale and perhaps geared at a more specialist market or product line. One other difference is that SME sites are often maintained in-house, although many are first set up by professional designers.

The audience for such a website is primarily the company's customers, whether they're resellers or end users, but don't forget that other people will use the site, too. Employees often depend on a company website for information when talking to clients on the telephone. This is especially true for newcomers, who may rely on it heavily during their induction.

# Planning

The planning stage is something you should never skimp on. Good planning always pays dividends in the end; not being too concerned with planning results in half-finished, sloppy sites with less appeal. Always give yourself plenty of time to research things, such as your audience, and to source and create content. Be sure to involve the relevant people from whoever you're creating the site for. Try circulating a questionnaire to the decision makers in the company, to discover their goals, what they want to achieve from the site, and how they'd like to make this happen. If possible, have a meeting with them, to discuss face-to-face their ideas for the site, and to provide your professional expertise.

People often assume that once the site's structure is complete, the content will only take a short time to deal with—it won't. Clients or co-workers are often notorious in taking their time to get content to you, and if you've set a deadline for the site's launch or relaunch, you could end up in a sticky situation. Under no circumstances use "under construction" pages if things are late; instead, temporarily remove the relevant pages from the site, along with their associated navigation elements. Whenever possible, set a number of deadlines for both yourself and your colleagues/client, to ensure collateral gets to you when requested, and also that sign-off occurs when it should, to allow you to continue working.

> *A good rule of thumb when planning is to give yourself twice the amount of time you think you'll need to do anything. Also, give other people deadlines that expire long before yours, so you end up with at least some content prior to working on the site.*

Also, beware of trying to do everything yourself in order to cut costs. Many companies assume that they're the only ones who should write their copy, as they know the marketplace, but a professional copywriter should be able to take your words and ideas, and make them more succinct, readable, and professional. Likewise, if you're branding from scratch, avoid having your director design your logo, as in all likelihood (unless they're a professional designer) it'll look "homemade," and your company will immediately look unprofessional. Hiring a photographer for half a day to take product shots, rather than getting someone to take them with a digital camera, is also a good idea.

## Our company

We'll be creating a website for the snappily named "Any SME Company," which was lucky enough to snap up the "anysmecompany.com" domain. This fictional organization, like many SMEs, has a small, core range of products and primarily relies on sales via the telephone.

## Aim

We need to decide what the site is for. Although this may seem obvious, you'd be surprised how often people fail to think carefully about such a thing, hence the number of websites that lack focus and structure.

Our SME company relies on sales over the telephone, so the site must first act as a "hook" to encourage people to get in touch. A visually appealing design, suitable for the audience, information on products, and easy access to contact details will all help with this.

Once hooked, the customer can be acquired through contact and sales. However, the site's purpose doesn't end there: you need to address visitor retention, an often-neglected area within SME websites. To keep customers coming back, ensure your site is kept up-to-date with the latest news, make use of the homepage in particular to release such information, and, if relevant, offer easy access to support information.

> *Although superfluous design that hinders more than it helps is to be avoided, don't underestimate the power of a visually appealing site. People are visually driven, and an unattractive site could see potential customers going elsewhere—to the competition. However, you must also take care to not alienate visitors. Don't do anything too radical if your intended market is a specific type or person with rather more conservative tastes.*

Finally, although you shouldn't port offline marketing material to the Web, you need to be consistent. Make sure your brand is unified across all such material, and that information isn't contradictory. Print design is typically too complex for the Web, but color schemes and photography can often be transferred, along with streamlined copy.

## Audience

I've mentioned that a typical SME audience comprises customers and employees, and these groups largely have the same requirements of the site. However, employees have time to become accustomed to the site, whereas end users don't; if things aren't up to scratch—the site slow, information hard to find, contact details buried ten levels deep—potential customers will simply go to a competitor.

You also need to take into account the technology visitors will be using—in other words, which browsers and what monitor resolutions. If you don't already have a site that enables you to access visitor logs, you can check out global statistics at the likes of `www.w3schools.com/browsers/browsers_stats.asp` or `www.upsdell.com/BrowserNews/stat.htm`. Typically, versions 6 and 5.5 of Internet Explorer for Windows account for well over 80% of users, and the most popular screen size is split between 800×600 and 1024×768, the trend being towards the latter. However, until the vast majority are using 1024×768, you still have to cater for the lowest common denominator when designing the site (or create a site that works on all monitor resolutions).

Another thing to bear in mind is accessibility: a small portion of your site's visitors may use alternative browsers, such as screen readers, so you should cater for them. One way of assisting them is to use Cascading Style Sheets instead of tables for page layout. The only problem with this is that some legacy browsers—notably Netscape Navigator 4—don't understand much CSS and therefore won't display the site as intended, or at all. However, a quick check of the browser statistics shows that usage of such browsers is negligible and in further decline, and there are workarounds that enable you to provide the site's content to *any* Internet-enabled device, but not the design. While this trade-off seems extreme, bear in mind that this way of working makes for faster downloads, more accurate rendering in modern web browsers, and easier maintenance for you. Although a few visitors won't see the design, all visitors will be able to access the *content*—and that includes those visitors with disabilities.

## Information collation

You need to glean information from as many people as possible, including your customers and clients. Ask different people what their requirements are and to prioritize them. If you already have a site, or an upcoming direct mail campaign, include a simple questionnaire with an incentive gift, such as a percentage off their next purchase once customers have responded. For those within your company, send a circular e-mail, so everyone at least knows they've had the opportunity to respond and have those views heard. Ensure that you ask employees at all levels—solely having the boardroom dictate the path and content of a website often leads to disaster. Its members may not be out of touch with the work-force, but they usually have very different ideas about how the company should be presented online. Of course, their ideas need to be taken into account, but so do those from the junior salesperson who just joined last week—in fact, their response may be more valid in some cases, because they'll be looking at things afresh and with an open mind.

Another thing to bear in mind is that you needn't use everything. Don't bombard your users with information; instead, keep things concise. Also, don't design around your company's organization chart, because this may confuse visitors.

In most cases, it's sufficient to put a synopsis of your usual marketing material online, because people tend to skip-read when using the Internet, and rarely scroll more than one or two screens. Also, you don't want to give everything away.

## Organization and site maps

Once you have sufficient information, you need to start organizing it. Ask people where they'd expect to find specific information, and group categories accordingly. You should now have the basis for a site map—a visual representation of your site's structure. Our site will have navigation on each page, controlled by a Dreamweaver template, so you need to consider what should be a "top-level" link—always available—and what might end up being a couple of clicks away.

While it would be wrong to suggest that every corporate site is the same with regard to categorization, there are many somewhat universal ideas. A typical SME site may contain the following, which you can use as the basis for your own site structure:

- **Information about the company:** General profile; information about senior staff; legal advice, including disclaimers; latest and archived news; case studies
- **Information about products:** General overview that leads to specific/in-depth details
- **Contact details:** Both for clients and support issues

Some of these are less important than others. Legal disclaimers don't need to be on the top level, nor does a news archive. However, case studies are "proof" that your company can perform and achieve, so they need to be easily accessible. Therefore, from the preceding list of items we might end up with a site map like the one shown in Figure 3-1.

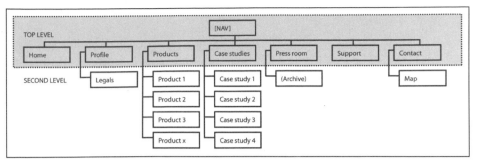

**Figure 3-1.** A site map, based on our content overview

> *Bear in mind that a site map isn't set in stone. In fact, with the methods we'll be using—CSS and Dreamweaver templates—you should be able to rapidly reorganize things. At this stage, a site map simply provides a foundation on which to develop the site in the early stages. Also, websites evolve as they're being developed. Don't be afraid to change things, if the end result will benefit.*

Upon creating a site map, content, design, and layout ideas should start to surface. For instance, we'll ensure top-level links are accessible at all times, or perhaps more prominent in some way should second-level links also be displayed. Most top-level links will be "overview" or "synopsis" pages, and the second-level links will contain in-depth information such as the products and case studies pages. "Profile" will contain a brief background on the company and senior staff, and also the company's vision or mission statement. However, it's worth noting that these pages can often come across as being very cheesy, so providing straightforward information about the company is of paramount importance, rather than just the mission statement (which is likely to sound like that of hundreds of other companies anyway). The homepage will likely contain numerous items, including an introduction to the company, customer quotes, and "pull-ins" to encourage people to explore further, such as news headlines, links to product pages, case studies, and so on.

Finally, as I've already mentioned, make sure you plan for content, giving yourself enough time to source or create it. People tend to think it'll be easy to rustle up some copy for web pages, but this takes longer than you might think.

# Design

For a corporate site, the design stage is often fairly brief. The overall look should be stylish, clean, and complement your brand, but flamboyance should be avoided. Many of the visual parts of a website can actually be developed with CSS later on, but you still need to work on a rough layout. Depending on your methods, you might start with paper and then work up your best ideas in a graphics package; alternatively, you may wish to start working right away on your PC or Mac. However, if you do, remember that simplicity is key—don't get carried away by lots of flashy effects.

> *Never underestimate the flexibility that working with paper affords you. It's possible to scribble down dozens of rough layout ideas, without getting distracted by software. From such basic layouts, you can then start working in a graphics package.*

## Working with layout

Web pages are typically built from rectangular sections, so try not to think in curves; don't try to mirror printed material, because it's often too complex—the Web and print are different mediums with different constraints and must be treated as such. Many printed brochures have text in columns or on curves, which doesn't work well online. For instance, text on curves has to be rendered as a graphic, and not as HTML text, so visitors won't be able to copy it or make a quality (readable) print of it. Columns should be avoided because of the way web pages work: unlike print, you often don't see the entire page at once, so if you use columns, visitors have to constantly scroll down and back up the page. Also, getting column-based content to be of equal length (without substantial intrusive editing) is nearly impossible on the Web.

> *One aspect of magazine columns worth bearing in mind is the use of narrow text columns. The human eye finds it easier to read text in relatively narrow columns, hence their use in magazines and newspapers. You should ensure your on-screen text is restricted in a similar way (albeit in a single column, not multiple ones); if your text spans the entire width of a 1024×768 browser window, visitors will simply give up on trying to read it and go elsewhere.*

Another print-based staple to be avoided is background images, which tend to obscure on-screen copy. When used with great care, a very subtle watermark can work online, but *never* make use of the Web's ability to tile backgrounds behind any content, unless you want visitors to flee. And if you do use a watermark, ensure that there is plenty of contrast between it and your text.

However, some ideas from your printed media should be retained, such as the brand, color scheme, and relevant copy and photography. That way, anyone who's already seen your printed material will straight away feel at home when first visiting the site.

Pages for corporate websites are classically broken down into the following areas:

- The masthead, which contains the main corporate identification, such as the logo
- The navigation (and subnavigation, if visible)
- The content area
- The footer, which usually contains a brief copyright statement, a link back to the top of the web page, and perhaps links to the homepage and disclaimer

Try scribbling a few basic layouts drawn on paper, just to get some ideas going. The final layout will largely depend on the relative dimensions on your corporate logo and how many top-level links you have.

## Mock-ups

The next step is to take a couple of sketched layouts and work them up in a graphics package. Don't worry about pixel-perfect precision—all we're after is a couple of rough layouts developed on screen. Instead of laboriously typing in lots of body copy, just insert "dummy" copy for now.

> There are various methods of getting dummy copy. For instance, you can use Dreamweaver's Latin extension, or grab some online from www.lipsum.com.

Note that you should be working with navigation links as defined in your site map. Also, if you're using a Mac and can change the color space in your graphics application, use sRGB, because this is the Windows standard, which most of your visitors will be using. The World Wide Web Consortium (W3C) provides a discussion of this topic at www.w3.org/Graphics/Color/sRGB if you'd like to know more.

Figure 3-2 illustrates the first design. It has horizontal navigation; a site built in this way would be easy to navigate, and the content area looks clean. Colors complement the brand, being the logo's color set at various opacities. However, although the design is in many ways suitable, it lacks the ability for us to easily add to it later. For instance, if a few more top-level links were needed, the design would have to be reworked, and corporate sites have a habit of being in a constant state of flux.

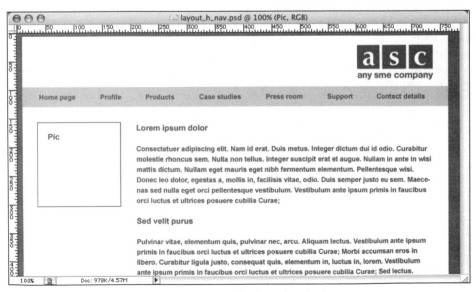

**Figure 3-2.** A rough website layout mock-up, with horizontal navigation

Figure 3-3 shows a design with vertical navigation. Links have been grouped under a colored heading, and several related top-level links from the site map have been combined into one section underneath the logo—a logical place for pages containing information about the company itself. Although it's subjective which of these initial designs looks better, the second one has more room for rapid expansion, and will be relatively simple to reorganize at a later date. It also provides access to some second-level links from the site map, which is handy if you want to give customers instant access to more content. Of course, the fact that ours is a fairly small site makes this possible, but the same concept can be applied to larger sites, if you logically group items.

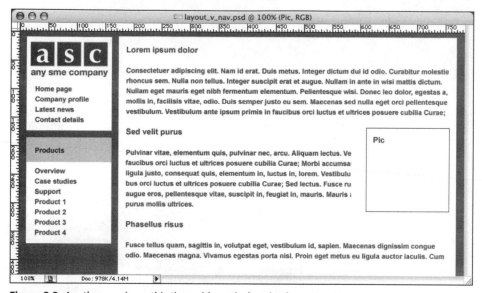

**Figure 3-3.** Another mock-up, this time with vertical navigation

However, from this mock-up, we can already see that some work will be needed with regards to the navigation area: for instance, the case studies and news areas should probably be grouped within a "Press room" section as per the original site map. We'll keep this in mind when developing our pages.

> *Remember to be flexible when designing a website. CSS and templates will enable you to amend various design, layout, and structural elements of the site fairly rapidly. Therefore, don't get too tied down at this stage about "perfecting" anything.*

Contrary to what you may have heard about how to make websites, we're not going to chop up this layout into a load of JPEGs and GIFs, and then put them all back together using a table. In fact, as we'll see later, only one graphic from this mock-up will be needed, and it won't be exported from the mock-up layout.

# Development

This is the longest part of the construction of our website, and we'll finally be getting to grips with Dreamweaver, along with delving into CSS. Prior to that, we need to get organized, in order to ensure important files don't go missing.

## File management

Some people claim they work better in a mess, but those people are usually the ones panicking because they accidentally trashed a file—virtual or physical—that has suddenly become essential. When working on websites, it pays to be organized and have everything within easy reach, including development and support files. Therefore, it's worth setting up a folder structure such as the one shown in Figure 3-4.

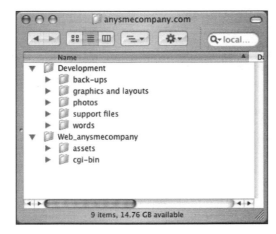

**Figure 3-4.**
An example of a typical website project folder hierarchy

The Development folder contains all development material, including original graphics and layouts prior to web optimization, scans of photos, and anything else you might need, such as Word documents, PDF files, and so on. Always keep these original files and don't overwrite them—you may need to refer to them again at a later date. Bear in mind that this is just a suggestion of how to organize your files—there are dozens of ways you can do so, and you have to discover which works best for you.

> *A general rule of thumb for website design is to never throw anything away. You never know when things might come in handy for the future. Keep backups of your site if things change significantly, not only for nostalgic reasons, but in case you want to reuse some previous ideas and information. It's also worth taking incremental backups when developing the website, in case something goes wrong—you can then revert to a previous version.*

The Web folder is your local website mirror. If you're working on several sites, append site names to the end of this folder; that way, you can easily differentiate between numerous Web folders when presented with a recent folders list.

The assets folder is where we'll keep website support files, such as images and things for download (for example, PDF files). The shared folder within the assets folder is for graphics used throughout the site, and is where we'll store the company logo and anything else that's used on every page. Note that a cgi-bin is the area on a web server where server-side scripts are placed, one of which we'll be looking at later to deal with feedback forms. Unless you're running a local web server, such scripts won't work on your PC. However, this won't be a problem when developing the site, so don't worry about it.

## Setting up Dreamweaver

Prior to working on the site, some of Dreamweaver's settings need checking. Dreamweaver is not geared towards legacy website design, and mostly adheres to W3C recommendations. However, we still need to ensure that certain settings are as they should be. By getting the preferences right before embarking on a project, you're more likely to wind up with an end result that's compatible across browsers and easier to edit.

> The World Wide Web Consortium, whose website can be visited via www.w3.org, makes the rules that govern web standards. Browser and web design application manufacturers are supposed to abide by these. Such rules and standards evolve, and obsolete legacy tags and attributes are marked as "deprecated" and should generally be avoided. Examples include the <font> tag, and the vast majority of attributes that you'd have previously placed within the <body> tag in order to control various default aspects of each page. All such things should now be controlled by Cascading Style Sheets.

### Preferences

Some of Dreamweaver's Preferences settings are down to personal taste (such as whether you want local files within the Files panel displayed on the left or right when it's expanded). Others are more important to ensure your site adheres to standards, so I've made some recommendations in the following text. Many of these settings are the defaults, but I'm going to mention them anyway, in case you've changed them.

As you can see in Figure 3-5, Dreamweaver's Preferences are grouped into categories, so you can keep track of how things are set up. You select a category from the list on the left, whereupon various options are displayed in the main area on the right of the panel.

General: There are few essential options here, but ensuring Use <strong> and <em> in place of <b> and <i> is checked is a good idea (this is Dreamweaver's default setting). Although the latter tags are more widely known, the former are more suitable for screen readers for the visually impaired; visual web browsers tend to render <strong> as <b> and <em> as <i> respectively. The Document options section also enables you to toggle the Start Page's appearance when opening the application.

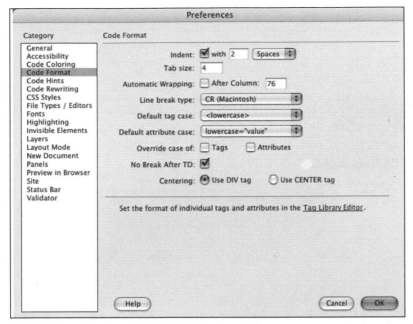

**Figure 3-5.** Dreamweaver's Preferences panel

Accessibility: Checking these boxes makes Dreamweaver prompt you for additional details when adding things like images, frames, and forms to your web pages. Note that on its own, these additions won't make your website accessible, but will at least enforce a few good habits. You should definitely ensure that at least the box for images is checked.

Code Format: Turn off Automatic Wrapping, because this can cause problems when working in Code view, making it tricky to edit body copy. (This is Dreamweaver's default setting, but I thought I'd mention it, in case you've messed around with the settings.) Ensure Default Tag Case and Default Attribute Case are set to lowercase (the recommended standard and Dreamweaver's default setting).

CSS Styles: Check all the shorthand boxes. This will streamline any Dreamweaver-created CSS rules. For instance, when defining margins, instead of margin-top: 10px; margin-right: 20px; margin-bottom: 5px; margin-left: 30px;, Dreamweaver will write margin: 10px 20px 5px 30px;.

Preview in Browser: You populate this list, as shown in Figure 3-6, with installed browsers by clicking the [+] icon and navigating to the relevant executable files on your hard drive. You can assign primary and secondary browser shortcuts to two of these browsers by selecting them and checking the relevant checkbox in the Defaults section.

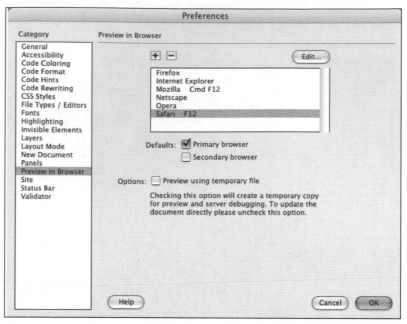

**Figure 3-6.** Dreamweaver enables you to select a number of browsers, to enable easy previewing of work-in-progress web pages.

## Building the layout

Now it's time to begin working on the first page, which upon completion will be transformed into a template. First, set up your site in Dreamweaver. Go to Site ➤ Manage Sites and select New ➤ New Site. Click Advanced and you will see the window depicted in Figure 3-7.

Under Site name, type in the website's name (anysmecompany.com) and then click the folder icon next to the Local root folder field, navigating to the Web folder created earlier (refer back to Figure 3-4). Click OK and Done to continue and Dreamweaver will set up the site.

Next, create a new document (File ➤ New or *CTRL/COMMAND+N*) and select the category Basic Page, then HTML from the Basic Page list, and check Make Document XHTML Compliant in the bottom right-hand corner, as shown in Figure 3-8.

> *XHTML is essentially the current version of HTML. There are a few differences to be aware of when using XHTML, such as the fact that all tags must be closed (including those without content, so* `<br>` *becomes* `<br />` *and* `<img src="an_image.jpg">` *becomes* `<img src="an_image.jpg" />)* *but by and large, you should have no problems adjusting and Dreamweaver automatically adjusts tags depending on what type of document you're creating.*

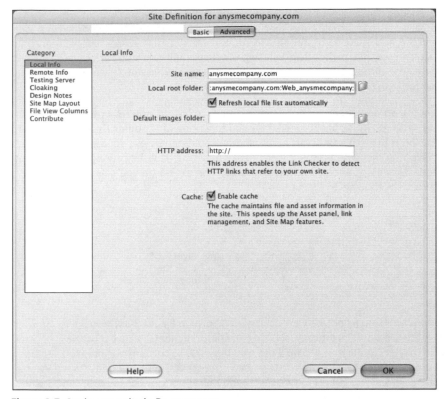

**Figure 3-7.** Setting up a site in Dreamweaver

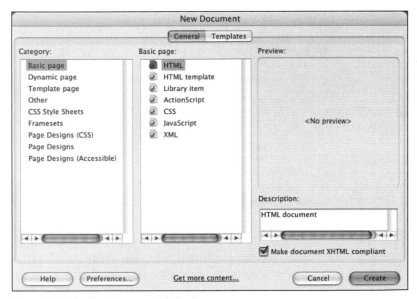

**Figure 3-8.** The New Document dialog box

Upon clicking Create, a new document will appear. Save this in the Web_anysmecompany.com folder as work_page.html. Note that we've replaced the space in the file name with an underscore and stuck to lowercase. This is a good system, because spaces are an illegal character in web file names, and by using lowercase and underscores only, file names will be consistent throughout the site, and therefore easy to remember; we'll be using it for all file names in this project.

Depending on how Dreamweaver is set up on your system, you may need to amend some display settings. The application enables you to work with Code or Design view, but I find Split to be more generally useful. This shows a split-pane view, so you can see code and your layout at the same time. You can change between views by clicking the buttons at the top-left of each document window, as shown in Figure 3-9. (If you can't see these buttons, go to View ➤ Toolbars ➤ Document.)

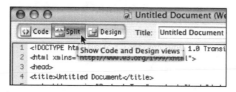

**Figure 3-9.**
Click these buttons to change the document view.

It's also worth turning on the view options, as shown in Figure 3-10. Visual aids (small icons within the Design view, mostly showing invisible elements) can be toggled on and off should they get in the way, but we'll use web browsers to confirm our site works rather than relying solely on Dreamweaver's Design view. The second set of options (Word Wrap, Line Numbers, and so on) relates to Code view and makes code easier to read. Unless you enjoy viewing a sea of black characters, ensure all of these options are turned on.

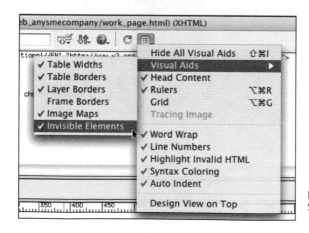

**Figure 3-10.**
Setting view options in Dreamweaver

## Page defaults

Now we're going to set up the page defaults for the web pages within our site. You might be used to defining such things via the <body> tag, but this is better controlled by CSS. This method means that should you later want to change, for instance, the entire site's background color, you can do so by editing and uploading a single CSS document, rather than every page of the entire site.

First, select Manage Styles from the Style drop-down menu in the Properties inspector, as shown in Figure 3-11.

**Figure 3-11.** Selecting Manage Styles in the Properties inspector

Upon seeing the Edit Style Sheet dialog box, click New and you'll see the New CSS Style dialog box (Figure 3-12). The Selector Type options enable you to create a new style for a class (which can be applied to multiple elements), tag (to redefine the look of a specific tag), or "advanced," which encompasses IDs and contextual selectors.

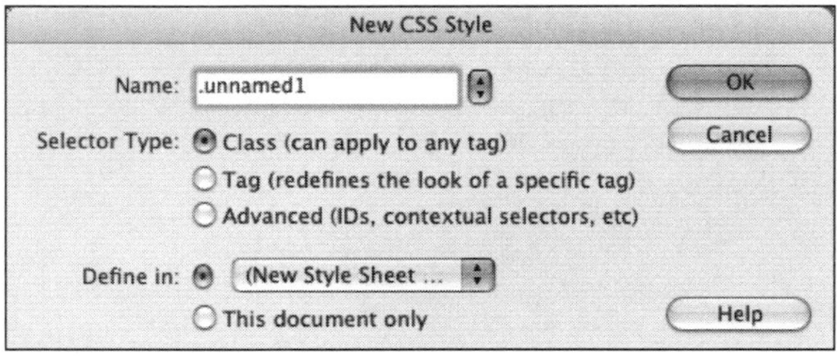

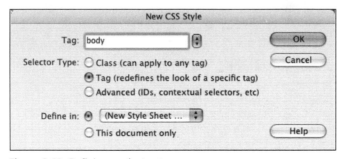

**Figure 3-12.** The New CSS Style dialog box

Choose Tag and you'll see the field at the top of the dialog box (Name in Figure 3-12) is now called Tag (this field label is context-sensitive). Either type body directly into the field or select it from the drop-down menu; ensure that Define in is set to New Style Sheet, because we don't yet have one (Figure 3-13).

**Figure 3-13.** Defining a selector type

Click OK and you'll be prompted to save the newly created CSS document. Call it anysmecompany.css and save it in the root of the Web_anysmecompany folder that was created earlier.

You'll then see the CSS Style Definition dialog box. Here, you can set various property values for the style (which in this case will affect the web page's <body> tag). Under the Type category, choose Georgia, Times New Roman, Times, serif for Font, 13 pixels for Size, and #111111 for Color, as shown in Figure 3-14. This hex value is a dark gray, which is more readable and professional than the blue text on the layout mock-ups produced earlier. The background color is set within the Background category, and should be #518bc1— this was taken from the mock-ups, using a graphics package's color picker.

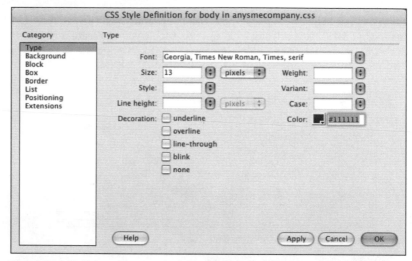

**Figure 3-14.** Defining property values for the body tag using the CSS Style Definition dialog box

> When defining colors in hex, don't neglect to include the pound sign (#). Although Dreamweaver's Design view may still display defined colors without this, not all web browsers do.

Although it's often recommended to use a sans-serif font on screen, such as Verdana, Georgia is also a good choice for body copy, as it's very readable when displayed at the size we're using. If you're not sure about this choice of font, don't worry about it. Extensive use of CSS means things like this can easily be edited site-wide at a later date just by amending the CSS document. This is, of course, a far more efficient method than having to change dozens of font tags on each page, and also ensures site-wide consistency.

Finally, the Box category (shown in Figure 3-15) enables you to set margins and padding for your website's pages. As you can see in the mock-ups, there is a 10-pixel surround, so we set Margin to 10 pixels (with Same for All checked) and Padding to 0, to ensure content sits flush to the browser window edges.

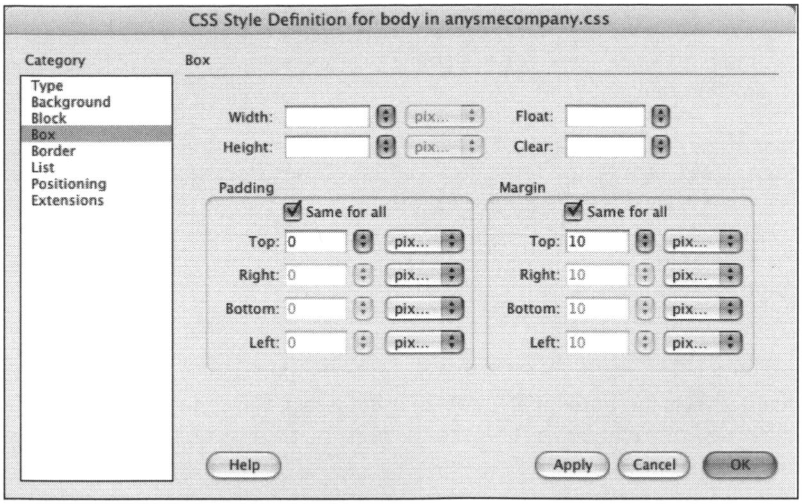

**Figure 3-15.** Defining box property values

Click OK and Done in the subsequent dialog boxes. Dreamweaver automatically saves the style sheet and attaches it to your web page. The results are visible in both Design and Code views—the former should now sport a blue background, while the latter will have the following code within the <head> section:

```
<link href="anysmecompany.css" rel="stylesheet" type="text/css" />
```

> *When you're working with multiple files, it's sometimes easy to forget to save them all. You should regularly save all of your open files, which Dreamweaver makes easy via* File ➤ Save All. *By default, this doesn't have a keyboard shortcut, but you can always add one by going to* Edit ➤ Keyboard Shortcuts (Dreamweaver ➤ Keyboard Shortcuts *on Mac*).

## Style sheet code explained

Style sheet rules are made up of two parts: a **selector** and a **declaration**. The former specifies the parts of the HTML document to which the style should be applied, and the latter is made up of property/value pairs that can be applied to the element defined in the selector. When a declaration has multiple property/value pairs, they are separated by semicolons:

```
selector {
property: value;
property: value;
}
```

The final semicolon in a declaration isn't required, but is good practice, because it means you don't have to remember to put one in should you add another pair later.

**139**

Open up anysmecompany.css, by double-clicking it in the Files panel (if this is not visible, go to Window ➤ File or press *F8*). Because style sheets are code-based, the document window defaults to Code view. After opening anysmecompany.css, you'll see something like the following code:

```
body {
font: 13px Georgia, "Times New Roman", Times, serif;
color: #111111;
background: #518bc1;
margin: 10px;
padding: 0px;
}
```

In this case, the selector is the HTML <body> tag, so the declaration (everything within the curly braces) affects the body of any web page we attach this style sheet to. The declaration is composed of a number of property/value pairs, each of which define some aspect of the web page's <body> tag.

```
font: 13px Georgia, "Times New Roman", Times, serif;
```

The preceding pair sets the default font for the website—13-pixel Georgia—and offers alternatives should that font not be installed: Times New Roman, Times, and then finally a generic serif font. Note that because the Times New Roman font name is made up of more than one word, it is surrounded by quotes in the style sheet.

```
color: #111111;
background: #518bc1;
```

The preceding two property/name pairs deal with the default color of web page content (namely, the default font color) and the default background color.

```
margin: 10px;
padding: 0px;
```

These final pairs are the settings for the margin and padding around the page's contents, set to 10 pixels and 0 respectively. It's worth stating both explicitly when styling the <body> tag, because some browsers don't default to 0 for these properties.

Using similar code, you can control most aspects of your web pages from this single CSS document. For instance, the following code would make the contents of all <h1> tags red:

```
h1 {
color: red;
}
```

The reason I've provided this CSS overview is because we'll sometimes be working directly with CSS rules, or just saying how to style a particular element. This is fairly easy once you get the hang of it, and quicker than working through the CSS Style Definition dialog box for every style you want to introduce or edit.

*For a more detailed explanation of CSS, check out* www.w3schools.com *or see the book* Cascading Style Sheets: Separating Content From Presentation, *2nd Edition, by Briggs et al. (Apress, ISBN: 1-590592-31-X).*

## Layout structure

The page design we're going to work with is essentially made up of two boxes: the navigation (which includes the logo), and the content. The site will have a footer, so that needs to be taken into account, too.

When working with CSS, it pays to work out your page's structure prior to designing, and decide how each of the elements will interact. Our design suggests a page structure like that in Figure 3-16.

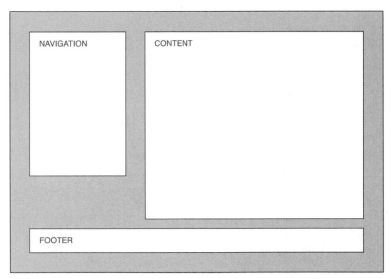

**Figure 3-16.** Our web page's basic structure

As of Dreamweaver MX 2004, this sort of structure can rapidly be built in Design view. Essentially, you create your structure by adding <div> elements to the web page, which are then styled in CSS, so they take on the required positioning, padding, margins, and so on.

These are added by clicking the Insert Div Tag button, found within the Layout section of the Insert bar (Figure 3-17). Doing so brings up the Insert Div Tag dialog box (Figure 3-18), which enables you to set a class or ID value for the <div> and also state where it is to be placed within the document.

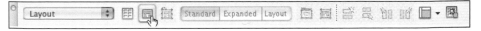

**Figure 3-17.** The Insert Div Tag button

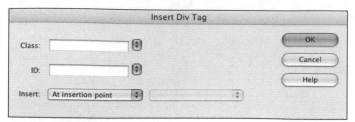

**Figure 3-18.** The Insert Div Tag dialog box

For our site, we want to add three <div> elements, each with an ID value that relates to its purpose. Therefore, first click anywhere inside Design view, then click the Insert Div Tag button. In the ID field, type navigation and then click OK. You'll see the <div> added to your web page, with some dummy content, as shown in Figure 3-19.

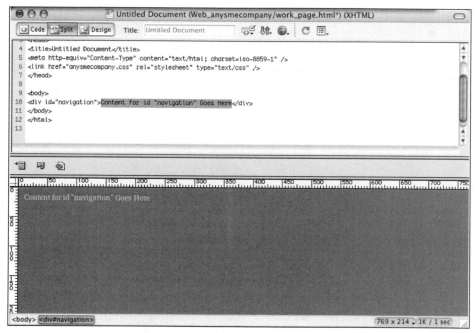

**Figure 3-19.** A <div> added to the web page

Click the Insert Div Tag button again, and this time type content in the ID field. If you check out the structural diagram again (Figure 3-16) you'll see that this <div> appears after the navigation one. Therefore, we must also state this in the Insert Div Tag dialog box. From the Insert drop-down menu, select After tag and then select <div id="navigation"> (the previous tag we added), as shown in Figure 3-20. Click OK and you'll again see the <div> added to the web page, and it should sit underneath the previous one.

**Figure 3-20.** Setting where a <div> will be placed on the web page

Follow this process one more time, to add the final <div>. This time, type footer into the ID field. This <div> needs to appear after the content one, so again we have to set Insert to After tag, but this time select <div id="content">. Upon clicking OK and returning to the web page, you should see something like what's depicted in Figure 3-21. The three <div> elements are displayed one under the other. If you mouse over one of them, a red border appears, showing the edge of the <div>. Now we need to style them, to make our web page resemble the mock-up.

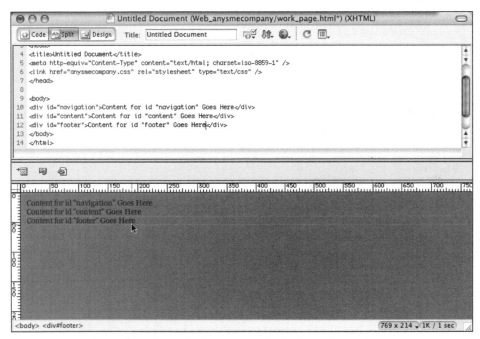

**Figure 3-21.** The three <div> elements that make up the structure of our web page

*You may be wondering why we're not using tables, which are perhaps more intuitive to use. CSS provides more control over layout, and each element within a CSS-based layout is independent of the others. Therefore, as we'll see later, we can rapidly edit and amend our web pages just by editing the CSS file, rather than having to merge table cells, use spacer GIFs, and so on.*

## Styling page divisions

For each of the <div> elements we need to create a new CSS rule in the anysmecompany.css file created earlier. Here's the procedure for doing so:

**1.** Select Manage Styles from the Properties inspector's Style drop-down menu.

**2.** When the Edit Style Sheet dialog box appears, click New.

**3.** In the New CSS Style dialog box, choose a selector type (I'll say which one in each case), and type its value in the field at the top of the dialog box.

**4.** Choose where to define the rule (by default, this selects the already attached style sheet) and click OK.

**5.** Use the CSS Style Definition dialog box to set property values.

Take care when typing the selector value into the field at the top of the dialog box. CSS classes must be preceded by a period (.), and IDs with a pound sign (#). Leaving these off can render the rule useless.

Okay, then: time to style our first division—the navigation <div>. In the New CSS Style dialog box, choose Advanced for the selector type and type #navigation into the field at the top of the dialog box (now named Selector). Click OK, and in the CSS Style Definition dialog box, set the following values:

■ In Background, set Background color to #ffffff (or use the color picker to choose white, as shown in Figure 3-22).

■ In Box, set Width to 160 pixels, and Float to left.

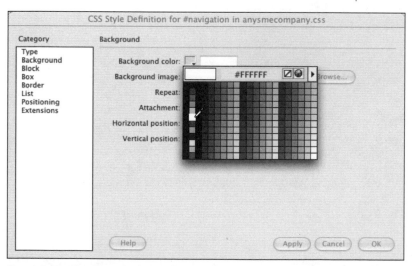

**Figure 3-22.** Choosing a background color

All of those properties should be familiar to you, with the possible exception of **float**. This is one of the most important properties to master when working in CSS. If you float an HTML element, other page content wraps around it. You can see this in Figure 3-23, which shows the newly styled navigation <div>, with the other content now appearing to the right.

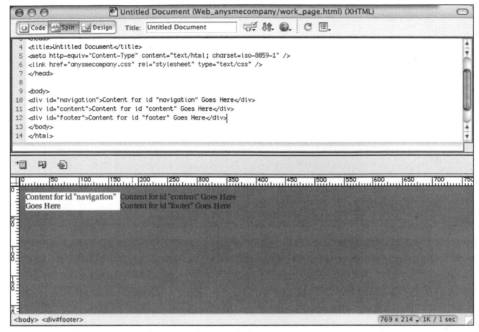

**Figure 3-23.** The navigation <div> after being styled

Next up is the content <div>. Again, choose Advanced for the selector type in the New CSS Style dialog box, but this time type #content into the Selector field. Click OK, and in the CSS Style Definition dialog box, set the following values:

- In Background, again set Background color to #ffffff.
- In Box, set Float to left.
- Set Padding to 10 pixels.
- Under Margin, uncheck Same for all and in Left type 10 (see Figure 3-24).

The difference between padding and margins should be obvious when you see the result in Design view. The content of the content <div> now has padding around it, and the entire <div> is now 10 pixels to the right of the navigation <div>. In this case, margins define space around a <div>, while padding sets padding within it.

Finally, the footer is defined. Choose Advanced for the selector type in the New CSS Style dialog box, and type #footer into the Selector field. Click OK, and set the following values in the CSS Style Definition dialog box:

- In Block, set Text align to right.
- In Box, set Padding to 10 pixels and Clear to both.

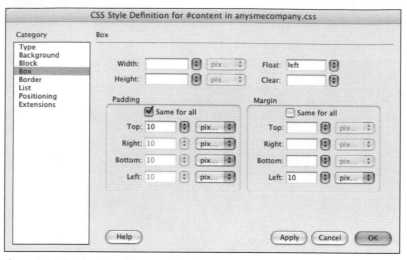

**Figure 3-24.** Setting Box property values for the content <div>

The last of those property/value pairs—clear: both—is one that positions the element its applied to underneath all floated content. Therefore, regardless of the amount of content in our content <div>, the footer will appear underneath it. As you can see from Figure 3-25, the page is now beginning to resemble the mock-up.

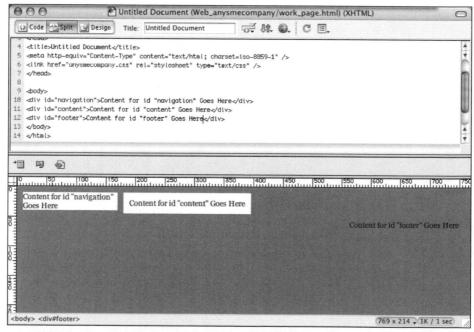

**Figure 3-25.** The web page, with styled <div> elements

## Editing invisible elements

Now we'll edit some invisible elements within the <head> area of our web page. The page needs a title, for the browser's title bar. Many people forget to add these, and so countless web pages online are titled untitled.html or something similar. Not only does this look unprofessional, but it compromises your standing in search engine results. The simplest way to add a title is to ensure the Document toolbar is on (View ➤ Toolbars ➤ Document) and add your page's title within the Title field.

The homepage title should usually include your company name and a few keywords about what you offer. It's usually best to title other pages with the name of the company and the name of the page/subsection as appropriate, such as "Any SME Company—Products—Product one."

We also need to create some meta tags, which are used to assist search engines. Due to these being abused at various points in the past, they are losing their importance, and many search engines simply use the content of your site to return results. However, they are still worth including.

Insert ➤ HTML ➤ Head Tags ➤ Meta brings up the dialog box depicted in Figure 3-26. For each new tag, you must add its value and content into the Value and Content fields respectively, as well as selecting the relevant Attribute from the drop-down menu.

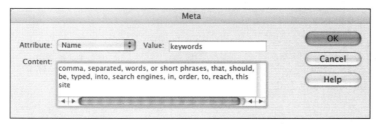

**Figure 3-26.** The Meta dialog box

The most important of these are the values keywords and description. The content of keywords should be a short, comma-separated list of keywords or short phrases that may be typed into search engines in order to access your site. The content of description should be a short, 20-word (or thereabouts) description about the website and what it offers; make it too long and search engines will crop it. Both of these require the Name attribute.

Two fairly useful tags that require the http-equiv attribute are pragma and imagetoolbar. Setting the former's content to no-cache instructs browsers to reload the page on each visit (although, frankly, with variable results), while setting the latter's content to false means that the image toolbar in the Windows version of Internet Explorer 6+ is cancelled.

## Adding the navigation bar

Now we're going to deal with the navigation bar, which includes the links to all the areas of the website, along with the company logo. The first thing to do is import the logo.

The navigation <div> has a width of 160 pixels, but the mock-up's navigation area has a gap of 10 pixels around its contents, so the final required width of the logo is 140 pixels.

### Editing the logo

Getting a version of your company logo at such dimensions can be done in many ways, but always make sure you start with the best quality image you have—preferably a copy of the original logo file (most likely an EPS or native Illustrator or Freehand file) rather than a scan or low-resolution bitmap. We've dropped the original logo file, as created in Illustrator, onto Photoshop and chosen the required width (see Figure 3-27). However, you could just as easily use another graphics package, such as Fireworks or the GIMP, for what follows.

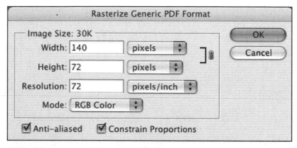

**Figure 3-27.** Rasterizing the logo in Photoshop

Once sizes are chosen, the logo is antialiased (made smooth, rather than having jagged edges). Should you need to change the size of the logo at a later date, reimport it rather than trying to resize the low-resolution bitmap generated here; otherwise the result will be poor in terms of quality. Also, never resize images by stretching them in Dreamweaver or HTML; otherwise, they will look distorted.

Depending on how the import into your graphics package goes, you might want to tidy up the logo. In Figure 3-28, we can see that antialiasing has blurred the edges of the squares, so we've selected square areas and colored them to make the edges solid once again. When saving an image like this, which is mostly made up of limited, flat colors, choose the GIF format. Conversely, photographic images should be exported as JPEGs. The image should be saved as any_sme_company_logo.gif in assets/shared within our Web_anysmecompany folder. The logo is placed in the shared folder because it will be used on all pages of the site.

> As I've already mentioned, keep a common naming convention across your entire website. Good practice is to use lowercase letters, and underscores instead of spaces. You should never use spaces within file names for the Web.

**Figure 3-28.** Tidying up the imported logo using Photoshop's Marquee and Brush tools

### Importing the logo

In Design view, click before the navigation <div> dummy text. Use the Insert bar's drop-down menu to access the Common selection, then click the Images button and select Image from the drop-down menu (Figure 3-29). In the subsequent dialog box, navigate to the any_sme_company_logo.gif and hit *ENTER* to add it to the web page.

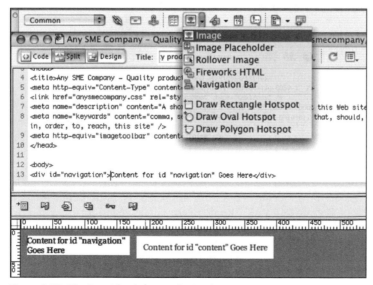

**Figure 3-29.** The Insert bar's Image button/menu

If you've turned on the accessibility preferences that I mentioned earlier (see "Setting up Dreamweaver"), you'll see the Image Tag Accessibility Attributes dialog box. In the Alternate text field, type something that's indicative of what the image is for (in this case, Any SME Company would suffice). Click OK and the logo will appear on the web page. Note that if you don't have accessibility preferences active, you can add alt text by selecting the image and adding your text to the Properties inspector's Alt field.

> Remember that alternate text, often referred to as alt text, is supposed to provide an indication of what the image is for. Keep such text succinct and helpful, and never just use the file name of the image, because that's of no help to anyone using an alternate browser.

It's perhaps worth noting one of Dreamweaver's odd quirks at this point. I said to click on Design view prior to adding the image. This is because Dreamweaver automatically includes useful attributes and values when doing so, such as the image's height and width. If you first click Code view and then insert an image, these attributes aren't included.

### Styling the logo

The logo is currently sitting flush against the sides of the navigation <div>, so we need to create a CSS style to add margins, and apply said style to the logo. Bring up the now familiar New CSS Style dialog box, and choose Advanced as the selector type. Type #navLogo into the Selector field. Click OK, and select the Box category of the CSS Style Definition dialog box. Uncheck Same for All under Margin and set Top, Right, Bottom, and Left to 10 pixels, 0 pixels, 10 pixels, and 10 pixels respectively.

> Note the convention we've used for multiple-word CSS rules: wordWord. This is down to personal preference—you could, for instance, just use lowercase. However, you should avoid underscores and spaces in such names, because certain browsers choke on them.

Applying the style to the logo is simple: select the image in Design view, then right/CTRL-click the <img> tag on the Status bar at the bottom of the document window. Navigate to Set ID ➤ navLogo, as shown in Figure 3-30. Upon selecting this style, you should see the margin appear around the logo in Design view. In Code view, you should also see a change in the <img> tag, which will now contain the attribute id="navLogo".

### Creating a navigation bar

The next stage of our project involves working on the navigation area—something that's crucial to every website's success. The popularity of animation, largely due to the Flash plug-in, means that many companies employ flamboyant interfaces on their websites. Unless this is totally relevant to your organization, I recommend that you steer clear of such things. Animated interfaces take time to update, and rely on plug-in technology being installed on the visitor's web browser. Furthermore, animations take time to execute, and people visiting SME sites often don't want to hang around: they want to access the site, get the information they require, and then go elsewhere. Wasting their time— even for only a niggling few seconds—only serves to put them off your company.

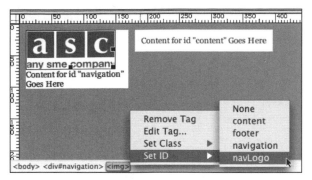

**Figure 3-30.** Applying a style to the logo

Instead, we're going to use some basic HTML for our navigation, and CSS to style it. In fact, existing HTML tags are perfect for navigation, which is effectively comprised of one or more lists of links. It therefore follows that we're going to largely use HTML lists as the basis for our navigation, with headings in between to title them and break up the list into visually manageable groups.

At the moment, underneath the logo should be the default "dummy" copy that Dreamweaver places inside any <div> added to a web page. Carefully delete this text (and not the logo), hit *ENTER*, and then click the Unordered List button in the Properties inspector, as shown in Figure 3-31. Add the following list items: Introduction, Company profile, Contact details, Legals. Then hit *ENTER* twice to terminate the list and create a new, blank paragraph.

The process of deleting the dummy copy and hitting *ENTER* has enabled us to insert our list, but also provided our logo with some unwanted formatting—an unfortunate quirk of working with Dreamweaver's Design view. If you select it, the Properties inspector will show the logo is formatted as a paragraph—something you can also see by looking at the code in Code view. This is redundant—we've already used CSS to position our logo where we want it. We also don't want subsequent CSS definitions of paragraphs to affect the logo, forcing us to make workarounds. Therefore, we need to remove this formatting. Doing so is a simple process: either

- Select the logo, right/*CTRL*-click the <p> tag in the status bar, and choose Remove Tag, or

- Select the logo, press *LEFT* on your keyboard to effectively select the paragraph, then use the Format menu of the Properties inspector to select None.

*This highlights why it's a good idea to work in Split view. Although Dreamweaver is a fairly intelligent application, it sometimes inserts tags that you don't want. Being able to catch such events as they happen is beneficial, and far better than trying to fix all such things once the site is nearing completion.*

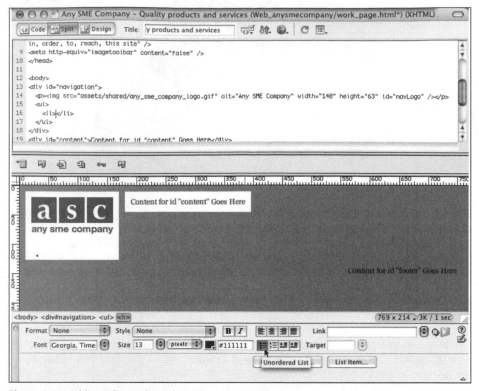

**Figure 3-31.** Adding a list to the web page

Now we can get on with adding the rest of our navigation bar. Earlier, you used Dreamweaver to create an empty paragraph underneath the list. Click inside it and type Products, then hit *ENTER* and create another list, with the items Overview, Product one, Product two, Product three, Product four, and Support. Hit *ENTER* twice to terminate this list and create a new paragraph, then type Press room. Hit *ENTER* again and create another list, this time with the items Case studies, Latest news, and News archive. Once done, there's no need to hit *ENTER* again, because we don't want another blank paragraph. The result should look like what you see in Figure 3-32.

### Creating and styling headings

At the moment, the headings that separate the lists—Products and Press room—are formatted as paragraphs, but we want to change this. As far as possible, we want to be working with **semantic mark-up**—that is, using the relevant and appropriate tags in every case. This aids alternate browsers when rendering a site, and also makes for more logical code. As I've said already, these two words are headings, used to introduce a group of links. Therefore, it follows that they should be marked up as such.

Doing so is easy: select each in turn and use the Properties inspector's Format menu to apply Heading 1 to each of them. Upon doing so, each will be displayed much larger in Design view (due to taking on the default appearance of a large heading); in Code view, you'll see the paragraph tags (<p>) replaced with <h1> tags.

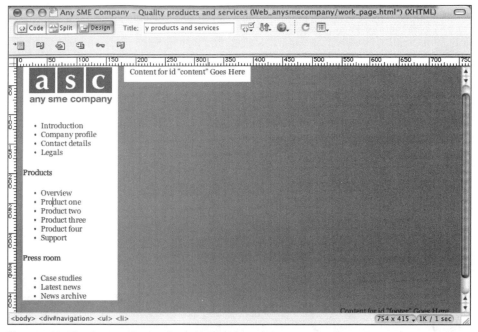

**Figure 3-32.** The three navigation lists added to the web page

We now need to style these headings. As we've seen earlier, when styling the <body> tag, HTML tags can be styled using CSS. In the case of our headings, we want to style <h1> tags. However, we will most likely be using such headings in the content area, too, and these will have a different style. Therefore, we need to use a **contextual selector**. A contextual selector effectively applies a declaration to a specific rule when in context. In our case, we need to apply a rule to <h1> tags that are inside the navigation <div>. The navigation <div> selector, as created earlier, was #navigation. Therefore, the contextual selector for <h1> tags within the navigation <div> is #navigation h1. Still with me? Good. (If not, have another read, and let it sink in.)

So, on to the styling. Open up the New CSS Style dialog box (if you've forgotten how, Style ➤ Manage Styles in the Properties inspector, then New in the Edit Style Sheet dialog box) and choose Advanced as the selector type (which, usefully, has contextual selectors listed as an example of what Advanced should be used for). Type #navigation h1 into the Selector field and hit OK.

In the CSS Style Definition dialog box, select the Type category. Set Font to Arial, Helvetica, sans-serif. This is a sans-serif font and will therefore make it easier to differentiate the navigation from the body copy, which we defined earlier as a serif font. Set the Size to 13 pixels, Weight to bold, and Case to uppercase. The last of those values is an interesting one, enabling you to "force" type to a certain case (in this instance, uppercase, but lowercase and capitalize are other options).

In the Background category, set Background color to #cbdff2, remembering to not omit the pound sign (#). This hex value was taken from the original mock-up. We next specify some padding around the headings, by going into the Box category and setting Padding to 10 pixels. (When setting padding here, ensure Same for all is checked prior to setting the Top value to 10 pixels—it's quicker than setting them all individually to 10 pixels!)

Finally, we're going to set a 10-pixel top border on each heading that's identical to the background color of the web page to provide the visual illusion that each set of headings and links is a self-contained block. This is done in the Border category: uncheck all of the Same for all boxes, then, for the Top border only, set Style to solid, Width to 10 pixels, and Color to #518bc1—the same as our body's background color. Click Done twice and the results should resemble those in Figure 3-33.

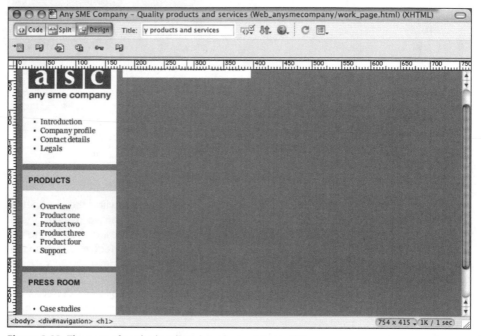

**Figure 3-33.** The page after the headings have been styled in CSS

### Creating and styling lists and links

We now need to turn all of our list items into navigable, styled links. To change the list items into links, select them, then enter a file to link to in the Properties inspector's Link field, and hit *ENTER*. Page names should relate to their contents, but with underscores replacing spaces, and all in lowercase. So for Company Profile, the linked page would be company_profile.html. The only exceptions in our site are Introduction, which links to the homepage (index.html) and the products overview page, Overview. Because overview.html would be too generic a name, we've gone for products.html as its name. All of these can be changed at a later date, which I'll show you how to do later.

These grouped of links are composed of three separate elements, each of which require styling in CSS:

1. The containing list
2. The list items
3. The links

Because we only want to affect each of these things within the navigation <div>, we'll again be using a contextual selector in each instance.

So, back to the New CSS Style dialog box, we choose Advanced as the selector type, and type #navigation ul into the Selector field and hit OK. In the List category, we set Type to none, which removes the default bullet from our list items. In Box, Margin is set to 0, to remove any default margins that browsers apply. In Padding, we uncheck Same for all and set all values to 0, except for Top, which should be 10 pixels.

> *You may be wondering why we don't just set all padding values on our list to 10 pixels. Typically, CSS-based design works well when you remove the top margins and then use the bottom ones to space elements. This ensures consistency across browsers and throughout the design. If you remember earlier, we set the margin underneath our logo to 10 pixels, so the "gap" between the logo and first list has already been dealt with. Similarly, the "gap" between each heading and list is dealt with by the default margin settings that browsers apply, although we'll likely change this later.*

Click OK and New to get back to the New CSS Style dialog box. This time, our selector is to be #navigation li and only one thing needs to be set: in the Box category, set Margin to 0. Setting margins around list elements is not strictly necessary, but some browsers—notably Opera—apply a default margin. Therefore, to ensure no margin, it's best to explicitly set it to zero.

For the links themselves, we must determine which properties we want to define site-wide, and which should only be applied to links within the navigation <div>. Things like font weight, color, and decoration can be defined site-wide, as can a background on the hover state. Navigation-specific elements for our site are a specific font and font size for navigation links, and any padding we want to place around the links to separate them out.

> *I refer to the hover state in the preceding text. As you may know, links have four states: link, visited, hover, active, the last two of which represent the link state when the cursor is over and clicking the link respectively. These days, it's common to merely style the default and hover states. However, if you wish, you can add additional rules for the other states, to differentiate links the visitor's already clicked on, and to create an effect when a link is clicked.*

In the New CSS Style dialog box, choose Tag as the selector type and type a into the Tag field. In the CSS Style Definition dialog box, select the Type category and set Weight to bold, Color to #003f8d, and Decoration to none, which removes the default underline from links.

> If removing the default underline from links, as we're doing, you must ensure that you still differentiate them from your other text. We've done this by making them bold and a different color than the body copy.

Go back to the New CSS Style dialog box, choose Advanced as the selector type, and choose a:hover from the Selector drop-down menu. In the CSS Style Definition dialog box, select the Type category and set Color to #111111; in the Background category, set Background color to #cbdff2.

Finally, create another new advanced selector in the New CSS Style dialog box, called #navigation a. In the CSS Style Definition dialog box, select the Type category and set Font to Arial, Helvetica, sans-serif and Size to 12 pixels. In Box, uncheck Same for all under Padding, and define the values as 2, 10, 2, and 10 respectively (all in pixels). Set Width to 120 pixels and in the Block category, set Display to block. The last of those rules means that the navigation links act more like buttons, so the visitor can mouse over the blank areas next to the links and still activate them. When viewed in a browser, the padding settings produce a gap around the link during the hover state, which looks better than having the content hug the sides of the background.

> You'll note that we set the width of the links to 120 pixels, rather than 140 pixels, which is the width of the logo. This is because of the way the CSS box model works. Padding values are added to the defined width, and are not a part of it. Therefore, our link elements are effectively 140 pixels wide: the 120-pixel width definition, plus the two 10-pixel padding definitions. Setting the width to 140 pixels would actually make the effective element width 160 pixels. This, in addition to our padding settings on the lists, would break the layout.

The result (seen in Figure 3-34) mostly looks fine, but there's some suspect spacing, due to default margins around the headings (which actually varies from browser to browser). Therefore, we need to explicitly define margins around our navigation area's headings.

To edit a style that already exists, we need to go to Style ➤ Manage Styles in the Properties inspector, select anysmecompany.css, and click Edit. We then need to select the rule we want to edit (in this case, #navigation h1) and click Edit. All we want to do is edit the margins; as you may remember, Margin is found in the Box category. Uncheck Same for all and set all margins to 0, apart from Bottom, which should be set to 10 pixels. This then results in much better spacing, which can be seen in Figure 3-35.

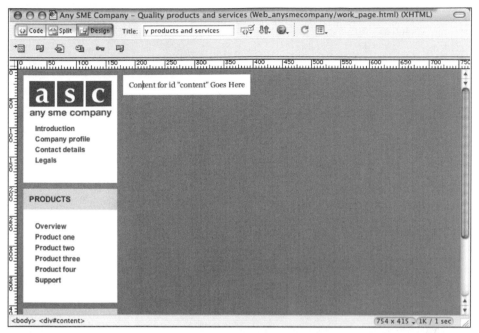

**Figure 3-34.** The styled navigation, albeit with some suspect spacing

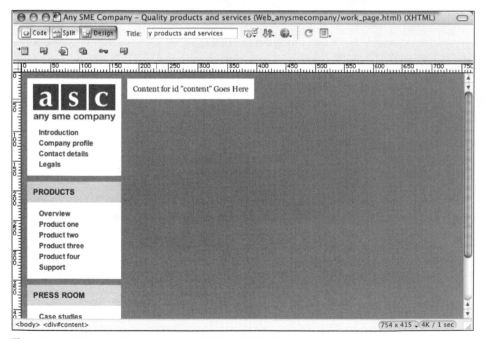

**Figure 3-35.** The styled navigation, with improved spacing

### Adding the footer

By comparison, working on the footer is simple. The footer for this site will include a copyright statement, and links to Home and the top of the page. In Design view, add the following content:

© 200X by Any SME Company | Home | Top

Link "Home" to index.html as we did earlier—click it, type index.html in the File field of the Properties inspector, and hit ENTER. Next, we'll turn "Top" into a "top of page" link. You may have seen links to #top, but this only works with Internet Explorer for Windows. You could place a named anchor at the top of your web page, such as <a name="top"> </a> and link to that instead, but this has a couple of problems. First, the space will be displayed as a styled link as per the settings earlier, and will also cause subsequent content to shift downwards.

Instead, we'll combine the #top method with JavaScript. There are a number of ways that we can add the code, but the simplest is just to type the following directly in Code view:

```
<a href="#top" onclick="javascript: scrollTo(0,0);"
onmouseover="window.status='Top'; return true;"
onmouseout="window.status='';">Top</a>
```

This JavaScript does two things when the link is clicked: scrollTo (0,0) scrolls the page to the coordinates (0,0), which is the top left of the page, and the window.status code places Top into the browser's status bar when you hover over the link, and removes this when you move the cursor off the link.

Some people turn off JavaScript, but such browsers have the #top link to fall back on. The chances of someone using a browser that doesn't understand #top *and* has JavaScript turned off is low.

## Testing the page

The basic web page, without content, is now complete. Note that although Dreamweaver MX 2004's Design view is much improved over previous versions (largely due to it using the Opera browser's engine to display everything), it's not perfect. And if you choose to flag invisible elements in the Preferences dialog box, the resulting icons will disrupt your layout. Also, various web browsers have their own quirks, so you should get into the habit of regularly testing your pages in them during development. Dreamweaver enables you to do this "on the fly" via its preview function (File ➤ Preview in Browser, or by using the primary and secondary browser shortcuts defined earlier). Alternatively, just drop the page directly onto a web browser for testing, making sure changes are saved first.

Some browsers can be problematic with regards to cache settings. Always ensure that you have their Preferences set to reload pages on each new visit, otherwise they might display an old version of your page, despite your having edited it since. Also, some—in particular the Macintosh version of Internet Explorer—hang onto style sheets within the cache for dear life. If your updates aren't appearing, force-reload (usually *ALT*-refresh for PCs or *OPTION*-refresh for Macs) or load the style sheet into a separate browser window and refresh it from there.

The most important browser to test in is Internet Explorer for Windows, versions 6 and 5.5, which command well over 80% of the market. However, don't stop there, as you wouldn't turn away a fifth of your visitors at the door, so you shouldn't online. You should also at least test in Mozilla (or Firefox) and, if possible, Internet Explorer on the Macintosh, which has some layout differences compared with the Windows version. Opera is worth installing, although its results should mirror those of Dreamweaver's Design view. Finally, Safari is the new default Mac OS browser, so it warrants testing in, too.

One disadvantage of Windows is the fact that you can only install one version of Internet Explorer, but there are marked differences between versions. To save buying multiple PCs, check out VirtualPC (available from www.connectix.com), which enables you to run multiple "virtual" PCs on a single machine, each of which can run their own operating system and version of Internet Explorer. VirtualPC is available for Macintosh and Windows. Alternatively, check out Insert Title Web Designs' method for installing various versions of Internet Explorer on a single PC: www.insert-title.com/web_design/?page=articles/dev/multi_IE. Zipped files for download are available at www.skyzyx.com/archives/000094.php.

## Creating a template

Assuming there aren't any major problems during testing, it's time to turn our page into a template. Once this is complete, we'll use this to create the site's pages. It also enables you to rapidly update your site: make changes to the template, and Dreamweaver automatically updates all pages based on it. In order to change the current document into a template, go to File ➤ Save as Template and name the file maintemplate.dwt. When asked whether you want to update links, click Yes. Dreamweaver automatically places the file into the Templates folder (which it creates) within the Web_anysmecompany folder.

> *Be aware that Dreamweaver templates are proprietary technology, so they won't work in other web editors, such as GoLive or FrontPage. However, they should work fine in other copies of Dreamweaver.*

Dreamweaver templates work by locking the entire page, and then enabling you to open up parts of it for editing by defining "editable regions." Doing so is a simple process: select an area in Design or Code view that's to be made editable, go to Insert ➤ Template Objects ➤ Editable Region, and give it a name. (Alternatively, you can right/*CTRL*-click selected content and choose Template ➤ New Editable Region, or even use the Insert bar, as shown in Figure 3-36.)

**Figure 3-36.** Using the Insert bar to add an editable region

For our main template, only the content area needs to be editable, so the dummy content is selected, and one of the methods outlined previously employed to create a new editable region. This prompts the New Editable Region dialog box (see Figure 3-37), within which you name the newly created region. As with CSS rules, it's a good idea to sensibly name editable regions, basing said names on the region's purpose. Also similarly, avoiding spaces and underscores is a wise move, leading us to use the wordWord convention again: thus our chosen name for this region is pageContent.

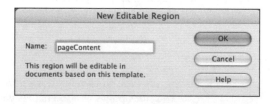

**Figure 3-37.**
The New Editable Region dialog box

Note that when adding such regions, Dreamweaver adds markup to your web page. Although this won't have much effect on download times (the amount of code it adds is negligible), don't panic when additional code suddenly appears in Code view.

As a slight aside, it's worth noting that Dreamweaver sometimes places the beginning or end of the editable region on the opposite end of a tag to what you intended. If this occurs (and this is usually easier to see in Code view), try selecting the template tag (something like `<!-- InstanceBeginEditable name="pageContent" -->`) and moving it to the other side of the HTML tag in question as in the following example:

Before:

```
<div id="content">
  <h1><!-- InstanceBeginEditable name="pageContent" -->A heading</h1>
```

After:

```
<div id="content"><!-- InstanceBeginEditable name="pageContent" -->
  <h1>A heading</h1>
```

# Adding page content

We have a template, so remember to save it; we shall now begin creating pages for our website based on the template. In this section, we'll be tackling pages in a specific order, because later ones will use ideas introduced earlier; this way, we can keep duplication to a minimum. On your own site, you can usually develop pages in any order, although many people will start with the homepage, because this is the first thing visitors see. You can then work down through the hierarchy.

Continue testing your pages in different browsers throughout in order to see what the changes do; as I've already mentioned, things may not look totally identical in all of them—font and letter spacing in particular can vary slightly from platform to platform.

To start working on a new page based on the template, go to File ➤ New and choose the relevant template from the Templates tab (see Figure 3-38). Ensure that Update Page when Template Changes is checked before clicking Create.

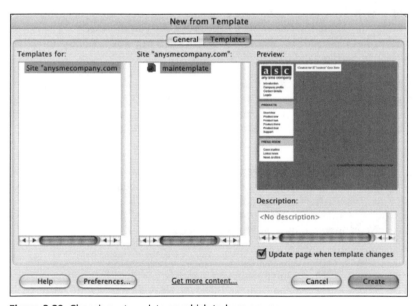

**Figure 3-38.** Choosing a template on which to base a page

## Company profile

The first page we're going to work on is the company profile page, which should immediately be saved as company_profile.html (the file name we earlier linked the relevant navigation link to). Upon creating a new page from a template, remember to change its title, using the Title field in the document window. This will include a brief introduction about the company along with some information about key members of staff. Copy for such things should be kept to a minimum. No one will care about your directors' exam results, or want to read an epic, 500-page opus on your company's history. One-liners should also be avoided—a couple of paragraphs on each is enough to get the message across.

> *Note that you have to manually apply the .html file suffix, because Dreamweaver defaults to .htm.*

Wherever possible, try to get some images onto your site. Avoid cheesy staff photographs, and get a professional photographer to take them rather than a member of staff with a cheap digital camera. Images should be consistent throughout wherever possible, perhaps by surrounding them with a thin border and giving them the same dimensions. Our two staff images are 130 pixels square and were saved as high quality JPEGs. Because the pictures are small, and there are no other graphics on the page, there's little point in saving them at a low quality—and this is true for the rest of the site.

### Working with copy

When working with words online, don't separate paragraphs with double carriage returns (<br /><br />): use normal paragraph tags instead. If using Design view, Dreamweaver does this automatically. Likewise, don't use styled paragraphs for headings—stick with standard <h1> to <h6> tags, which can be applied to text via the Format drop-down menu in the Properties inspector. Following these rules gives you more control over your site's copy and makes styling with CSS simpler. Also, watch out in Code view for unnecessary spaces prior to heading and paragraph end tags.

For our company profile page, we have its name as the main page heading, underneath which are a couple of paragraphs of text (see Figure 3-39). Following this introductory blurb is information about two key members of personnel, each with its own subheading. As both are of the same hierarchical standing, both are defined as "Heading 2."

> *Get into the habit of using a hierarchical text structure—<h1> tags for the main heading, <h2> for subheadings, <h3> for internal subheadings, and so on. If you do this and use standard paragraphs, restyling your site's copy at a later date is a simple task. More importantly, it ensures that your site makes logical sense and displays appropriately in browsers that can't deal with CSS.*

Upon adding text, you'll see the default web page font defined earlier has come into play, and all body copy is displayed in Georgia. However, we need to style the headings, because they are also currently being displayed in the serif font. We've not done so before, but selectors can be grouped if a number of tags are to have shared properties. This is the case for our headings; in the New CSS Style dialog box, this is done by choosing Advanced as the selector type and comma-separating the selectors (in this case, typing h1, h2, h3, h4, h5, h6 into the Selector field). In the CSS Style Definition dialog box, set Font to Arial, Helvetica, sans-serif in the Type category, Weight to bold, and Color to #111111; in Box, uncheck Same for all under Padding and set Left to 40 pixels.

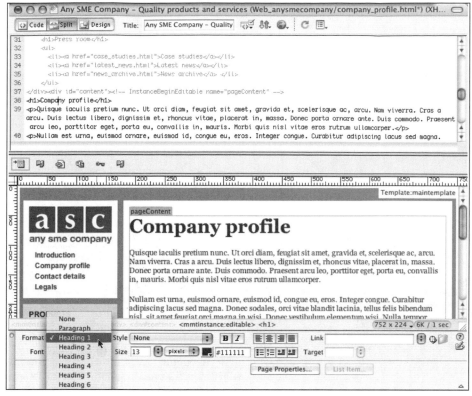

**Figure 3-39.** The Company Profile page taking shape

Specifics for individual tags are defined by choosing Tag in the New CSS Style dialog box, typing the relevant tag into the Tag field, and setting various property values in the CSS Style Definition dialog box. We're going to go over these quickly now, rather than in a step-by-step manner, because you should now be comfortable creating new rules.

- For h1, set Size within the Type category to 17 pixels and Margin to 0, except for Bottom, which should be 10 pixels.

- For h2, again set Size to 17 pixels, and Margin to 30 pixels, 0 pixels, 10 pixels, 0 pixels.

- For p, set Line height under Type to 1.4 ems. This increases the space between lines of text, making it easier to read. In Box, set the values as shown in Figure 3-40. Same for all needs deselecting for both Padding and Margin. The former needs Right to be set to 170 pixels, and Left, 40 pixels. Margin needs setting to 0, 0, 1 ems, 0.

> *Setting the bottom margin to 1 em means the space under paragraphs will be equivalent to the height of one character.*

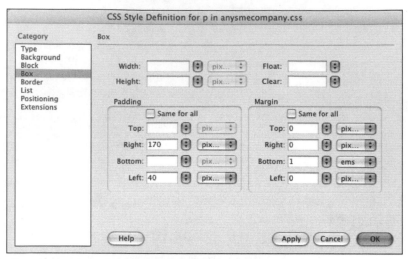

**Figure 3-40**. Defining Box property values for our paragraphs

Should you want your main page heading to stand out from subheadings, try changing the font size of the h1 rule to 20px. Because we're using CSS, <h1> tags throughout the entire site will be updated with this new setting whenever you change it.

Finally, padding has been set above in order to get some whitespace around the body copy and reduce the width of the text column, because people find it easier to read narrow columns of text. The padding-right value of 170 pixels on paragraphs is there to later accommodate images.

Applying these styles improves the look of the page, but the content would look better being in-line with the start of the navigation area. Therefore, the padding settings in #content are replaced by 85px 10px 10px 10px;, which increases the top padding to 85 pixels. Again, this shows the advantage of using style sheets, as we didn't have to edit table cells or invisible GIFs to alter the page's layout.

Sometimes it's advisable to make the padding-left setting of paragraphs 10-to-20 pixels bigger than that for headings, in order to differentiate more between them. With CSS, this is easy to achieve (for instance, just change the left padding to 60px in the relevant CSS rule). Try it out and see what you think.

### Adding images

Add the two portrait images to the page. In each case, add them as we did with the logo, and then use Code view to shift the tag above the copy that it's meant to float right of, as shown in Figure 3-41.

These now need to be styled, to add a border and float them to the right of the page, to the side of the text content. In the New CSS Style dialog box, choose Class as the selector type, and type .floatedImage into the Name field (remember not to omit the period prior to the selector's name).

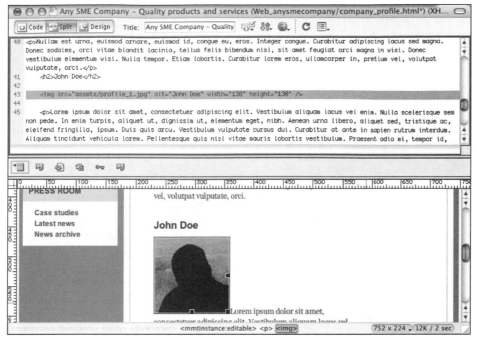

**Figure 3-41.** Repositioning the HTML `<img>` tag

> This CSS rule is different from the previous ones. The period preceding the selector makes it a class selector rather than an ID selector. Class selectors can be applied to multiple elements on a web page, unlike ID selectors, which can only be applied to one.

In the CSS Style Definition dialog box, select the Box category. Set Float to right, and under Margin, Left and Bottom to 5 pixels. Set Border to solid, 1 pixel, #111111. This style can then be applied to the images by selecting them and either

- Right/*CTRL*-clicking the `<img>` tag in the status bar and navigating to the style via Set Class, or
- Selecting the class from the Properties inspector's Class menu.

## Fixing the layout

Our site looks fine in Dreamweaver, so what fixing needs to be done? Well, like every good web designer, we've ensured this site has been tested as we've gone along, and we now have a problem. Although the site works just fine in Internet Explorer, the content area is now sitting underneath the navigation area in Safari, Mozilla, and Opera, as shown in Figure 3-42.

This highlights the importance of testing in a wide range of web browsers, and not just Internet Explorer, throughout your project.

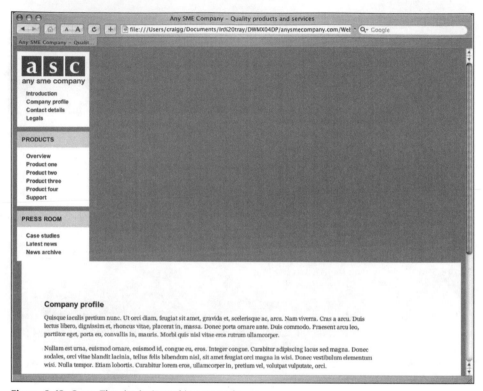

**Figure 3-42.** Oops. The site isn't working properly . . .

Apparently, because we've not defined a specific width for the content <div>, all browsers apart from Internet Explorer are making it the maximum possible width, therefore placing it underneath the navigation <div>. We now have a choice of setting a fixed width for this area, or a percentage width. The latter will enable the site design to continue "stretching" with the browser window, and the former won't. Setting the width of #content to 73% deals with this issue in all browsers, as shown in Figure 3-43, enabling the site to be correctly shown at screen resolutions down to 800×600. Due to this tweak, some amendments will be required later: for instance, the footer is now out of alignment.

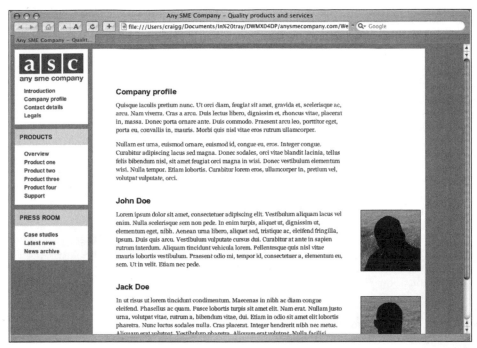

**Figure 3-43.** The site, fixed

## Products

Right, back to adding content. The copy for the products overview page (products.html) should be laid out in the same way as the profiles page, using a similar hierarchy with regards to headings. The opening paragraph needs to provide a brief overview about the company's products, and say to get in touch for further details. This should also be linked to the (not yet built) contact details page (contact_details.html), in case visitors want more information about your products (thus providing your sales staff with leads). This is shown in Figure 3-44.

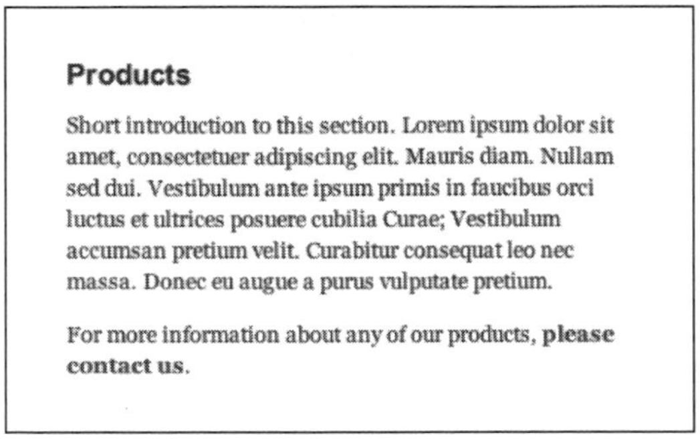

### Products

Short introduction to this section. Lorem ipsum dolor sit amet, consectetuer adipiscing elit. Mauris diam. Nullam sed dui. Vestibulum ante ipsum primis in faucibus orci luctus et ultrices posuere cubilia Curae; Vestibulum accumsan pretium velit. Curabitur consequat leo nec massa. Donec eu augue a purus vulputate pretium.

For more information about any of our products, **please contact us**.

**Figure 3-44.**
An internal link

Designers seem to have forgotten that links can be embedded anywhere in a web page—you often see bizarre copy such as "click the 'contact us' button to contact us." It's better to create links to pages from within your body copy.

To put images of the products on this page, we could use the floatedImage class on them that we've previously used. However, we have four images, and there's no guarantee that they won't overlap if the browser window is increased in size, pushing the paragraphs of text closer together vertically. Furthermore, it would be handy to annotate them. The solution is to add another <div> to our page and float that instead. The product images and annotations can then be placed within (and also linked to their relevant product pages).

We add another class to our style sheet in the same way that we did for .floatedImage. This one should be called .floatedDiv; the only things that need to be defined for this style are Float, which should be set to right, Width, 135 pixels, and Margin, where Left and Bottom should be sent to 5 pixels.

Click in Design view after the Products heading, checking in Code view that the insertion point is outside of any tags. Click the Insert Div Tag button to bring up the Insert Div Tag dialog box. Choose floatedDiv from the Class drop-down menu, and ensure Insert states At insertion point. The code should look like this:

```
<div class="floatedDiv">Content for class "floatedDiv" Goes Here</div>
    <p>Short introduction to this section. Lorem ipsum dolor sit amet,
consectetuer adipiscing elit. Mauris diam. Nullam sed dui. Vestibulum
ante ipsum primis in faucibus orci luctus et ultrices posuere cubilia
Curae; Vestibulum accumsan pretium velit. Curabitur consequat leo nec
massa. Donec eu augue a purus vulputate pretium.</p>
```

If the <div> tag is in the wrong place, move it manually in Code view. If not, add product images, with titles underneath, and a link to relevant product pages. The Properties inspector's Format menu can be used to separate each, by surrounding each set of image/title/link with paragraph tags. Testing the page now produces two problems: the <div> appears the wrong size and the images have a border color as per a default link (see Figure 3-45).

Two more contextual selectors deal with these problems.

The layout is thrown off because we earlier set padding on paragraph tags in the style sheet (padding-left of 40px and padding-right of 170px). This now needs to be overridden for these paragraphs. To do this, we create a CSS rule with the selector .floatedDiv p (thereby affecting paragraphs within any element that uses the floatedDiv class) and set padding to 0. You can do this via the CSS Style Definition dialog box, or, if you're feeling more confident about CSS, you can just type the following directly in your style sheet:

```
.floatedDiv p {
padding: 0px;
}
```

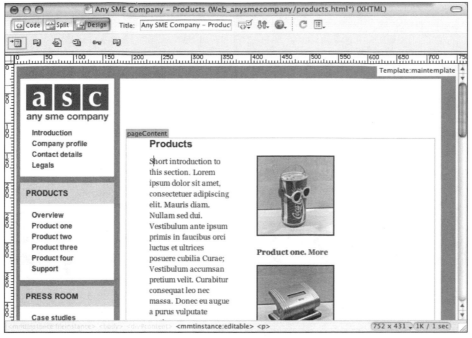

**Figure 3-45.** The floated area's paragraphs have padding that throws off the layout.

The issue with the borders is solved in a similar way, with a selector .floatedDiv a img (affecting images within links within an element using the floatedDiv class) and setting the border to be solid, 1 pixel in width, and to have a color of #111111. The CSS, if you want to type it directly, is

```
.floatedDiv a img {
border: 1px solid #111111;
}
```

The result is shown in Figure 3-46.

## Individual product pages

By and large, the products a company sells tend to have many common aspects, which enable us to use an advanced Dreamweaver feature for the individual product pages: embedded templates. The first thing to do is lay out the page.

Heading 1 is used for the product title, and Heading 2 is applied to subheadings. The relevant product image is placed immediately after the title and floated to the right, using the floatedImage class.

**Figure 3-46.** The floated `<div>` now sits correctly in the page.

Remember that to apply headings to text, we first select it, then choose the appropriate heading value from the drop-down menu in the Properties inspector. The resulting code should look like this:

```
<h1>Product one</h1>

<img class="floatedImage" src="assets/product_1_small.jpg" width="130"
height="130" alt="Product image" />
```

The page also has a section at the bottom for "specifications," as seen in Figure 3-47.

Once the layout is complete, save this page as a template called producttemplate and define editable regions for anything that will vary between each page, such as the title, image, product information, and the specification information. The original editable region will turn yellow, denoting that it's locked, and the new editable regions will be blue, as usual—see Figure 3-48.

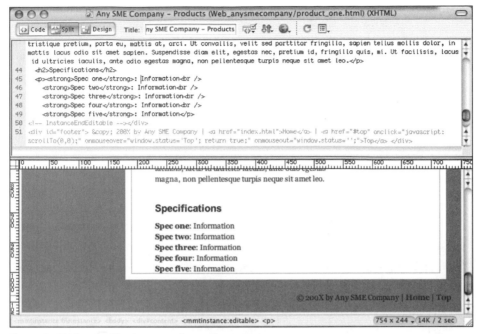

**Figure 3-47.** The specification area of a product page

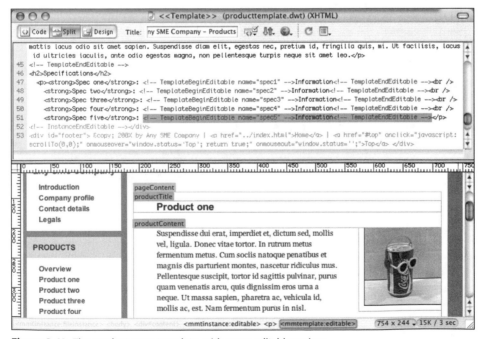

**Figure 3-48.** The product page template, with many editable regions

If you want to make the content of an element editable, but ensure its style remains constant, you can place the editable region within the tag. However, doing so will yield the warning seen in Figure 3-49. Don't worry about this; it's annoying, but only tells you what you already know: that users of this template will not be able to create new paragraphs in this region, and you don't want them to anyway.

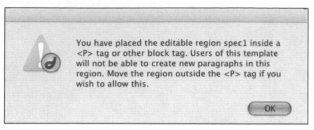

You have placed the editable region spec1 inside a <P> tag or other block tag. Users of this template will not be able to create new paragraphs in this region. Move the region outside the <P> tag if you wish to allow this.

OK

**Figure 3-49.** The warning shown when editable regions are placed inside block elements

If you update producttemplate, all its associated pages will be updated, but no others in the site. However, if you update maintemplate, all pages in the site and producttemplate will be updated accordingly. You can now use this template to produce the individual product pages (product_one.html, product_two.html, product_three.html, and product_four.html).

## Press room

The next set of pages we're going to work with are those relating to the "Press room" section. This contains the case studies and news pages.

## Case studies

Create a new page from the maintemplate template called case_studies.html. The copy within should introduce the section, and provide a brief synopsis of each case study, with an obvious "read more" link at the end of each, linking to the individual case study pages (case_study_one.html, case_study_two.html, and so on).

The structure is almost identical to the company profile page, with Heading 1 being applied for the main title, and Heading 2 being used for case study titles. The small image is placed alongside each case study in exactly the same way that we added the portrait shots (using the floatedImage class). This produces a page like the one in Figure 3-50.

The case study pages themselves (case_study_one.html and case_study_two.html) are built in much the same way. The main case study heading is defined as Heading 1, while subheadings (if any) are defined as Heading 2. In order for people to visually recognize where they are and that they clicked the right link, the relevant image from the overview page should also be included, and again styled, using the floatedImage class.

**Figure 3-50.** The case studies page

Like in the product pages, this should be placed directly after the title, so the resulting code in Code view looks like this:

```
<h1>Case study title</h1>
<img class="floatedImage" src="assets/case_study_1.jpg" width="130"
height="130" alt="Case study image" />
```

One further addition that some companies offer is a downloadable file of the printed version of your case study as a PDF. In Figure 3-51, you can see that we've used the PDF icon as a visual representation, so people know they're downloading an off-line file. We've also placed a link to Adobe's site for those who don't have Acrobat Reader. Figure 3-51 also shows a line of text smaller than the rest of the body copy. This was achieved by adding a class (.small) to the style sheet, with Size within the Type category set to 90%—or, if you prefer, the following CSS:

```
.small {
font-size: 90%;
}
```

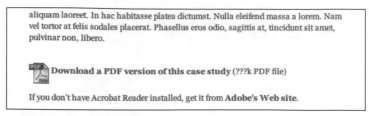

aliquam laoreet. In hac habitasse platea dictumst. Nulla eleifend massa a lorem. Nam vel tortor at felis sodales placerat. Phasellus eros odio, sagittis at, tincidunt sit amet, pulvinar non, libero.

**Download a PDF version of this case study** (???k PDF file)

If you don't have Acrobat Reader installed, get it from **Adobe's Web site**.

**Figure 3-51.** The PDF download section of a case study web page

Back in the web page, the relevant text was clicked, and the style chosen from the Properties inspector's Style drop-down menu, as shown in Figure 3-52. The font-size of any element this class is applied to appears at 90% size.

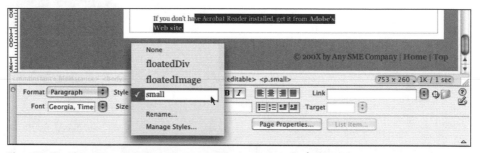

**Figure 3-52.** Choosing a style from the Properties inspector's Style menu

> *Classes can also be applied to in-line elements, such as a few words within a sentence. This is particularly useful for coloring a few words with a style such as* .red {color: red;}. *The method is the same as previously shown, except you precisely select the exact words you want to apply the class to. This results in a* <span> *tag being added to your code. Try it and see!*

## News pages

The latest news page (latest_news.html) should contain the latest story, and the date should be included in or near the heading. Many companies also choose to make the first paragraph bold, but that's obviously subjective, and you should do what you feel is best—just make sure you're consistent throughout the site.

The foot of a news page typically includes "about the company" and "press contacts" blurbs, the latter of which should include both telephone and e-mail contact details for whoever deals with your PR (see Figure 3-53). Don't just include just one or the other: people have very definite preferences as to how they contact people. To make an e-mail link, simply select the e-mail address, then type mailto: followed by the address in the Link field of the Properties inspector and hit *ENTER*.

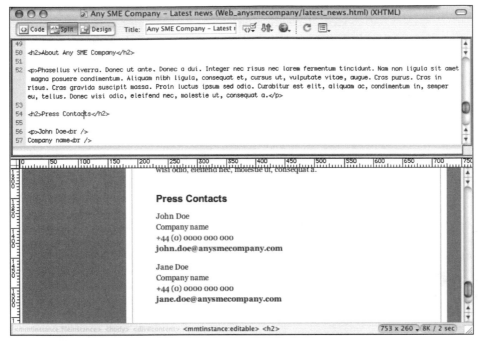

**Figure 3-53**. The contact section of a news page

> *Try creating another embedded template for your news pages, with editable regions for the headline, date, news content, and "about" blurb.*

At the foot of the story also provide a link to the news archive (news_archive.html). That page works in a similar way to the case studies overview page, with a brief overview of each news item linking to the full story. In turn, these pages are essentially archived versions of the latest news page.

> *See also Chapter 2 in this book, which describes a news portal project, for pointers on how to make this area of the site dynamic at a later date.*

## Support

Most SME companies tend to offer a brief introduction to how the company deals with support issues, and then an online form so customers can register problems that they have. The fields of said form on support.html will depend on your company, but I advise that you keep them to a minimum, otherwise people won't bother to fill them in. Keep them concise and they suddenly become preferable to a phone call.

### Building a form

Dreamweaver's built-in form elements, accessible under the Forms category of the Insert bar, are simple enough to use. All you have to do is click the relevant one on the tab and then give it a name in the Properties inspector (see Figure 3-54).

**Figure 3-54.** Naming a form element in the Properties inspector

For layout purposes, keep things simple when formatting input fields and adding titles. The name of each input field in bold, followed by a carriage return (*SHIFT+ENTER*), and then the field itself works well. Each title/field pair is then formatted as a paragraph via the Properties inspector, the results of which can be seen in Figure 3-55.

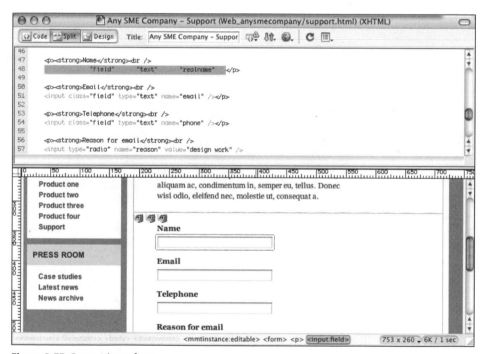

**Figure 3-55.** Formatting a form

Be sure to use the correct type of input field for the relevant details. Single-line details, such as Name, Email, and Telephone, require a text field (the second icon on the Insert bar), while multiline details, such as a general comments box, require a text area (the fourth icon).

Should you want to provide some method of enabling the visitor to state the purpose of their contacting you, use radio buttons or check boxes. The former force the user to choose one from a set, and the latter enable multiple items to be checked. The website www.w3schools.com provides additional insight into how to create forms.

3

**Styling a form**

The default look of form elements can be styled, although such settings are sometimes ignored by web browsers (for instance, at the time of writing, Apple's Safari ignores all border settings on form elements).

To style fields already added, we create two new classes. The first, .field, requires the following properties to be defined: Border set to solid, 1 pixel, #111111; Width set to 250 pixels; Color set to #111111; and Background color set to #ffffff. Alternatively, just add the following directly to your style sheet:

```
.field {
border: solid 1px #111111;
width: 250px;
background-color: #ffffff; color: #111111;
}
```

The second, .fieldSubmit, is specifically for the "Submit button". This mostly has the same settings as .field, but without a width property; the border's width needs to be 2 pixels instead of 1, and it also needs padding (4, 8, 4, 8). Again, here's the CSS, if you want to add it directly instead of using the CSS Style Definition dialog box:

```
.fieldSubmit {
border: solid 2px #111;
padding: 4px 8px;
background-color: #fff; color: #111;
}
```

As I've mentioned before, you can apply the styles by selecting the relevant element and using the Properties inspector's Class menu.

Note that it's not a good idea to apply styles to anything other than text fields; radio buttons and check boxes tend to be rendered in a very odd way if borders are applied. One other piece of advice concerns <textarea> tags: you should never have any content in the tag; otherwise, this will be the default content of the field when someone tries to use it, spaces included (you can remove such spaces in Code view, by deleting anything within the tags). You should also specify how many rows it needs, rather than a pixel height; this can be done by selecting the text area and placing a number within the Num Lines field in the Properties inspector:

```
<textarea class="field" name="comments" rows="5" style="width: 250px;"
wrap="wrap"></textarea>
```

Once you've built your form, you still have to make it work. Some advise using a mailto: link within the form's action attribute in order to send its contents, but this is a bad idea, because doing so relies on the user having a correctly configured e-mail client, and also requires this to boot in order to send the e-mail. You also don't get control over things like redirecting to a "thank-you" page. Elsewhere in this book, several methods are covered to work with forms. We're going to use a basic server-side CGI script, which assumes your site is hosted on Unix.

One of the most widely used is FormMail, freely available from `www.scriptarchive.com/formmail` and set up by default by many web hosts. (A superior script that does the same job and is set up in a similar fashion can be found at `http://nms-cgi.sourceforge.net/scripts.shtml`.) It's simple to get working, and many web hosts use it as a default, so it may already be set up on your hosting space. The script has a few things to configure, and you'll then have to add a few hidden input fields to your web page within the form tag (in Code view):

```
<input type="hidden" name="recipient"
value="emailaddresstosendto@anysmecompany.com" />
<input type="hidden" name="subject"
value="Contact form from Any SME Company Web site" />
<input type="hidden" name="redirect"
value="http://www.anysmecompany.com/thanks.html" />
```

They're all pretty self-explanatory: recipient is the e-mail address that the form gets sent to (you can specify multiple addresses by comma-separating them); subject is the subject line you want in resulting e-mails; redirect is the full link of the HTML page that the visitor will see once the form has been submitted. This should contain a short thank-you message and probably link to the standard contact details page to provide the user with alternatives.

The `<form>` tag itself needs amending as follows:

```
<form action='http://www.anysmecompany.com/cgi-bin/FormMail.cgi"
enctype="x-www-form-encoded" method="post">
```

Note that the action attribute is the full URL of where your FormMail file will reside within the `cgi-bin` of your hosting space.

### Configuring FormMail

Download the latest version of FormMail.pl and open it in a text editor (because CGI scripts tend to break with the slightest error). You can use BBEdit Lite on the Mac and NoteTab Lite or Notepad on Windows.

First, configure the path to Perl, which is on the first line of the script. Your ISP or whoever deals with your hosting should be able to tell you this. It will be something like `#!usr/bin/perl`.

Next, configure the `$mailprog` value with the location of sendmail (which deals with sending the resulting e-mail when the form is submitted). Again, you can get this from your ISP/hosting system administrator. This will be something like `$mailprog = '/usr/lib/sendmail -I -t';`.

As the instructions in the script state (anything after a # sign is a comment), the `@referers` value denotes what domain/ISP address the script is allowed to run from (in order to avoid anyone using your copy of FormMail from their web page form). Although this should only require your domain "as is," it's a good idea to add your IP address and domain with the www prefix. Therefore, the fully configured line for "anysmecompany.com" would look something like this:

```
@referers = ('anysmecompany.com', '212.3.333.222',
www.anysmecompany.com);
```

The @recipients value is usually set to the same as @referers and states which domains the resulting e-mail can be sent to. Assuming your e-mail has the same domain as your website, this won't need changing; otherwise, you'll have to add the relevant domains.

Now you need to save your changes, rename the file FormMail.cgi, and upload it to your cgi-bin. Be sure to upload the file as ASCII, not binary. Finally, change its permissions so that everyone can execute the script. Most FTP clients can do this, although the option might be called permissions, CHMOD, or you might have to select the file and "get info." Either way, you'll likely end up with a dialog box much like the one shown in Figure 3-56.

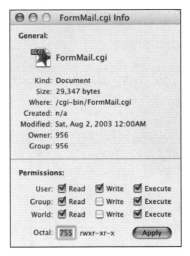

**Figure 3-56.**
Configuring permissions of FormMail.cgi

Set the permissions as shown: read, write, and execute for user, and read and execute for group and world (sometimes called all); if you can use CHMOD commands, CHMOD 755 is the one to go for.

Sometimes certain servers have problems with file extensions. This is why I suggested renaming FormMail.pl to FormMail.cgi, although this isn't always necessary.

Hopefully, everything should work fine—just don't forget to create your thank-you page, saved as thanks.html; otherwise, people will be redirected to an error page! Said page usually just includes a note thanking the sender for their interest, and saying you'll get back to them as soon as you can.

## Contact details

This page—contact_details.html—is pretty similar to the support page; again, form fields should be kept to a minimum; otherwise, people won't bother to fill everything in.

Some companies also choose to include a location map, or a link to an online service that shows their location. This is a very good idea if the company has visiting clients.

One problem that people come up against with the contact details page is what order to place them in. Should the form come first, and the address after? Perhaps the reverse? Maybe there should be two pages, one with a form, and one with other details?

Our solution is far more elegant: we'll create a <div> similar to that on the products overview page that will contain the address, telephone number, and fax details. Again, the paragraphs within have to have a class of noPadding so the <div> isn't wrecked by the default padding settings of paragraphs.

Just adding the <div> and applying the floatedDiv class isn't quite enough, though: after doing so, the page looks cluttered and the two sets of copy distract from one another. The solution is simple: add a subtle divide between the two. This can be achieved by editing the <div> tag within Code view, adding a style attribute as follows:

```
<div style="width: 170px; padding-left: 10px; border-left: 1px dotted
#111111;" class="floatedDiv">
```

The dotted border makes the division subtler than a solid line, and the padding means that the content doesn't hug the dotted line. The width setting overrides the one in the style sheet, meaning the phone and fax numbers can fit on a single line. As you can see from Figure 3-57, the result is pleasing.

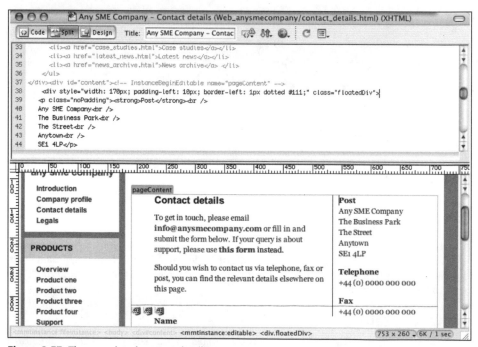

**Figure 3-57.** The completed contact details page

3

## Homepage

Finally, we reach the homepage. There's nothing new to teach you here: you should be able to use what you've learned so far to lay it out, although I'll provide some tips regarding content. A typical homepage serves many uses: it's an introduction to your company and your website; it can provide visitors with up-to-the-minute news and quotes from satisfied customers; it should contain "pull-ins" to make people want to explore the site further (and contact you); and finally, it's the best way of making the site look "alive." Change your homepage's content on a regular basis, and people will be more likely to make return visits.

Keep it clean, though. Don't clutter up the homepage, or people will get confused and go elsewhere. Also, remember to link through to other pages from each homepage section. This is saved as index.html.

Note that the homepage is often the first that people work on. However, as stated earlier, web pages for this site were created in a certain sequence in order to cut down on redundancy and repetition in the book.

## Amending the footer

As it stands, the footer is out of alignment with the rest of the site, because we defined a width for the content. Our effective width of navigation plus content is a combination of fixed and percentage values, so we cannot apply this to position the footer. The best alternative is simply to move the footer inside the content <div>. This is done by editing maintempalte.dwt.

In Code view, find and cut the following:

```
<div id="footer">&copy; 200X by Any SME Company |
<a href='../index.html'>Home</a> | <a href="#top" onclick="javascript:
scrollTo(0,0);" onmouseover="window.status='Top'; return true;"
onmouseout="window.status='';">Top</a></div>
```

Then paste it at the end of the content <div>, but *after* the end of the editable area. The end of the document should then look like this:

```
<div id="content"><!-- TemplateBeginEditable name="pageContent" -->
Content for id "content" Goes Here<!-- TemplateEndEditable -->
<div id="footer">&copy; 200X by Any SME Company | <a
href="../index.html">Home</a> | <a href="#top"onclick="javascript:
scrollTo(0,0);" onmouseover="window.status='Top'; return true;"
onmouseout="window.status='';">Top</a></div></div>
</body>
</html>
```

Save the template and you'll be prompted to update all associated files. Upon doing so, the footer will sit inside the content area. This needs to be better differentiated from the other content, so amend the #footer padding settings to 60px 10px 10px 10px;, which, if directly editing the CSS, makes the footer rule look like this:

```
#footer {
padding: 60px 10px 10px 10px;
clear: both;
text-align: right;
}
```

The first setting applies to the top padding, putting 60 pixels of space between the footer and the other content.

## Legacy browsers

For most intents and purposes, our site is complete, and works in modern web browsers, but there are other changes we can make. For instance, we can hide the style sheet from legacy browsers, because they don't understand much CSS.

Figure 3-58 shows the site in Netscape Navigator 4. This browser's market share is almost nonexistent today, and authoring for it requires using much older methods that aren't future-proof and potentially increase maintenance time. Obviously, we cannot cater for this browser with regards to design, but there's no excuse for not enabling users of such browsers access to the *content*. We do this by amending our main template file, maintemplate.dwt, and changing the line `<link   href="../anysmecompany.css" rel="stylesheet" type="text/css" />` to the following:

```
<style type="text/css" media="screen">
@import url(anysmecompany.css);
</style>
```

This is the @import method, and it imports the style sheet in a way Netscape Navigator 4 and other legacy browsers don't understand, so the style sheet is ignored. Note that the path to the CSS file is equivalent to that from the pages this tag will be placed on, not the template itself, which sits within the Templates folder. Once this method is employed, the result in legacy browsers is like that shown in Figure 3-59. Although it doesn't look pretty, you can access all the content in any Internet-enabled device. This also highlights why you should order your website content in a logical way, as obsolete browsers will simply display one <div> after another.

If you'd like to enhance this look slightly, you can use multiple style sheets. Basic settings, such as those relating to background colors and font family/font size, can be placed in a CSS file and then attached via the link method that we originally used. The remaining CSS, such as anything relating to positioning, borders, padding, and margins, would then be placed in a second CSS file, which would be attached via the @import method.

The upshot would be legacy browsers only reading CSS that they understand, while modern browsers would read the information from both style sheets, thus rendering the site as intended.

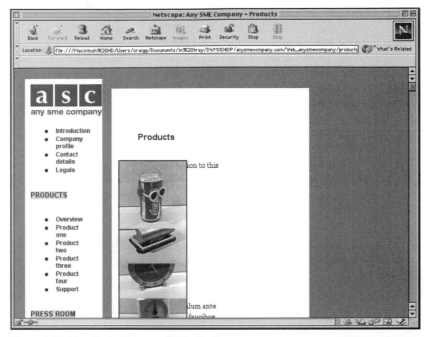

**Figure 3-58.** The site in Netscape Navigator 4

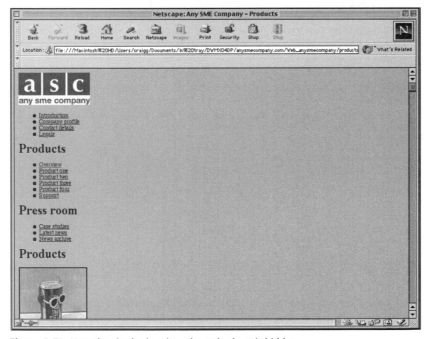

**Figure 3-59.** How the site looks when the style sheet is hidden

# Printing

Most web pages look terrible when printed out, but many people regularly do so anyway. Some designers create "print-friendly" web pages alongside the standard ones, but this just doubles your workload. Similarly, ensuring your site is 600 pixels wide so it will print is too much of a compromise.

The best method of enabling printing is to use another style sheet. This would be attached to the `maintemplate.dwt` file via the `link` method, with the `media` attribute set to print.

```
<link href="../anysmecompany_print.css" rel="stylesheet"
type="text/css" media="print" />
```

The simplest way of creating the print style sheet itself is to duplicate your standard one and then edit it. Anything that doesn't need to be printed (such as the navigation) should have a sole declaration of `display: none;`:

```
#navigation {display: none;}
```

The body declaration should be amended to have a white background, and the default text color is usually best set to black (#000000). The margin should be set to 5%, which provides a small margin around all printed content. Font sizes should also be defined in points (pt), as this style sheet is for print, not screen.

```
body {
font: 13pt Georgia, "Times New Roman", Times, serif;
color: #000;
background: #fff;
margin: 5%;
padding: 0px;
}
```

*The preceding example uses shorthand for hex color values—#000 instead of #000000 and #fff instead of #ffffff. This can be done whenever a hex color is paired. If you're uncomfortable doing this, just write out the values in full. And to convert from shorthand to standard, just duplicate each character (so #f2c would become #ff22cc).*

Changes also need to be made to font definitions. Headings and paragraphs should be resized according to your requirements, colored black, and padding set to 0.

If you've used a sans-serif font for your main body copy, change it to a serif font in the print style sheet, as serif fonts are easier to read on paper.

Links are obviously of less use in print than on screen, but it's still perhaps useful to provide an indication of where they were in the web page. Changing the `text-decoration` value to underline and the `color` to #660000 can do this. This dark red shows up on a color output, but is close to black when printing in grayscale.

One problem you may face is values "leaking" through from other style sheets. While this tends to happen when a site's main style sheet is attached with an all media attribute value, it can happen at other times, due to browser bugs. If you find this occurring, duplicate all the original's values in your print style sheet, to override the main style sheet. Many will have to be set to none or 0px.

Also, remember to print a page for various web browsers, as all interpret print style sheets in a slightly different way. However, once everything works satisfactorily, you can tweak the printed output from your site without ever touching a single page of HTML.

3

> *Be aware that support for print style sheets is incomplete in most web browsers, so you'll need to do plenty of trial and error in various browsers to get your print CSS working satisfactorily. Despite this, they're sometimes still worth using. Keep things simple and the output will mostly be usable.*

# Experimentation and enhancements

A website is never finished. There are always improvements that can be made, but unlike printed collateral, a change to a website can be painless and cost-effective. While you may have your own ideas about how to improve what's already been created, I've outlined a few in the following text, most of which take advantage of the power of Dreamweaver, the flexibility of a CSS-based layout, or both.

Prior to experimenting on what is a completed site, back up your work, preferably to CD. If you make a copy of the site on your hard drive, make sure it's outside the site folder as defined within Dreamweaver; otherwise, template changes may overwrite your work so far.

## Folder-based navigation

Many companies make use of direct links on their brochures, and the easier they are to remember, the more successful they are. One method that tends to work quite well is to make things accessible via the likes of www.domain.com/word/, so to access our main products page, we could use www.anysmecompany.com/products/, and to access the contact details page, www.anysmecompany.com/contact/, and so on.

This is extremely easy to do within Dreamweaver. Simply use the Files panel's menu to create folders in the root of the site (File ➤ New Folder). These should be given the name you require for each link (making sure they're all in lowercase). Then drag the relevant web page into each folder and rename them index.html.

Take care when you have multiple index.html files though, as it's easy to overwrite ones by mistake. Work within one folder and not across folders, and only edit one at a time.

Dreamweaver will periodically want to update links site-wide. Allow it to do this, otherwise all your links to the amended page will be broken.

The advantage of this style of organization is that the sections of your website have more memorable addresses; the disadvantage is that your site's organization on your hard drive becomes more complex. However, Dreamweaver does most of the grunt work, making the job easier for you.

## Switching sides

This tip highlights the flexibility of CSS, enabling us to amend several aspects of our website, just by changing a few CSS rules and not even touching our web pages—something that's not possible with tables.

Open up anysmecompany.css and change float: left to float: right in both #navigation and #content, and also change margin-left to margin-right in #content. As shown in Figure 3-60, that's all you need to do to switch the navigation to the right of the browser window, instead of the left.

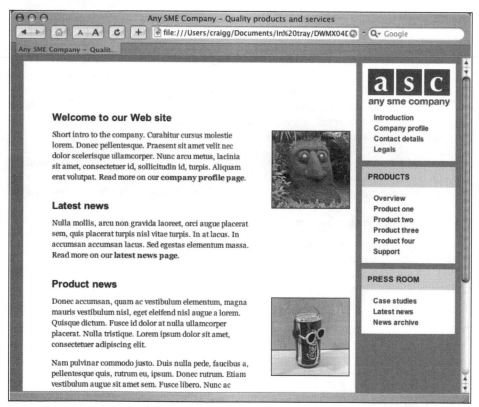

**Figure 3-60.** The navigation on the right of the page

This is much quicker than working with table cells, even if they were within a template that Dreamweaver could automatically update. We can also shift the photos to the left, in order to create a mirror of our original layout. In most cases, you need to seek out things within the style sheet that were floated left, and float them right, or amend padding. This applies to all the following classes, which should be updated as follows:

```
.floatedImage {
float: left;
margin-bottom: 5px;
margin-right: 5px;
border: 1px solid #111111;
}
.floatedDiv {
float: left;
width: 135px;
margin-bottom: 5px;
margin-right: 5px;
}

h1, h2, h3, h4, h5, h6 {
font-family: Arial, Helvetica, sans-serif;
font-weight: bold;
color: #111111;
padding-left: 170px;
}

p {
padding-right: 40px;
padding-left: 170px;
margin: 0px 0px 1em 0px;
line-height: 1.4em;
}
```

Figure 3-61 shows the end result.

## Hiding e-mail addresses

Everyone hates spam, so it's often a good idea to "hide" the e-mail addresses on your site, particularly if you offer direct addresses to staff members. Perhaps the best way of doing this is remaking the address in a mixture of HTML entities and JavaScript that stumps most address-harvesting spiders. This is a tedious thing to do yourself, but many online services exist, such as the excellent one at http://hiveware.com/enkoder_form.php.

## Working with Word

In a word, don't. (Excuse the pun.) Microsoft Word's HTML output is terrible and will always need significant cleaning up; even Dreamweaver's internal tools to streamline terrible Word code often cannot cope, so don't rely on them. The upshot of trying to integrate Word-originated code is an inconsistent site: headings and body copy will likely not react correctly to any style sheet changes you might make, and the web pages themselves will be much larger than necessary due to Word's bloated code. If you do find yourself lumbered with a number of duff Word HTML documents, check out Textism's Word HTML cleaner at www.textism.com/wordcleaner/.

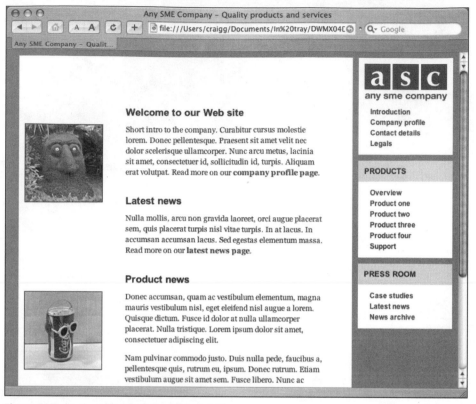

**Figure 3-61.** A mirror image of the original design

For best results, always build pages from scratch, and only use Word when you need the content—and be sure to paste this as text, not HTML.

# Testing and debugging

Once you've made any changes, tweaked your copy, shown the site to people, and responded to their comments, it's time to perform some final checks and then make it live.

## Checking links

It's important not to have broken links, because this makes the site and your company look unprofessional. Dreamweaver's built-in link checker, found under Site ➤ Check Links Sitewide, is more than satisfactory for reporting on broken links and orphaned files.

In our site, we found broken links, although this is because we don't actually have any PDF files to link to from the case study pages that we made earlier! As for orphaned files, they can usually be removed, but not always. For instance, Dreamweaver regards thanks.html as an orphaned file, because it's not directly linked to anything. However, it's essential to our site: our contact forms redirect to it.

## Checking code

Although Dreamweaver is a pretty good tool, mistakes are made, and mistakes can cause problems with browsers, especially with CSS. File ➤ Check Page ➤ Validate Mark-up enables you to use Dreamweaver's internal tools to check your code. Alternatively, check out the validation services at W3: http://jigsaw.w3.org/css-validator/ (CSS validator) and http://validator.w3.org/ (HTML validator).

Note that for CSS there are two levels of compliance: errors and warnings. The former must be fixed, but the latter can often be recommendations rather than changes you must make.

There's also a standalone offline application for (X)HTML checking called Tidy, available from http://tidy.sourceforge.net/, plug-in versions (such as for BBEdit) and even a Dreamweaver extension (Windows only—see www.macromedia.com/software/dreamweaver/special/extensions/#dmx_tidy). Be aware that this is a very powerful application, so read the documentation prior to using it and configure it according to your needs. Also, use Tidy on a backup of your site, not the original. Finally, always check "Tidied" code, because it sometimes introduces a few problems of its own; for instance, if you choose to indent tags, it will place tabs between <textarea> tags that need to be deleted.

## Browser checking

Our site seems to work fine in all currently shipping browsers, and we also used the @import method to cater for alternate and obsolete devices. However, there is one browser out there that is still in use and thinks it's compliant when it isn't: Internet Explorer 5.5 for Windows. As you can see in Figure 3-62, the navigation bar doesn't work correctly in this browser.

The problem occurs due to Internet Explorer 5.5 misinterpreting the box model. As I stated earlier, padding should be placed outside an element's width, but Internet Explorer 5.5 places it inside. Our navigation links are set to 120 pixels width, with 10 pixels of padding on each horizontal edge, making a total of 140 pixels in compliant browsers. Internet Explorer 5.5 instead takes the 120 pixels, and places the padding inside that width, thereby creating navigation links that are shorter than they should be.

Tantek Çelik's box model hack enables you to get around this problem by exploiting parsing bug in Internet Explorer 5.5 for Windows. Here's our original CSS rule:

```
#navigation a {
font-family: Arial, Helvetica, sans-serif;
font-size: 12px;
padding-top: 2px;
padding-right: 10px;
padding-bottom: 2px;
padding-left: 10px;
display: block;
width: 120px;
}
```

**189**

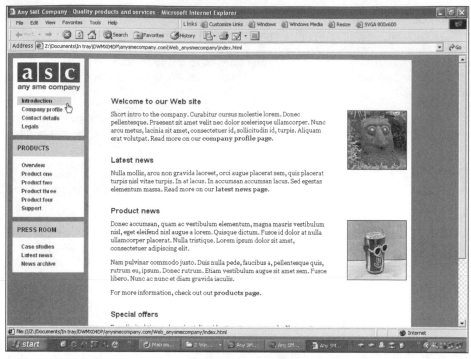

**Figure 3-62.** The navigation bar in Internet Explorer 5.5 for Windows

Before we get to the width property for compliant browsers, we insert a second width rule for Internet Explorer 5.5, and then follow this with the voice-family lines shown here:

```
#navigation a {
font-family: Arial, Helvetica, sans-serif;
font-size: 12px;
padding-top: 2px;
padding-right: 10px;
padding-bottom: 2px;
padding-left: 10px;
display: block;
width: 140px;
voice-family: "\"}\"";
voice-family:inherit;
width: 120px;
}
```

Due to the parsing bug, Internet Explorer 5.5 for Windows terminates the rule before reaching the correct width measurement, and therefore displays the width of the navigation links at 140 pixels. Compliant browsers go on to complete the rule, displaying the navigation links at 120 pixels. The only problem is compliant browsers that also suffer from the same parsing bug (such as Opera 5). We cater for them by adding another rule after the preceding one, confirming the correct width of the element in question:

```
html>body #navigation a {
width: 120px;
}
```

Although this is a hack, it works, as shown in Figure 3-63. Also, it only requires a few lines of code in the style sheet, as opposed to messing around with the design. A more in-depth look at the hack can be found on Tantek Çelik's website: www.tantek.com/CSS/Examples/boxmodelhack.html.

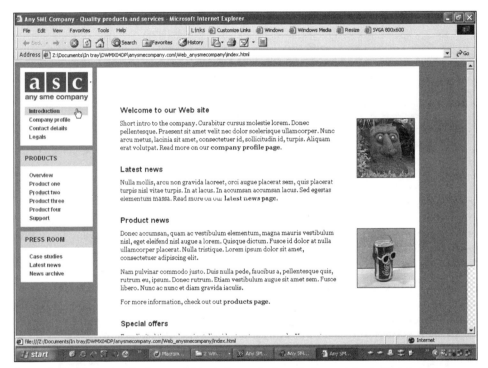

**Figure 3-63.** After using the box model hack, the navigation displays as intended in Internet Explorer 5.5.

## Updating the site

Sometimes upon completing your site, you'll find some pages haven't picked up additional edits you may have made to the templates. This is primarily due to operator errors, but Dreamweaver provides a simple way of ensuring everything's up to date. Prior to uploading your site, force Dreamweaver to check and update all the files by going to Modify ➤ Templates ➤ Update Pages (see Figure 3-64). Even if nothing needs updating, the whole process only takes seconds, and is well worth doing.

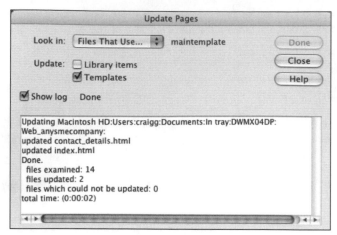

**Figure 3-64.** The Update Pages dialog box

# Deployment and maintenance

Finally, it's time to put your site online, by using your favorite FTP application, or Dreamweaver's built-in FTP client (see Dreamweaver's Help for more on how to use this).

However, this isn't the end for your website. Make sure that you keep it up to date with the latest news and products from your company. If relevant, set aside time every week or month to update content—sites that are left to stagnate soon lose traffic, but those that are updated tend to gain visitors over time. Due to the way we've constructed the site, using Dreamweaver templates and a lot of CSS, updates should be relatively quick and painless. Many visual things, such as font types, sizes, and colors, and new navigation colors, can be amended by editing the CSS file alone.

As I've already mentioned, should the situation arise where several people—and some without expertise in Dreamweaver—need to update the website, then it might be worth checking out Macromedia's Contribute. With this software, nontechnical users can rapidly make changes to a site while automatically respecting website standards for style, layout, and code—without knowing any HTML. More information can be found at www.macromedia.com/software/contribute/.

Once your site is live, don't forget to shout about it! Publicity is key, so don't forget to include your site address on business cards, press releases, all offline material, and company vehicles.

# Summary

We have a completed website that adheres to web standards and presents the company brand in a professional manner. Although we partook in a little hand coding, the vast majority of the development was done using Dreamweaver's built-in tools, proving that you can use such an application to create CSS-based layouts. We've seen that the application also excels in site management, and that using templates massively speeds up site maintenance. This, in tandem with CSS and a little knowledge of hand coding, enables you to create a cutting-edge website that's future-proof.

Also, you've no doubt noticed that certain things changed as we progressed. That's because I wanted to present a *realistic* case study, and sites do evolve as they are created, which is part of the fun. Don't be afraid of changing course slightly if the end result will benefit.

So finally, here's an overview of what we've learned:

- We've researched the background of SME websites and the likely potential audience, worked on an aim for the site, and collated information to use.
- Information was organized into categories and a site map built, from which we developed some mock-up layouts.
- We looked at file management and setting up Dreamweaver.
- The site's layout was constructed, and we learned about page defaults, CSS, layout structure, creating a navigation bar, importing and editing a logo, and styling various page elements.
- We created a template from this design, and added content, which included working with copy and images, positioning "floated" elements, such as images and sidebars, and we also created embedded templates.
- The site was amended to take into account legacy browsers.
- Finally, we looked at some possible experiments and enhancements before testing and debugging the site, ready for uploading.

3

# 4 INTRANET DESIGN PROJECT

**In this chapter**

- What is an intranet and why might you need one?
- How to plan and design an intranet application.
- Creating a layout and using Server-Side Includes to make page creation easy.
- Creating an Access database.
- Connecting to a database.
- Creating a news page—adding, editing, and deleting records.
- Creating a simple document management system—the FileSystemObject.
- Managing users—security and user levels.
- Using Dreamweaver extensions to create a dynamic events calendar.

# What are intranets and extranets?

An intranet is a web-based system that enables the sharing of information and resources on a local level. A company intranet, while it feels to the user as if it is part of the Web, contains information that is not accessible to the outside world. The intranet does not have to be based in one physical location, however; an excellent use is to keep employees working at different branches of one company informed and able to collaborate and share knowledge. It can also be a way to ensure that employees who work from home are kept in touch with the rest of the company and able to feel part of the organization despite being located remotely.

An extranet is an intranet that is open to more people, perhaps to partner companies, or the clients of your company. A design firm may have an extranet that allows people within the company to post new designs or project progress reports for clients who log on to the system. Again, this system would not be fully open to the Web, but to people who have been given the right to log on to it.

Many large companies have huge intranets or extranets and use them in order to keep vast numbers of employees in touch with information and resources that are helpful to their day-to-day work. There are commercial options that can be purchased in order to implement a quick large-scale solution. A commercial system may be a good idea for a large company without the in-house ability to implement such a system, although they can be expensive and require a lot of server resources. Out-of-the-box solutions can also come with many features that you will never need, and may lack features that would be useful for specific needs within your company.

# Planning an intranet

A company intranet, if implemented well, will become an important part of the working day for the people who work in the company. Therefore it is important to plan the project carefully in order that as many people as possible are represented in the final project.

# The brief

It's Monday, the coffee machine is broken, there are several hundred e-mails to read, and your boss has called you into the office because Stephanie, who has just started in marketing, was very surprised that the company did not have an intranet. "Is this something we should implement?" Of course the budget will be minimal, the time that you have to do the work will have to fit around all your other jobs as company web designer and general computer person, and no one really knows what the intranet needs to do. From your meeting you come away with something that reads like this:

- Give everyone access to important news and information.

- Make the intranet secure so that employees cannot read data that is confidential to another employee and so that people without login details cannot access company information.

- Enable employees to view and edit their own personal information (such as home address).

- Allow people in different departments to share documents.

On coming out of that initial meeting, it will be very tempting to just sit down, open Dreamweaver, and start playing with ideas. However, this approach has a high likelihood of failing to produce an application that will fully serve the needs of your company. Your first step should be to talk to the different departments within the company to find out what would be helpful to them—what information would they like to be able to access when they are out of the office, what kind of documents would they find it useful to share. Grab some paper and a pen and go talk to people.

The decision to develop an intranet may come from many sources—company growth may bring with it the need to have an easy-to-use, accessible point for information and resources; the number of people working from home and feeling isolated from the main company might be the starting point; you may have a very basic system that is not fulfilling your needs—whatever the starting point, you probably don't have all of the information you will need at hand!

# Gathering information

At this point it is a good idea to call a meeting with key people in each department of your organization, or speak to them individually, so that you can explain the project in general terms and how you see it being helpful to them. Find out how they currently deal with sharing documents, where the current company contact lists are stored, and how these are updated and by whom.

## Different departments

The different departments in your company will have different uses for an intranet—some departments and individuals may not be interested in the project initially, others may see the benefits or have worked in an organization that has such a tool before. Quite possibly many people will not initially see the use for an intranet, but it is important to chat to people in order to find out what their possible concerns might be.

## Hosting

An intranet for a small company is unlikely to take up a huge amount of system resources; if you already have an internal server that acts as a central file server, then it is perfectly possible to host your intranet on that. If the server is accessible only to your internal network and situated behind a firewall, then it alleviates some of the security concerns inherent in running a web server. It is also possible to host an intranet on a remote server, in the same way that you might host any other web site, although this is more of an extranet situation. For the purposes of this chapter, we will assume that the intranet is to be hosted on a local, in-house web server and that you are developing on IIS on your local computer.

However you are hosting the intranet, the platform, web server, and technologies available to you will dictate the database and server technology that you can use. As many small to medium-sized companies currently have a Microsoft Windows 2000 Server in-house performing other tasks, we are going to develop this application using ASP and an Access database.

I have used Access in my examples as, unless your company is very large or has the need for a SQL Server database in other areas, it is unlikely that they will initially wish to pay out for the licensing. Access can be very easily upgraded to SQL Server, and should your intranet grow beyond a small-scale application it is not a difficult job to move an application from Access to SQL Server at a later date.

I have also opted to use VBScript as the scripting language because, while you can write ASP in a variety of scripting languages, most tutorials and help sites for ASP presume the use of VBScript. JScript is the commonest alternative language used by ASP developers, and it is also supported by Dreamweaver MX 2004. The concepts described here would convert well to JScript if you are already confident in that language.

## Security

When looking at the security of the application, you should consider

- How you will authenticate users to allow them to log on and use the resources of the intranet
- How you will prevent users from seeing or editing data that they should not have access to
- Whether users will be accessing the intranet from outside your firewall

The first two considerations we will be addressing within the design of this application. If you already have the ability to allow remote users access to the company network, then you should be able to work with the individual who set up this access to enable access to the intranet for these users. This will depend on your individual network and firewall setup and is outside the scope of this chapter to discuss fully; however, as you plan your intranet it is worth considering, as having access to the intranet is very useful to those who work from home.

# Designing the application on paper

Once you have spoken to and gathered the opinions of people who will be using the intranet, you need to sit down and work out what will be included.

## User administration

- Add, edit, and delete users to, in, and from the system.
- Users need to be able to log on to the system and log out again afterwards.
- There are currently to be three levels of user—users, management, and site administrators:
  - **Users:** The basic user level with few access rights to change data
  - **Management:** Will have the right to view all data added to the intranet
  - **Site administrators:** Will have the right to add content but not necessarily see all privileged information (such as full employee details)
- There must be a way for the system to differentiate between these user types.

## The homepage

- Should show the user only the options they have the rights to access
- Should display the latest company news items
- Should give an easy way to navigate to the rest of the intranet functionality

## Employee information

- This data will be taken from the users database.
- All users should be able to access lists of employees, with their internal phone numbers and e-mail addresses.
- Management should be able to access full employee details including home address.
- Employees should be able to edit their own details.

## Resources—document sharing

- Site administrators can add and make new documents live and available to all users.

## Company events calendar

- A calendar that can be added to by site administrators so that all users can easily see upcoming events

## Site administration

- Site administrators will have additional menu options in the navigation.
- They have rights to edit and delete any information that has been posted to the intranet.

## Ensuring the proposed application meets its requirements

Once you have refined your plan, it is time to present it to the relevant people in order that you can get a feel as to whether the proposed functionality is going to be suitable. If people in the company have come up with lots of good ideas that you have not been able to include at this point, reassure them that the intranet can and should develop over time and new functionality added to it as people use it more frequently. The application we will create in this chapter would be very easy to expand on to add all sorts of new functionality.

## Interface design

"Easy to use" should be your mantra when designing the look and feel for the company intranet. This is not the place to show off your Flash and DHTML skills, but can be an excellent place to showcase your abilities in creating a usable interface. If you succeed, you will have fewer problems to sort out as users learn how to use the system.

A second and related objective to keep in mind is the accessibility of the site, more so in those countries with legislation forcing web sites to comply with published guidelines of how to make sites accessible to those with a variety of disabilities. This includes accommodating users with visual impairments through sensible choices of colors and the inclusion of alternative text for images. Check out www.webaccessguides.org/accessguide/toc.htm and *Constructing Accessible Web Sites* by Jim Thatcher et al. (Apress, July 2003, ISBN 1-59059-148-8) for more guidance on building for accessibility.

# Creating an initial layout

If you are working on a machine that is running a version of the Windows Server family, then you will be able to set up a separate IP address for each site that you create. Professional versions of Windows do not allow for this, however, and so I tend to set the application I am working on as the default web site. Then to browse the site I simply need to type http://localhost or http://computer_name to get to my homepage. To work on a different application you just need to browse for a different home directory.

The first stage in actually implementing our intranet is to create a design that will be used as the basis for all pages created for the intranet. In practice you may need to create your intranet using the design of your main company web site or taking parts of that design. You should have no problems in working through the steps in this chapter with Dreamweaver MX templates taken from an existing site design. As we are designing from scratch, however, we shall use a simple CSS-based layout for our intranet, utilizing includes that help make the creation of new pages simple and quick.

## Layout

When working on a new project I usually begin by creating a layout and CSS style sheet that contains all my basic layout and text-formatting elements. I will add to the style sheet later as I develop forms and display data. My layout for the GNN intranet project looks like what you see in Figure 4-1.

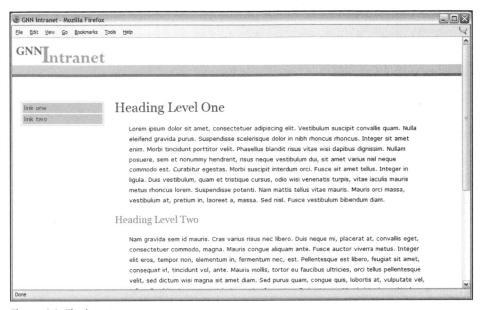

**Figure 4-1.** The layout

This layout is created with the following structural XHTML markup (with the Latin filler text removed for brevity!), which I've called master-layout.asp:

```
<!DOCTYPE html PUBLIC "-//W3C//DTD XHTML 1.0 Transitional//EN"
        "http://www.w3.org/TR/xhtml1/DTD/xhtml1-transitional.dtd">
<html xmlns="http://www.w3.org/1999/xhtml">

<head>
<title>GNN Intranet</title>
<link href="/inc/old.css" rel="stylesheet" type="text/css" />
<style type="text/css" media="all">
@import "/inc/global.css";
</style>
</head>

<body>
```

```
<div id="logo">
<p class="logo"><img src="/images/logo.gif" width="199" height="36"
border="0" alt="GNN Intranet" /></p>
</div>
<div id="banner">
</div>
<div id="content">
<h1>Heading Level One</h1>
<p>Content here </p>

</div>
<div id="nav">
<p><a href="#">link one</a></p>
<p><a href="#">link two</a></p>
</div>

</body>
</html>
```

Note the location of the CSS files: they're both specified as being in the inc subfolder. The GIF for the logo can be found in the images folder. Personally, I find it helpful to put includes and CSS files into a separate folder so I can easily see what they are. The main CSS file (global.css) provides the layout information and text styling for newer browsers:

```
body {
  margin:0px;
  padding:0px;
  background-color: #ffffff;
  color: #000000;
  font-size: 1em;
}

#logo {
  width: 100%;
  height: 60px;
  padding:0px;
  margin:0px;
}

.logo {
  position: absolute;
  top: 6px;
  left: 10px;
}

#banner {
  width: 100%;
  height: 20px;
```

```
  background-color: #cccccc;
  color: #668099;
  border-bottom: 6px #668099 solid;
}

#content {
  margin-left:230px;
  margin-top: 50px;
  margin-right: 80px;
}

#nav {
  position: absolute;
  top: 140px;
  left: 20px;
  width: 180px;
  border: 1px solid #BDC8D3;
  padding-top: 2px;
  padding-left: 2px;
  padding-right: 2px;
}

#nav p {
  margin-bottom:2px;
  margin-top: 0px;

}

#nav a{
  color: #39396F;
  background-color: #BDC8D3;
  display: block;
  font-weight: normal;
  text-decoration: none;
  padding-left: 4px;

}

#nav a:hover {
  background-color: #E4E9ED;
  text-decoration: none;
  color: #39396F;
}

p, td, li, dd, dt {
  font: 80%/1.8em Verdana, Geneva, Arial, Helvetica, sans-serif;
}
```

```
#content p {
  margin-left: 2.5em;}

h1 {
  font: 1.8em Georgia, "Times New Roman", Times, serif;
  color: #39396F;
  background-color: transparent;


}

h2 {
  font: 1.4em Georgia, "Times New Roman", Times, serif;
  color: #668099;
  background-color: transparent;
}

h3 {
  font: 1.2em Georgia, "Times New Roman", Times, serif;
  background-color: transparent;
  color: #668099;
  width: 60%;
  border-bottom: 1px solid #BDC8D3;
  padding-bottom: 0px;
  margin-bottom: -10px;
  margin-left: 1.7em;
}

a:link, a:visited, a:active {
  color: #668099;
  background-color: transparent;
  text-decoration: underline;
  font-weight: bold;
}

a:hover {
  background-color: #cccccc;
  text-decoration: none;
  color: #39396F;
}
```

*A note on browser compatibility:* When creating an intranet that will only be accessed by people within your company, you may find yourself in a situation where you are working mainly for one major browser, or at least know that everyone accessing the intranet is using relatively up-to-date browsers. In this situation you may not need to be too concerned with supporting the troublesome older browsers such as Netscape 4.

The preceding layout uses the @import method to attach a style sheet. @import is not recognized by Netscape 4 and so is a good way to hide the CSS from any older browsers that happen upon it. If you are creating an extranet and you do not have control or knowledge of which browsers people will use to access it, then you would be wise to either hide the CSS in this way or provide a simple cut-down style sheet for older browsers. This is particularly true where you are using CSS to style form fields, since older browsers have a great deal of trouble in rendering this and can make the form unusable. This is also a good point to validate your CSS and (X)HTML either within the Dreamweaver validator or at the online validator at http://validator.w3.org. Once you have added ASP you will not be able to use the internal Dreamweaver validator, and knowing that you have a valid layout to start with will decrease the likelihood of introducing problems later on.

# Creating includes

In order to simplify new page creation and to ensure a consistent look and feel across our intranet, we are going to use includes. Includes, as we shall discover, mean that you can place parts of your page layouts that are repeated across the site into a single file. For instance, if you have navigation that remains the same on all pages of your site, you can make that navigation a single file, so when you need to add another item you simply add it to the one file as opposed to needing to add it to all pages of the site. If you have used Dreamweaver Templates before, you might feel that you can achieve the same thing with those. However, with templates, although you only need to add the item once in your template, you still need to then transfer all the files of your site to the server to make the change rather than transferring one include file. Static includes are also cached by the web server which assists in making the pages quick-loading, and their use in cutting down possible inconsistencies in the layout cannot be overemphasized.

Additionally, the Template feature is Dreamweaver-specific. To work on a site using the templates, someone must have Dreamweaver. By using includes you can create a site that is not reliant on one particular development environment.

## What are includes?

Even if you are new to ASP you may have come across **Server-Side Includes** (SSI) in the past, as they are a feature of many languages and server platforms. SSI, through its include directive, enables the inclusion of a file within another file. There are other SSI directives, but include is the one that you are most likely to have come across and is the only one implemented by ASP.

Our layout can be split into three areas—top, content, and bottom. The only part of the page that will change is the content area; the top and bottom of the page are layout and will not change. This makes them ideal to be placed in an include file, meaning that any change needed to the top banner or navigation need only be made in that one file for it to be replicated across every page that includes the file.

With your layout open in Dreamweaver, switch into Code view, so that we can create the top include file. Now we need to select the portion of the markup that will make up this include file. I usually start with the markup that includes the CSS files, underneath the title tag. Leaving the title tag out of the include will enable you to have a different title on each page. I then select down to, and including, the opening of the first content `<div>` tag as you see in Figure 4-2.

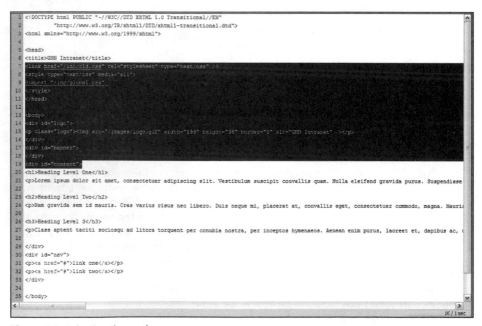

**Figure 4-2.** Selecting the markup

Copy this selected text and paste it into a new, empty file. The only markup in this file should be what you paste into it here (delete the standard markup that Dreamweaver MX always adds for you when you create a new blank page). Here's what the file should look like now:

```
<link href="/inc/old.css" rel="stylesheet" type="text/css" />
<style type="text/css" media="all">
@import "/inc/global.css";
</style>
</head>

<body>
<div id="logo">
<p class="logo"><img src="/images/logo.gif" width="199" height="36"
border="0" alt="GNN Intranet" /></p>
</div>
<div id="banner">
</div>
<div id="content">
```

Save this file as top.asp (I have created a new directory for all includes, CSS files, etc. and so I save the file there).

Return to your layout page, and delete all the markup that you just placed into top.asp. Now, leaving your cursor in the same place in the markup, select the ASP tab of the Insert toolbar. On this tab you should find a button for Server-side Include:

Clicking this button will enter the following markup in your document:

```
<!--#include virtual=""-->
```

Edit this to become a root relative link to top.asp:

```
<!--#include virtual="/inc/top.asp"-->
```

> **Why root-relative links?** *Creating your links relative to the root of the site as opposed to relative to various documents is generally a good plan when building a web application that may grow and change over time. Root-relative links mean that the links to pages are the same all over the application; this ensures consistency, means that they are easily human-readable (you aren't having to mentally step through your directory structure to work out where something is), and there is less likelihood of broken links resulting from a page being moved from one folder to another. Dreamweaver does handle this kind of scenario very well, but there is no guarantee that your application will stay within Dreamweaver, and so using root-relative links will enable the application to be worked on outside Dreamweaver in the future.*

After saving the document, switch back into Design view, or preview the page in a browser; it should still display as before, with all of the top part of the document in place.

We can do the same with the bottom of the document; in my case this includes the navigation. Depending on your layout, your navigation may be part of the top include, or you could even have a separate include for the navigation. As this is a very simple layout, we'll take the whole bottom part of the document as one include. The markup that I have copied out of my document looks like this:

```
</div>
<div id="nav">
<p><a href="#">link one</a></p>
<p><a href="#">link two</a></p>
</div>

</body>
</html>
```

I have taken the closing `</div>` tag of the content area right down to the closing `</html>` tag, placed it in a new file, and saved it as bottom.asp. Again, I have used the Server-Side Include button on the Insert toolbar to insert the markup that calls this file. My completed layout document now contains the following markup:

```
<!DOCTYPE html PUBLIC "-//W3C//DTD XHTML 1.0 Transitional//EN"
        "http://www.w3.org/TR/xhtml1/DTD/xhtml1-transitional.dtd">
<html xmlns="http://www.w3.org/1999/xhtml">

<head>
<title>GNN Intranet</title>
<!--#include virtual="/inc/top.asp"-->
<h1>Heading Level One</h1>
<p>Content here </p>

<!--#include virtual="/inc/bottom.asp"-->
```

You will now find that you are unable to edit the areas that are in the includes from within the Design view; however, the main content area of the page is still available for editing (see Figure 4-3). To make changes to the include files you need to open up the actual include document.

We can use this page as a master layout page and create new pages for our intranet from it. To create a new page, simply open up your layout page and save it with the new filename. When I ask you to create a new page in this chapter, you will be creating a new page by saving this master layout page as the new filename unless I state otherwise.

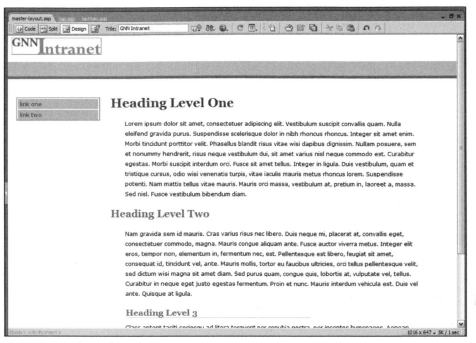

**Figure 4-3.** The layout in Design view

# The homepage

Create a new page from your layout page and name it default2.asp. This will be the main homepage of the intranet, and users will come to this page once they have logged in successfully.

# The database

The data for our intranet will be stored in an Access database. We will start by creating that database and some of the tables that we will need later in the process. So, open Microsoft Access and create a new database file—save this as gnn_intranet.mdb. The first table that we are going to create relates to our users, the company employees. In Access's Design view, create a table that contains the schema shown in Figure 4-4 and save it as tblUsers.

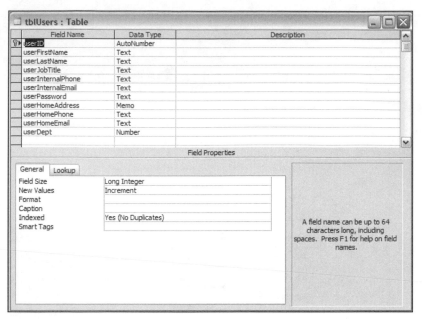

**Figure 4-4.** tblUsers in Access

The first field, userID, is the primary key and set to AutoNumber; the following table shows the field names and sizes for the remaining fields:

| | |
|---|---|
| userFirstName | 100 |
| userLastName | 100 |
| userJobTitle | 255 |
| userInternalPhone | 16 |
| userInternalEmail | 100 |
| userPassword | 10 |
| userHomePhone | 16 |
| UserDept | LongInteger |

Any field that you do not need the user to complete must be set in Field Properties to accept zero length strings. In the Field Properties, General tab, with your field selected locate the label Allow Zero Length and set it to Yes; if you don't do this you will get an error if you try to enter information and haven't completed all the form fields. If there are fields that must be filled in, then use JavaScript to ensure that the user does complete them—we will cover using the Form Validation Behavior later in this project.

The field userDept refers to the department the user works in. Instead of putting the name of the department directly into this table, we will create a separate list of departments and link the two tables by way of inserting the primary key of the table of departments into the userDept field in tblUsers. This will make it easier to display all users from one department and saves us duplicating the department name in every record.

I called this one tblDepts, and it looks like what you see in Figure 4-5.

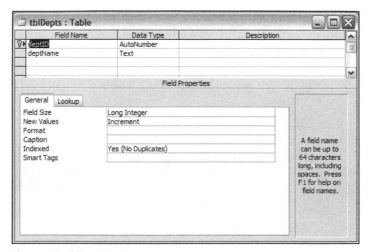

**Figure 4-5.** tblDepts in Access

The deptName field has a size of 80.

Once we have built the application, we will be adding data directly from our web forms; for now, however, it will be helpful to have some data already added to this table. Switch to Datasheet view in Access and add three rows of data by adding the following department names to deptName:

- Management
- Marketing
- Editorial

## Creating relationships

To link the two tables we need to create a relationship between them. In Access, select Tools ➤ Relationships as shown in Figure 4-6.

You will be presented with the Show Table dialog box, which should have both your tables listed. If you do not see this dialog box, right-click the blank gray area that will have opened up and select Show Table from the context menu.

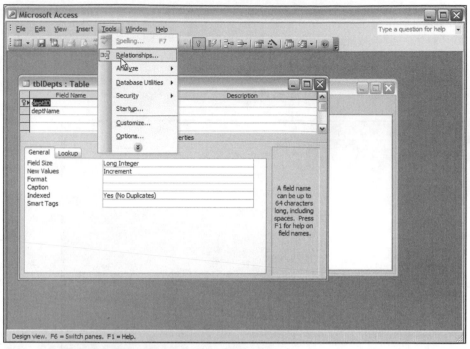

**Figure 4-6.** Selecting Relationships from the Tools menu

Select both tblUsers and tblDepts from this menu and click Add. Then close the dialog box.

Your blank Relationships canvas should now contain two boxes, tblDepts and tblUsers, which list the fields in each table (see Figure 4-7).

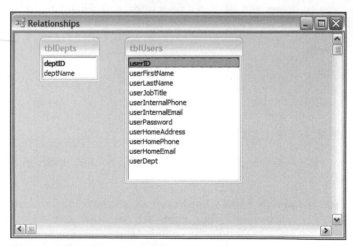

**Figure 4-7.** The tables in the Relationships window

Click the field deptID in tblDepts and drag it until it is over the userDept field in tblUsers, then release the mouse button and the Edit Relationships dialog box, shown in Figure 4-8, should appear for you to edit the details of this relationship.

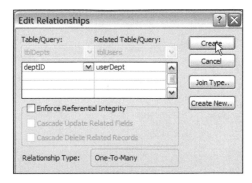

**Figure 4-8.**
Edit Relationships dialog box

For this particular relationship, the defaults as shown in Figure 4-8 are all we need and so you need to simply click Create in order to create this relationship. You will see a linking line drawn between the two tables to show that there is a relationship between the fields.

We also need to create a table that will contain the information about user levels, allowing us to set the level of access for a particular user. This table is called tblLevels and looks like what appears in Figure 4-9.

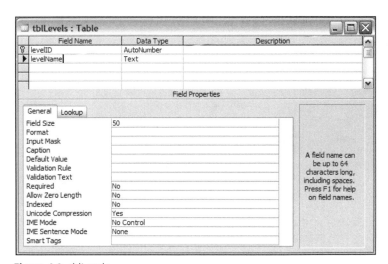

**Figure 4-9.** tblLevels

As with the department table, we want to add a few records to this table:

- Management
- Admin
- User

When we joined the department table to the users table, we used a one-to-many join. Many users records from tblUsers could be joined to one department. Joining tblLevels to tblUsers requires a slightly different approach because it could be a possibility that a user could have rights on more than one level. For instance, a user may be both management, allowed to access all the data on the system, and an administrator, allowed to add content. In the future, new levels or groups could be introduced. In this situation, you have a many-to-many relationship. Many users could be linked to one level, and many levels could be linked to one user.

To deal with this situation, we will create a joining table in order to link users and levels; this is sometimes known as a **lookup table** by Access developers, but are more generally known as **linking tables**. Create a new table in Design view and save it as tblUser_levels as shown in Figure 4-10.

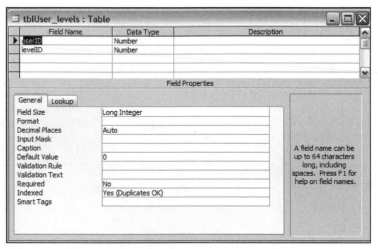

**Figure 4-10.** tblUser_levels

Now return to the Relationships diagram.

Right-click the diagram and select Show Tables. In this dialog box, select and add tblLevels and tblUser_levels to the diagram. Drag the objects around the diagram so that tblUser_levels is between tblUsers and tblLevels as shown in Figure 4-11.

We need to create a relationship between the userID in tblUsers and userID in tblUser_levels, and a relationship between levelID in tblLevels and levelID in tblUser_levels (see Figure 4-12).

Create the relationships by clicking the field name and dragging it to the corresponding field in tblUser_levels.

We will return to Access later to further develop our database, but first let's connect our web application to the database. Before moving on to the next stage, you will need to close down Access as you will get error messages if you attempt to create an ODBC connection to it while it is open.

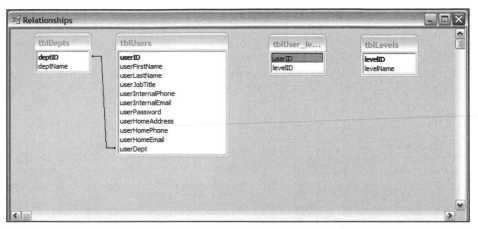

**Figure 4-11.** The Relationships diagram

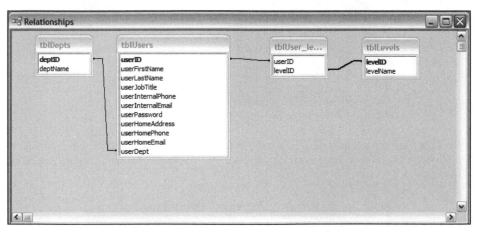

**Figure 4-12.** The relationships created

# Connecting to a database

To start work on the project, Dreamweaver needs to know how to connect to our database. In an intranet situation, where we are likely to have access to our web server, in order to create a database connection we will use the simplest method of database connection, connecting via a **D**ata **S**ource **N**ame (DSN). Using a DSN means that you will not need to change the connection details if you move the intranet from your own computer or a development server to the live site, as long as the DSN has the same name on each machine.

## To create a DSN

Select Start ➤ Settings ➤ Control Panel ➤ Administrative Tools, then select Data Sources (ODBC). The ODBC Data Sources Administrator should appear. Select the System DSN tab and click Add. The Create New Data Source wizard will ask you to select a driver for which you want to set up a data source; you need to select Microsoft Access Driver (*.mdb) as shown in Figure 4-13.

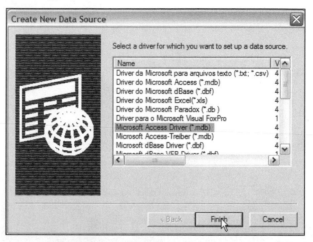

**Figure 4-13.** Selecting Microsoft Access Driver

Then click Finish. A new dialog box like the one in Figure 4-14 will appear which will allow you to name your data source and browse for the database that we created earlier by clicking the Select button.

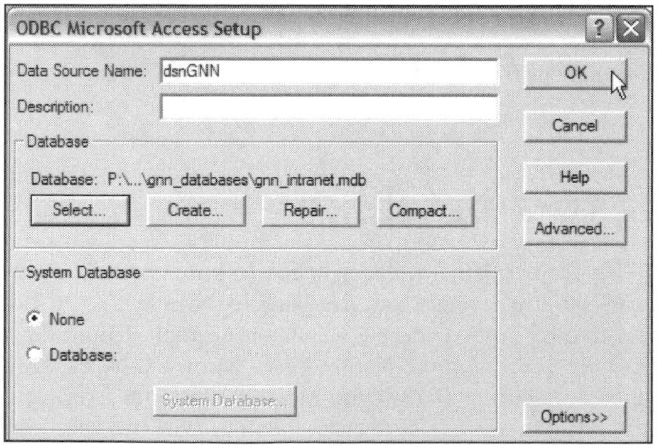

**Figure 4-14.** Create the DSN.

Click OK and you should find your DSN in the list of System DSNs. Close the ODBC Data Sources Administrator.

# Making a database connection in Dreamweaver MX

Now that we have set up a DSN, we need to let Dreamweaver know where our connection is in order that it may set up the database connections for our application.

Make sure that you have opened your intranet site within Dreamweaver MX, and open the `default2.asp` file that we created earlier. Select the Databases panel of the Application Panel Group, expand the +, then select Data Source Name (DSN).

In the dialog box that launches you need to name this connection; if you are using a DSN on the local machine (the one on which Dreamweaver is installed), then select the radio button Using Local DSN and select the DSN from the drop-down list. If you have set up a DSN on another server such as your intranet server, then select Using DSN on Testing Server as shown in Figure 4-15 and click the DSN button to select your DSN from the list. If you have a password-protected database, you will need to enter the username and password here too.

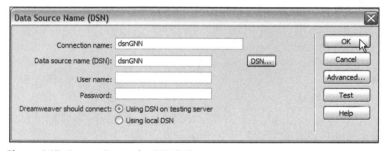

**Figure 4-15.** Connecting to the DSN in Dreamweaver

You can click the Test button to check that your connection is successful. If you have any problems, it is most likely that your DSN is not set up correctly, so check back through the previous steps.

Click OK to confirm this connection and in the Databases panel you will see the connection name as in Figure 4-16; if you click to expand it you will see an object for tables; expanding this will show you the tables that you have already created in your database.

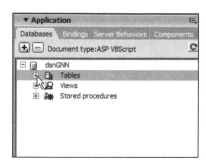

**Figure 4-16.**
The database can now be viewed in Dreamweaver.

# A news page

On the homepage that our users arrive at after logging in to the intranet we will display some latest news headlines. These headlines can be added to by anyone who has administrator privileges and are a good way to ensure that everyone notices some important piece of office information. Clicking the news headline will take the user through to a page that will display more details about this headline and also an archive of older information.

First we need to create a database table for the news items called tblNews. In Design view in Access create a new table with the fields shown in Figure 4-17.

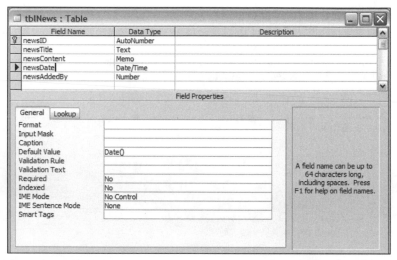

**Figure 4-17.** tblNews

newsTitle has a size of 255. In the Field Properties section for the field newsDate, enter Date() as the Default Value. This will mean that every time you insert a record into this table, the database will add today's date automatically.

Save the table as tblNews. Create a new page from the master layout page and save it in the admin directory as addnews.asp.

Create a form on this page that contains a text input field named newsTitle, a multiline textbox named newsContent, and of course a Submit button (see Figure 4-18).

Call the single-line text field newsTitle and the multiline text area newsContent. This not only makes the code easier to read and understand what it's doing, but it also means Dreamweaver will match the form fields up with the same fields in the database, saving us some time.

**Figure 4-18.** The News Item form in Dreamweaver

## Inserting data into the database

We can now use a Dreamweaver MX Server Behavior to insert data entered into this form into our database.

In Dreamweaver, select the form, then select the Server Behaviors panel of the Application Panel Group. Expand the + and select Insert Record. Fill in the box, shown in Figure 4-19, as follows:

- Connection: The connection that we defined earlier (dsnGNN).
- Insert into Table: We want to insert the data into the table tblNews.
- After Inserting, Go To—editnews.asp: We haven't created this page yet so just type editnews.asp into the field, it will also be saved into the admin directory.
- Get Values From: If you had several forms on the page you need to select the one you are using here.
- Form Elements: Because we named our elements the same as the fields in the database, Dreamweaver will have presumed that we want to match them up. You can change which element matches to which field here.

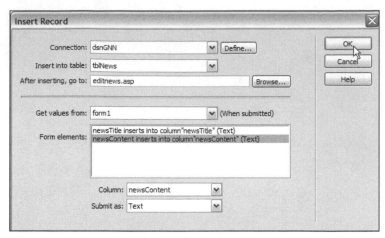

**Figure 4-19.** Insert Record dialog box

Click OK. You should now be able to preview your page in a browser; add some data into the form fields, which will be inserted into the database when you submit the form. If you get an error message that says something like this:

Error Type:

Microsoft OLE DB Provider for ODBC Drivers (0x80004005)

[Microsoft] [ODBC Microsoft Access Driver] The table 'tblNews' is already opened exclusively by another user, or it is already open through the user interface and cannot be manipulated programmatically.

check whether you have the table tblNews open in Access's Design view. Closing the table should release it for you to use.

> **Error messages:** *When working with any server-side scripting language, it is helpful to understand what the error messages mean when you do something that causes an error message to appear in the browser. Internet Explorer by default does not show the full error message. To see full error messages in Internet Explorer select Tools ➤ Internet Options ➤ Advanced and uncheck Show Friendly HTTP Error Messages.*

## Styling the form

When starting work on a site that is going to contain a lot of forms, I like to set up rules in a style sheet that I can apply to forms as I create them in order to maintain a consistent look and feel. As this is our first form, let's create those styles now.

As you can see in Figure 4-20, my form currently looks quite plain in a web browser.

**Figure 4-20.** The addnews.asp page containing the form

By adding simple style rules to the style sheet we can easily create styles that we can apply to any form in the site. I added the following rules to my global.css file.

```
.text {
  width: 180px;
  background-color: #DDE2E8;
  color: #000;
  border: 1px solid #AAAAAA;
}

.textarealarge {
  width: 320px;
  height: 200px;
  background-color: #DDE2E8;
  color: #000;
  border: 1px solid #AAAAAA;
}

.textareasmall {
  width: 220px;
  height: 100px;
  background-color: #DDE2E8;
  color: #000;
  border: 1px solid #AAAAAA;
}
```

**4**

221

```
select {
  background-color: #DDE2E8;
  color: #000;
}

.submit {
  background-color: #DDE2E8;
  color: #333333;
  border: 1px solid #333333;
  font-size: 80%;

}

label {
  font-weight: bold;
}
```

These simply add some color and size to the form fields. To apply the classes, select the field in Design view in Dreamweaver and use the Properties inspector to apply the class as shown in Figure 4-21.

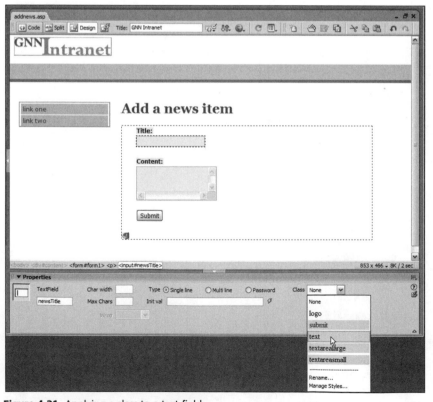

**Figure 4-21.** Applying a class to a text field

In a web browser, my form now looks like the one in Figure 4-22.

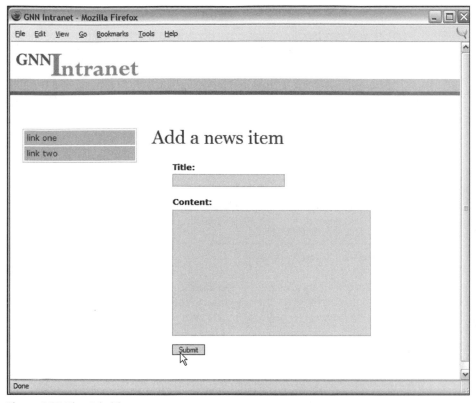

**Figure 4-22.** The styled form

# Listing the items

We now need to create the page editnews.asp that our insert page redirects to after doing the insert. This page will also list all the news items in order to allow us to edit or delete items. Save a page from master-layout into the admin area as editnews.asp.

## Creating a Recordset

In order to list the news items that are stored in our table tblNews, we need to retrieve that data from the table.

To create a Recordset, open Bindings ➤ + ➤ Recordset(Query). In the New Recordset dialog box you need to give your Recordset a name (rsNews) and select the connection that you want to use (dsnGNN). Then select the table in the database from which you wish to pull the data—tblNews.

Next to the label Sort select newsDate and then in the next select menu choose Descending (see Figure 4-23). This will mean that our Recordset will have the most recent record first.

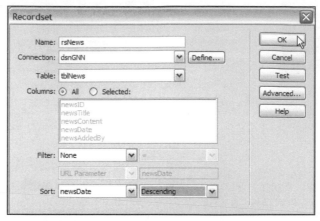

**Figure 4-23.** Recordset rsNews

You can test your Recordset by clicking the Test button. If you have already tested your insert form, you should see the data that you inserted. In the Bindings panel you should now be able to expand a tree view of your Recordset as shown in Figure 4-24.

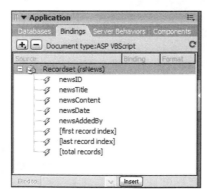

**Figure 4-24.**
The Recordset in the Bindings panel

To insert dynamic data onto your page, first click your cursor onto the position in Design view where you would like the title of the first news item to be displayed. Then, in the Bindings panel with the Recordset expanded, select the field newsTitle and click the Insert button at the bottom of the panel. You should see a placeholder, highlighted in blue, appear on the page, which looks like

```
{rsNews.newsTitle}
```

If you have entered data into the table tblNews by way of our form, you should now see the latest title appear on the page if you switch to live data view.

# Repeat regions

To display all the data from our Recordset on the page, we need to add some code that will loop through the rows in the Recordset and display them on the page until it gets to the end of the data. We'll use the Dreamweaver MX Repeat Region Server Behavior.

To create a repeat region, you need to select the text and markup that you wish to repeat. If your text is between two `<p></p>` tags, make sure that you have selected the opening and closing tags as well; switch into Code view to make sure.

In Design view, with your text and markup selected, select Server Behaviors ➤ + ➤ Repeat Region. In the dialog box that opens you need to simply select the name of the Recordset that you wish to repeat and how many records to display. In this case I want to display all records, as Figure 4-25 shows.

**Figure 4-25.**
The Repeat Region dialog box

Your code block should now be flagged up with a Repeat Region label in **Design** view. Save this page as editnews.asp.

With your browser go to http://localhost/admin/addnews.asp.

Fill in some data into the news form and submit it; all being well, you should be taken to the editnews.asp page and see your news items added to the top of the list.

# Editing news items

Save a new page from your template page as editnews2.asp. This page will contain a form that loads the selected entry in order that it may be edited. We need a way to tell that page which entry we wish to edit. To do this we need to send the field newsID to that page.

We use the field newsID because we know that it will be unique, as it is created by the database as an AutoNumber. Other databases that you may come across have similar functionality, and this is the best way of ensuring that you have a way of identifying each record in the database.

We can send the newsID to editnews2.asp by way of a querystring. To do this, open the page editnews.asp, and select the placeholder for newsTitle.

In the Link field in the Properties inspector browse for the page editnews2.asp. Once you have selected the page in the Select Page dialog box, click the Parameters button to launch a new dialog box. Under Name type newsID as shown in Figure 4-26.

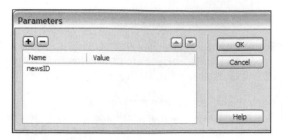

**Figure 4-26.**
The Parameters dialog box

Tab to the Value column and click the lightning bolt icon in the box in that column. A dialog box like the one in Figure 4-27 will open with the fields of your Recordset listed, just as they are in the Bindings panel. Select newsID and click OK.

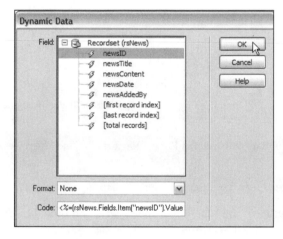

**Figure 4-27.**
Select newsID.

Click OK on the next two dialog boxes. In the Link field of the Properties inspector you should now see something that looks like

/admin/editnews2.asp?newsID=<%=(rsNews.Fields.Item("newsID").Value)%>

Save the page and preview it in your browser. The titles should now all be links with a querystring that contains newsID= and a number which is the AutoNumber from your database. Clicking these links should take you through to editnews2.asp with the querystring displayed in the browser location bar.

Open editnews2.asp; we now need to create a new Recordset on editnews2.asp. Create the Recordset in the same way as you created the one for editnews.asp and call it rsNews. This time we need to add a filter. In the New Recordset dialog box shown in Figure 4-28, under Filter, select

newsID    =

URL Parameter  newsID

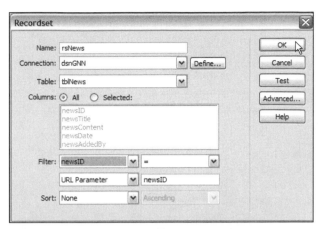

**Figure 4-28.** Create a Recordset filtering on newsID.

Here we are saying that we want the Recordset to select only the record where the field newsID matches the value of newsID in the querystring (the "URL Parameter" as Dreamweaver calls it). You can test this by clicking the Test button. A dialog box will appear asking you to input a test value. If you input a value that exists in the database, you should get one record displayed. Click OK.

Create a form on the page that contains the same fields as the form on addnews.asp.

Select the form field newsTitle, then in the Bindings panel select the corresponding field newsTitle. Click the Bind button at the bottom of the Bindings panel. You should see the placeholder *rsNews.newsTitle* appear in the form field. Repeat these steps for the form field named newsContent. Save the page.

To test this page go to http://localhost/admin/editnews.asp and click one of the linked titles. You should find yourself on editnews2.asp with the title and content of this news item displayed in the form fields (see Figure 4-29).

If this doesn't work check that the ID is present on the querystring and that your Recordset is created correctly on the page editnews2.asp.

If all is well, return to editnews2.asp in Dreamweaver to apply the Server Behavior, which will update the record in the database. Select the form, and, in the Server Behaviors panel menu, select Update Record (see Figure 4-30).

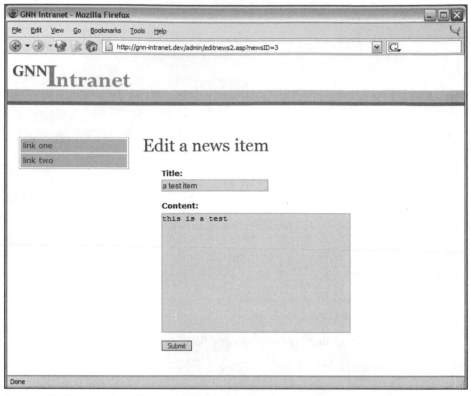

**Figure 4-29.** The news item displayed for editing

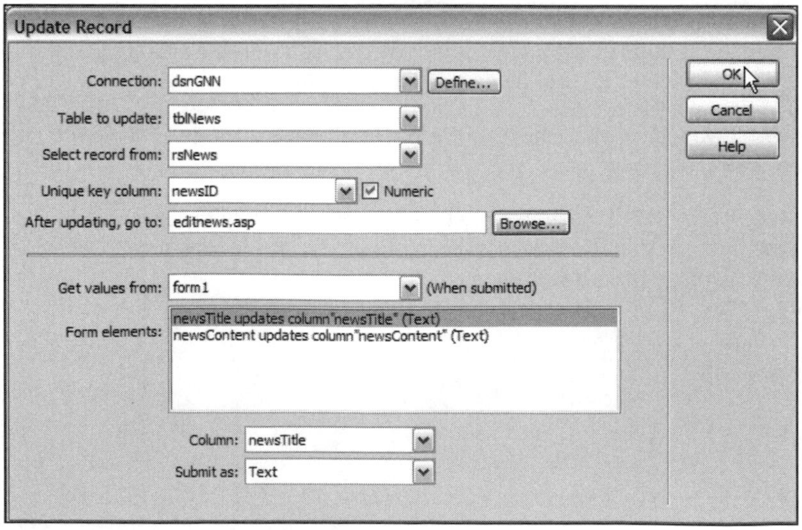

**Figure 4-30.** Update Record dialog box

You should find that many of these fields are similar to those of the Insert Record dialog box. The additional fields are to ensure that you update the correct record. Select Record From needs to be set to the Recordset from which you have taken your form data; the Unique Key column is newsID.

Click OK and test your script by selecting a record from the list of entries on editnews.asp, editing the values, and clicking Submit, and you should find that the record has been updated.

# Deleting records

The final stage in the functionality for the news administration is to allow items to be deleted.

Create a new page in the admin folder called deletenews.asp.

On the page editnews.asp, next to the title placeholder add the text DELETE, select it, and create a link to deletenews.asp that includes the value of newsID in the querystring, just as we did for the link to editnews2.asp.

On the page deletenews.asp create an identical Recordset to the one we created for editnews2.asp, a Recordset that selects the record based on the value of newsID. Instead of binding the fields in the Recordset to a form, on this page all we want to do is display them so that the user knows they are about to delete the correct record. With the cursor in the place that you would like the title to appear, select newsTitle in the Bindings panel and click Insert; do the same with newsContent.

Create a form on this page; the form simply needs a submit button with the label Delete.

To delete the record when this form is submitted, apply the Delete Record Server Behavior by selecting it from the list in the Server Behaviors panel. The result is shown in Figure 4-31.

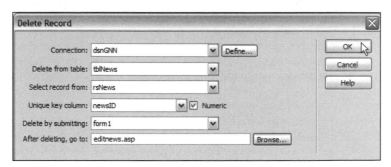

**Figure 4-31.** Delete Record Server Behavior

You should now be able to add, edit, and delete records with your administration pages.

On `editnews.asp` add a link to `addnews.asp`. `editnews.asp` will be the main news administration page linked from our menus, which we'll do next.

## Add the news administration to the menus

Open the include file `bottom.asp`; at the moment this simply contains two placeholder link items. Replace those with a link to `/admin/editnews.asp`. Later in the project we will be applying access restrictions on these pages, but for the time being just simply add it to the menu so that you can easily get to it for testing.

# Displaying the news on the homepage

Now that we have a way of administering our table of news items, we need to be able to display them on the homepage. Open `default2.asp` and create a new Recordset in the same way as we created the Recordset for `editnews.asp`—sorting by newsDate descending.

Before closing the Recordset dialog box, we don't want to display every record in the database but only the three newest records. To only select the top three records we will need to click the Advanced button. In the box labeled SQL you will see

SELECT *

FROM tblNews

ORDER BY newsDate DESC

This is **S**tructured **Q**uery **L**anguage (SQL), which is the language that we use to send queries to our database. It is not difficult to learn basic SQL, and so if you are new to working with databases, a good SQL book will be of great use to you as you work on more complex applications. While much of SQL is common to all DBMSs, some syntax is database-specific such as the SELECT TOP in the syntax that follows, which is common to Access and MS SQL Server's dialect of SQL. In MySQL, for instance, you would need to use LIMIT to get the same result. Once you have learned the basics of SQL, however, a good reference book will explain these differences. A couple of good examples are Practical Web Database Design *by Chris Auld et al. (Apress, July 2003, ISBN 1-59059-194-1), and* Beginning SQL Programming *by John Kauffman et al. (Apress, March 2001, ISBN 1-861001-80-0).*

As shown in Figure 4-32, we need to change this SQL to

```
SELECT TOP 3 *
FROM tblNews
ORDER BY newsDate DESC
```

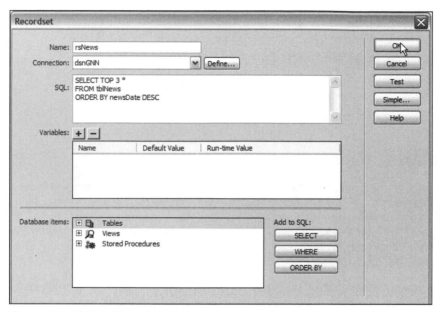

**Figure 4-32.** Advanced Recordset dialog box

TOP 3 requests only the first three records from the table. Click OK.

With this Recordset created, you can now add the title to the location on the page where you would like the news items to appear.

Some of our news items might be quite long, so we don't want to display the whole thing on the page, but just a few words to get the user's interest. To display only a few words without having to handcode, we need to use a Dreamweaver extension. Download the Crop Sentence Server Behavior from www.dmxzone.com/showdetail.asp?TypeId=3&NewsId=1645 (you will need to create a free account and log in first). Install the extension with the Extension manager and restart Dreamweaver.

Place your cursor on the location in the page where you would like the extension to be applied and then expand the + in the Server Behaviors panel and select Ultra Dumb ➤ Crop Sentence.

In the dialog box that opens, select the Recordset rsNews and the field newsContent. Then add 50 (characters) in the Length input box and ... under Characters as shown in Figure 4-33—these will appear after the content to show there is more.

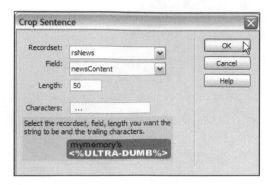

**Figure 4-33.**
The Crop Sentence dialog box

Click OK and your content field placeholder will display.

## Formatting dates

We want to display the date the entry was made on the page so that users will know when the item was posted. You can insert the date in the same way you insert any other field. This will display on the page in the format month/day/year or day/month/year (12/14/2002 or 14/12/2002 is 14th December 2002). This can be confusing with UK and American formats displaying dependent on the user's system settings, so it is a good idea to display the date in a way that will not be misunderstood, for example as 14th December 2002.

To format the date in long date format, insert your date field as normal, then look at the Format column in the Bindings panel. If you click the arrow in this column for our date field, there are a variety of ways to set the format. Select Date Time ➤ Long Date Format as shown in Figure 4-34.

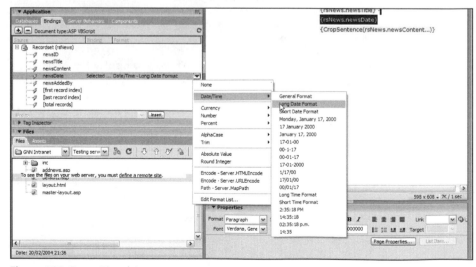

**Figure 4-34.** Formatting dates

To complete this news section, return to Design view in Dreamweaver and add a repeat region to the section containing the news item, so that all three items will be displayed, and preview this in the browser—you will need to ensure that your items are longer than the number of characters specified in the Crop Sentence extension, in order for you to see that this is working.

# Create the news page

Save a new page from your template as news.asp. This will be the page that users who wish to read the full news article will go to. On this page create a Recordset that filters on newsID—just as you did when creating the page delete.asp. Insert the news title and content onto the page as dynamic data.

To create the links to this page, select the title of the article on default2.asp and create a link, giving it a querystring of newsID, just as we did when linking to the edit and delete pages. You should now be able to launch default2.asp in the browser and click through to read the full article on news.asp.

## Preserving line breaks

If you have added lengthy text to the newsContent field, which included line-spacing, you may have now realized that this text all runs together as one big block when displayed on the page. The database will preserve the spacing so we just need to use a VBScript function to replace the line breaks with HTML. Switch to Code view and find the location of your newsContent field.

```
<h1><%=(rsNews.Fields.Item("newsTitle").Value)%><h1>
  <p> <%=(rsNews.Fields.Item("newsContent").Value)%></p>
```

Wrap this with the VBScript Replace function. This function replaces one string with another. We want to replace Chr(13), which is the newline character, with </p><p>. Because I have wrapped my dynamic text with <p></p> tags, this will ensure that they are opened and closed in the right places. The new code looks like this:

```
<h1> <%=(rsNews.Fields.Item("newsTitle").Value)%></h1>
<p><%=Replace((rsNews.Fields.Item("newsContent").Value),Chr(13),
➡ "</p><p >")%></p>
```

If you view an article that contains line breaks, you should now find that they are displayed in the browser. If you haven't surrounded the news article with <p></p> tags, you'll find this doesn't produce the desired effect. You could alternatively replace the breaks with <br /> tags. Replace can be used for any scenario where you wish to not change the content of the database but change the way that it is displayed on the screen.

**233**

# News archive

Finally we want to create a news archive page that will allow us to browse through old news items. Create a new page called newsarchive.asp.

Create a Recordset on that page which selects newsID, newsTitle, newsContent, and newsDate, and sorts by newsDate descending (see Figure 4-35).

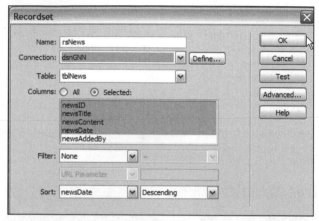

**Figure 4-35.** Creating the Recordset

Add the data to the page in the same way that you did for the homepage, except this time you have all of the records in the table and not just the top three. Make the article titles link back to our news.asp page to display the full article.

When you get to the point of adding the repeat region, select to only show 5 Records at a Time as shown in Figure 4-36; this will stop the page taking too long to load once you have a lot of records in the database.

**Figure 4-36.**
Displaying 5 records

To show the rest of the records, we need to add some forward and back links, which will allow us to page through the records. This is a simple process within Dreamweaver.

Underneath and outside your repeat region add the following text:

```
<< previous    next >>
```

Select the text next >>. In the Server Behaviors menu select *Recordset* paging ➤ Move to Next Record. In the dialog box that launches, check that the field Link is listing your selected text and that the Recordset is rsNews (see Figure 4-37). Click OK.

**Figure 4-37.**
Move to Next Record dialog box

Keeping this text selected, return to the Server Behaviors menu and select Show Region ➤ Show Region If Not Last Record, make sure that the Recordset rsNews is selected in the dialog box that displays as shown in Figure 4-38, and click OK. This will ensure that if you have come to the last news item it does not show a next link.

**Figure 4-38.**
Show Region If Not Last Record dialog box

Repeat the process with the << previous text selected. You will need to select Server Behaviors Recordset paging ➤ Move to Previous Record and Show Region ➤ Show Region If Not First Record.

If you have more than five news articles in the database, you will be able to see this in action if you open the page in your web browser. Add News Archive to your navigation menu.

# Document sharing

There are often documents within a business that are needed by all employees, such things as travel directions to the office, the training manual, or other documents. These can be uploaded to a central place on the intranet, from where they can be accessed by everyone. The advantage of these being stored in one place is that if they need to be updated there is no risk of old copies lurking around the place, which could cause problems if you have updated some terms and conditions, for example, and an old version was sent out.

If you were using a remote web server, then you would need to provide some method of uploading files via the web browser. In ASP there is no built-in way to do this, and we need to either rely on using third-party components or writing a lot of code! There is a Dreamweaver extension available to accomplish this, and should you wish to add upload capability to your extranet you might like to look at the extension **Pure ASP Upload** available from www.dmxzone.com—search for "Pure ASP Upload" (this extension costs $49 at time of publication)—or at the upload component **ASPUpload** available from www.aspupload.com. The advantage of the Dreamweaver extension is that it does not require a component to be installed on your server. However, installing components such as ASPUpload is not difficult, and there is a free trial available of that particular component, so that you can test whether it will be suitable for your needs before making a purchase. Both the extension and the component mentioned have excellent help, installation, and usage instructions.

As we are working on an intranet that is hosted locally, we can take the route of simply requesting that people place documents into a certain directory on the web server. We can then write a small piece of code which uses the **FileSystemObject** to locate these files and list them on the intranet itself for download.

The **FileSystemObject** (FSO) is a component that allows you to access the filesystem of the web server. Using the FSO means you can read from and write to files within the directory structure, move and copy files, and check that files exist.

First create a directory within your web site; this is where documents will need to be placed for download. The directory will need to be shared for users with rights to place documents into this directory in the same way that any directory is shared on that server. Note down the full system path to the directory (such as C:\1web\GNN_intranet\intranet_docs, or C:\Inetpub\wwwroot\GNNIntranet\intranet_docs). Note that you will also have to map this in as a virtual directory of the server.

Open Access and create a new table called tblDocs in Design view with the fields you see in Figure 4-39.

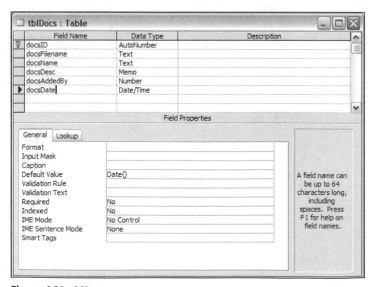

**Figure 4-39.** tblDocs

As with the table tblNews, give the field docsDate a default value of Date() so that Access automatically inserts the day's date when a new record is added. docsFilename and docsName have a size of 255.

In Dreamweaver create a new page in the admin section called adddocs.asp. This page will allow administrators to locate the file they have just placed into the intranet documents directory and add some details about it before it becomes available for download. You should add some text here explaining that they should have already placed their file into the correct directory before continuing.

Add a form on this page, with the fields docsName and docsDesc (see Figure 4-40). Add one radio button named docsFilename and some placeholder text. This is where we will display all the files in the intranet_docs directory so that the user may select the file they placed there.

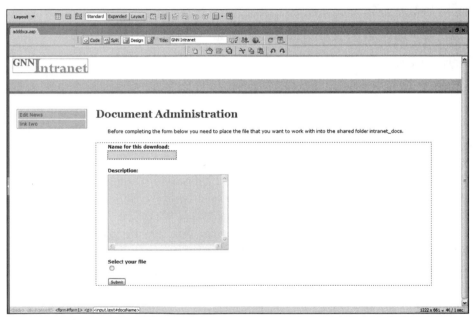

**Figure 4-40.** The Document Administration page

# Using the FileSystemObject

Switch into Code view. At the very top of the document, before the DOCTYPE add the following code:

```
<%@LANGUAGE="VBSCRIPT"%>
<%
Dim thePath, fso, theFolder, theFiles, myFile
thePath = "C:\1web\GNN_Intranet\intranet_docs"
```

```
Set fso = CreateObject("Scripting.FileSystemObject")
Set theFolder = fso.GetFolder(thePath)
Set theFiles = theFolder.Files
%>
```

Don't forget that ASP only allows one @LANGUAGE statement on a page, so don't add one if it's already there.

You will need to change the location for the variable thePath to the folder on your system in which files will be stored for download. This code simply opens an instance of the FileSystemObject, gets the folder from the path that you give it, and then gets all of the files in that folder and puts their details into an array called theFiles. We now need to display this information on the page.

Scroll down through the code to the place where you put your radio button and place-holder text:

```
<input type="radio" name="docsFilename" value="" /> [filename]
```

Replace that with the following code:

```
<%
For Each myFile in theFiles
%>
<input type="radio" name="docsFilename" value="<%=myFile.Name%>" />
➥ <%=myFile.Name%><br />
<%
Next
Set fso = Nothing
%>
```

If you insert some documents into the directory and then view this page in the browser, you should see the names of your documents.

All that is left to do is insert this data into the database. The selected radio button will give the filename as the value for the field docsFilename. Use the Dreamweaver Insert Record Server Behavior. After inserting this record we want to be redirected to the page /document.asp, which we are about to create.

All we need to do now is create a page that will allow users to download these documents. Save a new page as documents.asp and create a Recordset that selects everything from the table tblDocs. Call this new Recordset rsDocs.

Use the Bindings panel to put the dynamic data for the name of the download, the description, and the date onto the page as you would like them to be displayed. To create a link to the file, select the name of the download and switch into Code view. We need to create a link that references the folder where all downloads are stored and then uses the dynamic data docsFilename as the file to download. This will look like the following:

```
<a href="/intranet_docs/<%=(rsDocs.Fields.Item("docsFilename").
➡ Value)%>">
<%=(rsDocs.Fields.Item("docsName").Value)%></a>
```

Now create a repeat region using the Server Behavior in order to display all files that have been added and given details in the database. You can now add Download Documents and Document Administration to the menu. Ensure that your users understand that simply placing the file into the directory will not make it live on the intranet; they need to go through the steps of selecting and adding the details for this file before it becomes listed.

This simple method could, of course, allow people to create multiple descriptions for the same file by selecting the same file and adding another entry for it. If a large amount of document sharing is to take place on your intranet, then a more complex solution may need to be investigated. However, for a small system where people can be made aware of this type of issue, it should not cause a problem.

# Adding new users

Save a page into the admin directory from your template page as useradd.asp.

On the page useradd.asp we need to create a form that contains the following fields from the table tblUsers in our database.

- userFirstName
- userLastName
- userJobTitle
- userInternalPhone
- userInternalEmail
- userPassword

We also need to create a list of the departments so that we can select the department to which our user belongs, and also select which levels of access this user has.

## A dynamic select menu

Using the Forms tab of the Insert toolbar, add a menu form object into your page. Name it userDept.

We need to create a Recordset that contains the data about our departments.

In the New Recordset dialog box you need to give your Recordset a name (rsDepts); select the connection that you want to use, which is the one we created earlier. Then select the table in the database from which you wish to pull the data—tblDepts (see Figure 4-41).

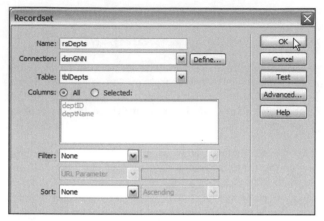

**Figure 4-41.** Creating the Recordset rsDepts

Click the Test button and you should see the data that we input into the table tblDepts when we created it. Click OK and you should see your Recordset in the Bindings panel; we can now use this Recordset to create our menu.

In the Properties inspector, with your menu object selected, click the Dynamic button; the Dynamic List/Menu dialog box will open (see Figure 4-42).

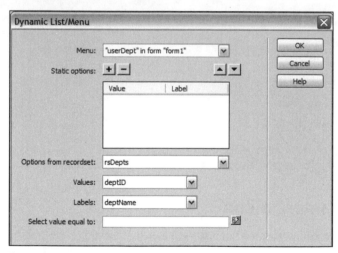

**Figure 4-42.** Dynamic List/Menu dialog box

In this dialog box, you need to select your Recordset in the drop-down list Options from Recordset, then select which field from that Recordset should make up the value, and which should be the label (the text that appears in the list). We want the value to be the ID from this table but want to show the user the actual name of the department, so in Values select deptID, and for Labels select deptName as shown in the preceding image. Preview your page in the browser to see the select menu in action.

When the form is submitted, the value of the option will be sent along with the name of the select list. For instance, if the HTML (after being processed by the web server) for the list looks like this:

```
<select name="userDept" id="userDept">
          <option value="1">Management</option>
          <option value="2">Marketing</option>
          <option value="3">Editorial</option>
</select>
```

and the user selects Marketing, when the form is submitted userDept=2 will be sent from this form object. When we set up the database, we joined the table tblDept to the table tblUser, so by inserting the deptID into tblUsers we will link this user with the correct department.

## Checkboxes for user levels

Create a new Recordset in the same way as we created the Recordset for the list of departments. Call this Recordset rsLevels and select the data from tblLevels.

What we are now going to do is loop through the data in this Recordset creating a label and a checkbox for each level of access that we have in our database.

In the Design view of Dreamweaver MX, place your cursor in the position you would like the label for the checkbox to go.

In the Bindings panel, expand the tree for the Recordset rsLevels. Select the field levelName (see Figure 4-43).

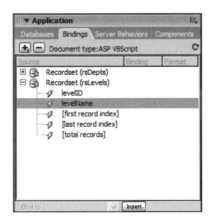

**Figure 4-43.**
Select levelName.

Click the Insert button at the bottom of the Bindings panel and Dreamweaver will insert {rsLevels.levelName} into the page, highlighted. If you switch into Code view you can take a look at the VBScript that has been inserted by Dreamweaver.

```
<%=(rsLevels.Fields.Item("levelName").Value)%>
```

This snippet of code is requesting the data from the field levelName from the Recordset rsLevels.

Back in Design view, insert a checkbox. Name the checkbox levelID. With the checkbox selected, return to the Bindings panel, and this time select the field levelID. You will notice that the Insert button is named Bind when you are working with an object such as a checkbox or form field, as it will bind the dynamic data to the value. Click the Bind button and you should see that the checkbox is faintly highlighted in the same color as the dynamic data you placed on the page.

Preview the page in the browser and you should see that the first row of your table tblLevels has been pulled out onto the page. Use the Repeat Region Server Behavior to repeat each record in tblLevels, including both {rsLevels.levelName} and the checkbox, and don't forget we're using rsLevels as the Recordset. Your completed form should look something like the one in Figure 4-44 in the Dreamweaver Design view.

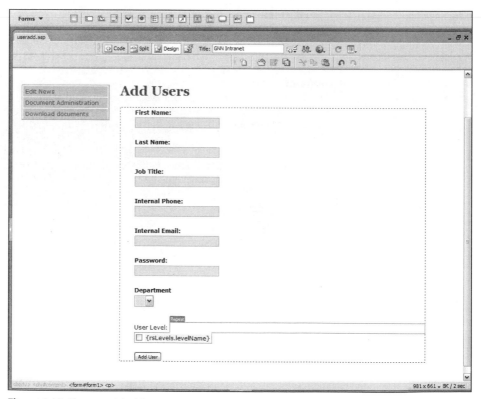

**Figure 4-44.** The completed form

## Inserting the user data into the database

Now that we have our form, we need to insert data collected by it into the database. Our previous inserts have been simple enough to do using the Dreamweaver Insert Record Server Behavior. This behavior is excellent if you are just doing a simple insert into one table. However, we need to not only insert the data to the table tblUsers, but also insert the information about which levels of access this user has into tblUser_levels. In this case it is easier to hand code the insert than it is to try and edit the Dreamweaver Behavior.

Create a new blank page in Dreamweaver and save it as useradd_script.asp in the admin folder. We don't need any HTML on this page, as it will simply be a script page to do our insert. Following is the code in its entirety:

```vbscript
<%@LANGUAGE="VBSCRIPT"%>
<!--#include virtual="/Connections/dsnGNN.asp" -->

<%
'dimension variables
Dim userFirstName, userLastName, userJobTitle,
➥ userInternalPhone,
➥ userInternalEmail, userPassword, userDept, levelID, rsAddUser,
➥ aLevelID, i, strSQL, userID, adoCon

'function to remove single quotes from input
Function stripQuotes(strQuotes)
Dim strOutput
strOutput = Replace(strQuotes, "'","''")
stripQuotes = strOutput
End Function

'put the values from our form into variables,
' using the function stripQuotes to remove quotes
userFirstName = stripQuotes(Request.Form("userFirstName"))
userLastName = stripQuotes(Request.Form("userLastName"))
userJobTitle = stripQuotes(Request.Form("userJobTitle"))
userInternalPhone = stripQuotes(Request.Form("userInternalPhone"))
userInternalEmail = stripQuotes(Request.Form("userInternalEmail"))
userPassword = stripQuotes(Request.Form("userPassword"))
userDept = stripQuotes(Request.Form("userDept"))
levelID = stripQuotes(Request.Form("levelID"))

'create a recordset in order to insert the record using addnew
Set rsAddUser = Server.CreateObject("ADODB.Recordset")
rsAddUser.ActiveConnection = MM_dsnGNN_STRING
rsAddUser.Source = "SELECT * FROM tblUsers"
rsAddUser.CursorType = 2
rsAddUser.CursorLocation = 2
rsAddUser.LockType = 3
```

```
rsAddUser.Open()
rsAddUser.AddNew

rsAddUser("userFirstName") = userFirstName
rsAddUser("userLastName") = userLastName
rsAddUser("userJobTitle") = userJobTitle
rsAddUser("userInternalPhone") = userInternalPhone
rsAddUser("userInternalEmail") = userInternalEmail
rsAddUser("userPassword") = userPassword
rsAddUser("userDept") = userDept
rsAddUser.Update
rsAddUser.requery
rsAddUser.MoveLast

userID = rsAddUser("userID")
rsAddUser.Close
Set rsAddUser = Nothing

'insert the levels
Set adoCon = Server.CreateObject("ADODB.Connection")
adoCon.Open MM_dsnGNN_STRING
'split the values sent for levelID into an array
'using the VBScript Split function
alevelID = Split(levelID, ",")
'loop through that array inserting the levelID and userID
For Each i In alevelID
  strSQL = "INSERT INTO tblUser_levels (userID, levelID) VALUES (" &
➥userID & ", " & i & ")"
  adoCon.execute(strSQL)
Next
adoCon.Close
Set adoCon = Nothing

Response.Redirect "/list.asp"
%>
```

In the preceding code, we use the addnew method of inserting rows into the database as this allows us to easily retrieve the ID of the newly inserted record (userID). We need this ID in order to populate the table tblUser_levels with this ID and the values from the array of selected levelIDs.

After the script has run, we redirect to /list.asp; we will create this page later in the project. Before testing that your form can add users to the database, set the method of the form on useradd.asp to POST and the action to useradd_script.asp.

# User authentication

We can now use our user database in order to create our login system for the intranet.

Save a page from the template page, and name it `default.asp`. This will be the initial page that visitors to your intranet will arrive at.

As this will simply be a page with the login form on it, we want to remove the navigation include from this page. Switch into Code view and replace this markup:

```
<!--#include virtual="/inc/bottom.asp" -->
```

with

```
</div>
</body>
</html>
```

This will give us a page with no navigation but which retains the top banner and logo.

In the content area of this page, we need to create a form that has a text input field for the username or e-mail address, one for the password, and a Submit button.

Give these form fields the same name as the relevant fields in the database—userInternalEmail and userPassword. In Code view my form looks like this:

```
<form name="login" id="login" method="post" action="">
  <p>
    <label>Email Address:<br />
    <input name="userInternalEmail" type="text"
    ➥ id="userInternalEmail" />
    </label>
  </p>
  <p>
    <label>Password:<br />
    <input name="userPassword" type="password"
    ➥ id="userPassword" />
    </label>
</p>

    <p>
      <input type="submit" name="Submit" value="Submit" />
    </p>
  </form>
```

To enable users to log in we will use the User Authentication Server Behaviors.

Select the form. Select Server Behaviors ➤ + ➤ User Authentication ➤ Log in User. Complete the fields as shown in Figure 4-45.

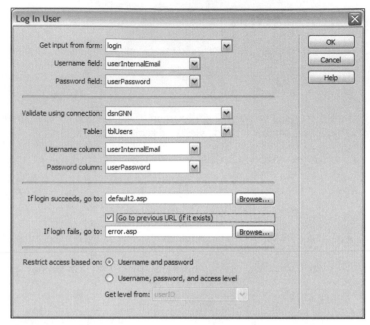

**Figure 4-45.** Log In User dialog box

Click OK. As long as you have already added a user with an e-mail address and password into your database, you should be able to log in and be redirected to default2.asp. You will need to create a page, /error.asp, that tells users that they have logged in incorrectly and give a link back to the login form to try again and the details of someone who can help them.

## Restricting access to pages

On all pages of the intranet you will need to ensure that only logged-in users can access the page. To do this open the page default2.asp and select the User Authentication ➤ Restrict Access to Page Behavior from the Server Behaviors menu. You will simply need to select the username and password radio buttons and add the page that users who are not logged in will go to—I usually use the login page here as it is likely that a user who is not logged in has bookmarked a restricted page and just needs to be reminded to log in (see Figure 4-46). This is why we checked the box on the login Server Behavior dialog box that enables the user to return to the page they were attempting to go to when they were redirected.

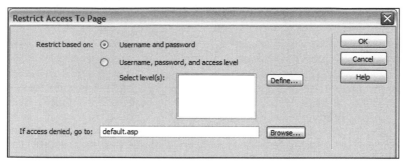

**Figure 4-46.** Restrict Access To Page dialog box

## Logging out users

To log out users we can use the Dreamweaver User Authentication Log out Server Behavior. I am going to place the logout link in my include file `bottom.asp` as the final menu item—this means I don't need to add it to every page, as by adding it to the include it will appear everywhere that the menu does.

Open the `bottom.asp` include. Place your cursor where you would like the new menu item to be. Select User Authentication ➤ Log out user from the Server Behaviors menu. The dialog box as shown in Figure 4-47 will open; select the options shown.

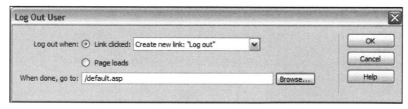

**Figure 4-47.** Log Out User dialog box

Click OK and the new link should be created and the logout ASP will be at the top of the include. Before you reload your page to see this in action, you will need to scroll to the top of the `bottom.asp` include file and remove this line:

```
<%@LANGUAGE="VBSCRIPT"%>
```

otherwise you will get an error because the @LANGUAGE command can only be used once in the page, and we already have one in the page that calls this include—Dreamweaver cannot distinguish between regular pages and include pages and so will add this at the top of the page.

## Checking user levels

We also need to check the user level of our user after they have logged in; this check will enable us to display the correct options in the menu and also restrict logged-in users from viewing pages or using functionality that they do not have access to. The Dreamweaver Login Behavior does have the functionality to include a user level, but this level needs to be stored in the same table as the user details, and because our users could have multiple levels this is not the situation we find ourselves in.

I am going to create a new include file, checklevels.asp, in the inc directory, and, in this include, set a couple of variables: isSiteAdmin and isManager. These will be set to true if the user is either a manager or a site administrator. Then, when I have a situation where I need to hide content from users who do not meet one or other of these criteria, I can just check whether they are true or false.

Create a new blank file, save it as checklevels.asp, and add the following block of VBScript to that file:

```
<%
Dim rsCheckLevels, aLevels
Set rsCheckLevels = Server.CreateObject("ADODB.Recordset")
rsCheckLevels.ActiveConnection = MM_dsnGNN_STRING
rsCheckLevels.Source = "SELECT userID, levelID, levelName
➥ FROM qUserLevels
➥ WHERE userInternalEmail = '" & Session("MM_Username") & "'"
rsCheckLevels.CursorType = 1
rsCheckLevels.CursorLocation = 2
rsCheckLevels.LockType = 1
rsCheckLevels.Open()
isSiteAdmin = False
isManager = False
Do While Not rsCheckLevels.EOF
  if rsCheckLevels("levelName") = "Admin" Then
    isSiteAdmin = True
  elseif rsCheckLevels("levelName") = "Management" Then
    isManager = True
  end if
rsCheckLevels.MoveNext
loop
rsCheckLevels.Close
Set rsCheckLevels = Nothing

%>
```

You will see that I am selecting not from one of our tables but from qUserLevels. This is a query that I have created in Access. Queries (called **Views** in most other Relational Database Management Systems, such as SQL Server) allow you to combine data from several tables where that data is linked. To create the query, open your database file in Access and select Queries, then Create Query by using Wizard.

In the wizard, select your table and then select the fields that you would like to have in the query. From tblUsers select userID, userInternalEmail, and userPassword as shown in Figure 4-48.

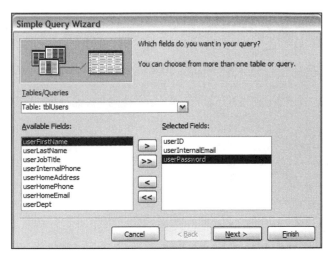

**Figure 4-48.** Select fields from tblUsers.

From tblUser_levels select levelID and from tblLevels select levelName. Then click Finish. You will see a datasheet that includes multiple entries for each user, depending on how many levels they can access, as shown in Figure 4-49. Save this as qUserLevels.

| userPassword | levelID | userInternalEm: | userID | levelName |
|---|---|---|---|---|
| 1234 | 3 | joeb@gnn.com | 1 | User |
| 1234 | 2 | admin@gnn.co | 2 | Admin |
| 1234 | 1 | manager@gnn. | 4 | Management |
| | | | (AutoNumber) | |

Record: ◄◄ ◄ 4 ► ►► ►* of 4

**Figure 4-49.** qUserLevels

Add this include to all pages of the site (you could add this to top.asp):

```
<!--#include virtual="/inc/checklevels.asp" -->
```

To only display menu items to users that they are allowed to access, open the include bottom.asp. Currently I have six links to functionality in my bottom.asp include; three of them are for site administrators only:

```
<p><a href="/admin/useradd.asp">Add Users</a></p>
<p><a href="/admin/editnews.asp">Edit News Items</a></p>
<p><a href="/admin/adddocs.asp">Document Administration</a></p>
<p><a href="/documents.asp">Download Documents</a></p>
<p><a href="/newsarchive.asp">News Archive</a></p>
<p><a href="<%= MM_Logout %>">Log Out</a></p>
```

To prevent anyone other than site administrators seeing these options, wrap these links in an if statement that checks that isSiteAdmin = true.

```
<%If isSiteAdmin = true Then%>
<p><a href="/admin/useradd.asp">Add Users</a></p>
<p><a href="/admin/editnews.asp">Edit News Items</a></p>
<p><a href="/admin/adddocs.asp">Document Administration</a></p>
<%End If%>
<p><a href="/documents.asp">Download Documents</a></p>
<p><a href="/newsarchive.asp">News Archive</a></p>
<p><a href="<%= MM_Logout %>">Log Out</a></p>
```

If you now log in as a regular user or a manager, you will only see the option to download a document or view the news archive; log in as a site administrator and you will get all the other options.

We can also use these variables to check that users are of the right level to use certain pages. Open the page useradd.asp.

After the markup that calls the include <!--#include virtual="/inc/top.asp" --> (as this is where our variable are set to true) add the following:

```
<%If isSiteAdmin <> true Then
  Response.Redirect "/error.asp"
end if
%>
```

This checks the variable isSiteAdmin and if it is anything other than true it redirects to the error.asp page. All of the pages that we have created now need to have the Dreamweaver Restrict Access Server Behavior applied and the following pages

- /admin/adddocs.asp
- /admin/addnews.asp
- /admin/deletenews.asp
- /admin/editnews.asp
- /admin/editnews2.asp

need the code to check levels.

# Employee information

Now that we can create a user list, we can use this list to create an employee list so that employees can look up the internal phone and e-mail details of members of other departments. We can also give managers the rights to view more complete employee details and enable the editing of details, both of the basic details by the site administrator, and the full details by the employees themselves.

## List of employees with internal phone/e-mail details

Create a new page, accessible to everyone who is logged in, that contains a Recordset that is the data from tblDepts, and name it list.asp. Place the dynamic name deptName onto the page and create a repeat region to display all department names on this page.

Now create a Recordset that contains the data from tblUsers. Sort these by userLastName—ascending.

Staying within the repeat region of tblDepts, insert the userFirstName, userLastName, and userJobTitle to the page. Now switch into Code view. What we need to do is loop through only those employees from rsUsers who are in the department we are in. Dreamweaver won't do a nested repeat region for us so we'll need to do it by hand. Near the top of the document, after the Recordsets have been created, find this section:

```
Dim Repeat1__numRows
Dim Repeat1__index

Repeat1__numRows = -1
Repeat1__index = 0
rsDepts_numRows = rsDepts_numRows + Repeat1__numRows
```

Edit this to add a duplicate set of code that references Repeat2 and rsUsers.

```
Dim Repeat1__numRows, Repeat2__numRows
Dim Repeat1__index, Repeat2__index

Repeat1__numRows = -1
Repeat1__index = 0
rsDepts_numRows = rsDepts_numRows + Repeat1__numRows

Repeat2__numRows = -1
Repeat2__index = 0
rsUsers_numRows = rsUsers_numRows + Repeat2__numRows
```

Now scroll down the page to where the repeat region for rsDepts is located. Find the place in the code where you place your dynamic data from rsUsers onto the page:

```
<p><%=(rsUsers.Fields.Item("userFirstName").Value)%>
➡ <%=(rsUsers.Fields.Item ("userLastName").Value)%> -
➡ <%=(rsUsers.Fields.Item("userJobTitle").Value)%></p>
```

Edit this so that you wrap it in a repeat region and a conditional statement. What we are saying is that if the field userDept and deptID match, then this user is in this department, so print out their details; if no match, don't print anything. The full code block, including the initial Recordset rsDepts, looks like this:

```
<%
While ((Repeat1__numRows <> 0) AND (NOT rsDepts.EOF))
%>
    <h2><%=(rsDepts.Fields.Item("deptName").Value)%></h2>
      <%
    While ((Repeat2__numRows <> 0) AND (NOT rsUsers.EOF))
    if rsUsers("userDept") = rsDepts("deptID") Then
    %>

    <p><%=(rsUsers.Fields.Item("userFirstName").Value)%>
➥ <%=(rsUsers.Fields.Item("userLastName").Value)%> -
➥ <%=(rsUsers.Fields.Item("userJobTitle").Value)%></p>
      <%End If
    Repeat2__index=Repeat2__index+1
      Repeat2__numRows=Repeat2__numRows-1
      rsUsers.MoveNext()
    Wend
    rsUsers.MoveFirst()
    %>

    <%Repeat1__index=Repeat1__index+1
    Repeat1__numRows=Repeat1__numRows-1
    rsDepts.MoveNext()
Wend
%>
```

Note that after the second repeat region we do rsUsers.MoveFirst(). This is because we have got to the end of the Recordset looking for users that match this department, so we need to move the cursor back to the start in order to look through it again for the next department. What we have just created is a **nested repeat region** and something that cannot be done just using Dreamweaver Server Behaviors.

Once you have edited Dreamweaver ASP code, you are not advised to then reopen the Server Behavior dialog box by double-clicking it in the Server Behaviors panel; it will more than likely edit your code. Edited Behaviors may also disappear from the panel or appear with a red exclamation mark. Save a copy of the page first if you are not sure!

From the employee name, create a link to employeedetail.asp and add the userID as a querystring parameter, as we did earlier in the chapter when creating the news administration functionality. In Figure 4-50, you can see this section in Design view. In Dreamweaver, the yellow ASP shields show that there is ASP code in the page that Dreamweaver cannot display.

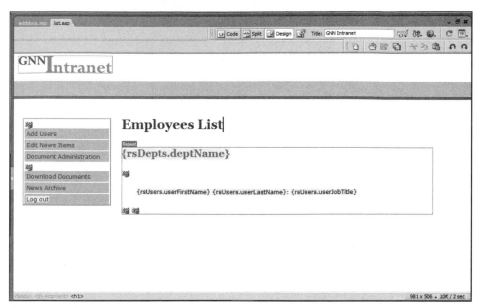

**Figure 4-50.** The document in Design view

# View and edit employee details

Create the page employeedetail.asp. This page should be accessible to all logged-in users. Create a Recordset that selects all from tblUsers filtering on the URL parameter userID.

Depending on the status of the user who comes to this page, they will see a different set of options. If I was visiting the page and I was the user whose details were displayed, I would see all my details in a form so that I could edit my details. If I had a userLevel of management, I would see all the details (including the home address details) but they would not be editable. If I had a user level of administrator, I would be able to see and edit only the job-related details for this user. All other users will just be able to view the job-related details.

We will need to use a conditional statement to create this functionality, but first let us just display the data on the page. Add the users first and last name as the heading for the page as shown in Figure 4-51.

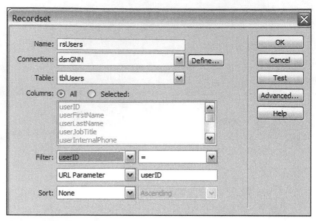

**Figure 4-51.** The Recordset filtering on userID

First add a form to the page and display all of this user's data (apart from name and last name), just in text format (not in form fields). Add a hidden form field named userID, click the lightning bolt next to the value in the Properties inspector with the hidden field selected, and set the value to the userID from your user details Recordset (see Figure 4-52).

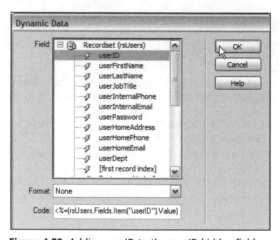

**Figure 4-52.** Adding userID to the userID hidden field

Next display all of the user's data, but in form fields so that it can be edited, with a Submit button underneath.

Now display only the user's data that the administrators originally entered on the page useradd.asp. In this section we also want to display the list of departments and user-level checkboxes that are on the useradd.asp. Create these in exactly the same way as on that page.

Select the drop-down userDept and switch into Code view. Find the <option> tag for the userDept menu and change it to look like the following:

```
<option value="<%=(rsDepts.Fields.Item("deptID").Value)%>"
➥ <%If (rsDepts.Fields
➥ .Item("deptID").Value) = (rsUsers.Fields.Item("userDept").value)
Then%>
➥ selected="selected"<%end if%>>
```

The conditional statement here will mean that the selected item in this menu will be the item selected when the record was last updated.

Create a Recordset that selects from tblUser_levels named rsUserLevels filtering on the URL parameter userID. Find the checkbox levelID, and add a similar conditional statement to check which levels this user has been assigned (see Figure 4-53).

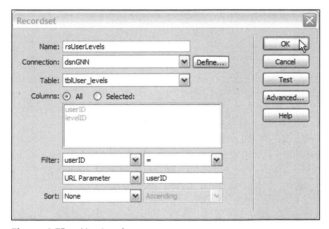

**Figure 4-53.** rsUserLevels

```
<input name="levelID" type="checkbox" id="levelID"
➥ value="<%=(rsLevels.Fields
➥ .Item("levelID").Value)%>" <%If
➥ (rsLevels.Fields.Item("levelID").Value) =
➥ (rsUserLevels.Fields.Item("levelID").Value)
➥ Then %> checked="checked"<%End If%> />
```

Add a Submit button underneath this section.

Now display only the job-related details—userJobTitle, userInternalPhone, and userInternalEmail in text. The page should now look like Figure 4-54 in Dreamweaver.

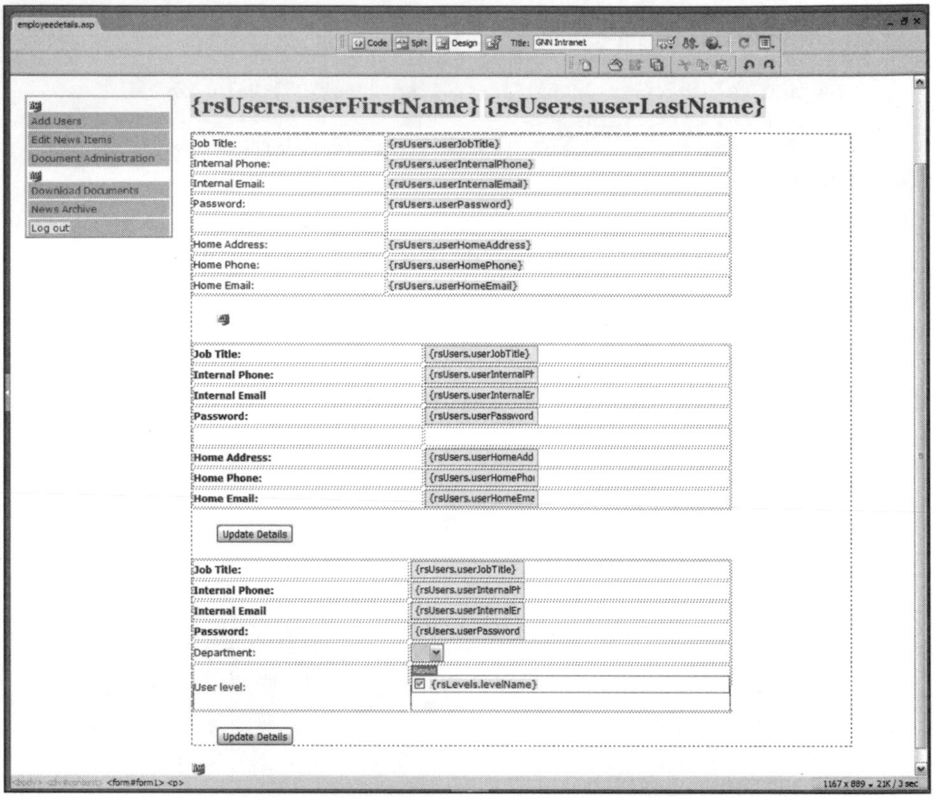

**Figure 4-54.** The employee details page

## Displaying employee data conditionally

To display only that data relevant to the particular user level, we need to wrap each section with conditional statements. The logic of the statements is as follows (the accompanying comments explain what is being tested for and deduced, in each case):

```
<%If isManager = true And Session("MM_Username") <>
(rsUserDetail.Fields.Item
➥ ("userInternalEmail").Value) Then %>

'If the user is a manager but we're not displaying the manager's own
'details, display only the details

<%End If
If Session("MM_Username") =
(rsUserDetail.Fields.Item("userInternalEmail").Value)
➥ Then%>
```

```
'This is the user viewing their own details, so allow them to edit them

<%End If
If isSiteAdmin = true And Session("MM_Username") <>
(rsUserDetail.Fields.Item
➥ ("userInternalEmail").Value) Then%>

'This is a site admin, allow editing of user's details

<%End If
If isSiteAdmin = false And isManager = false And Session("MM_Username")
➥<> (rsUserDetail.Fields.Item("userInternalEmail").Value) Then %>

'This person is neither a manager or site admin and these are not their
'details, so display only basic details

<%End If%>
```

Let's see the full code for this page, including all the forms. Note the addition of a hidden field, formuser; we will use on our update page shortly to record the fact that a user was updating their own records, rather than an administrator doing so, and thus control what can be updated in either case:

```
<h1><%=(rsUsers.Fields.Item("userFirstName").Value)%>
<%=(rsUsers.Fields.Item
➥ ("userLastName").Value)%></h1>
<form name="form1" id="form1" method="post" action="">
<input name="userID" type="hidden" id="userID"
value="<%=(rsUsers.Fields.Item
➥ ("userID").Value)%>" />
<%If isManager = true And Session("MM_Username") <>
(rsUsers.Fields.Item
➥ ("userInternalEmail").Value) Then %>
  <table width="60%"  border="0">
    <tr>
      <td>Job Title: </td>
      <td><%=(rsUsers.Fields.Item("userJobTitle").Value)%></td>
    </tr>
    <tr>
      <td>Internal Phone: </td>
      <td><%=(rsUsers.Fields.Item("userInternalPhone").Value)%></td>
    </tr>
    <tr>
      <td>Internal Email:</td>
      <td><%=(rsUsers.Fields.Item("userInternalEmail").Value)%></td>
    </tr>
    <tr>
      <td>Password:</td>
```

4

```
              <td><%=(rsUsers.Fields.Item("userPassword").Value)%></td>
          </tr>
          <tr>
            <td> </td>
            <td> </td>
          </tr>
          <tr>
            <td>Home Address: </td>
            <td><%=(rsUsers.Fields.Item("userHomeAddress").Value)%></td>
          </tr>
          <tr>
            <td>Home Phone: </td>
            <td><%=(rsUsers.Fields.Item("userHomePhone").Value)%></td>
          </tr>
          <tr>
            <td>Home Email: </td>
            <td><%=(rsUsers.Fields.Item("userHomeEmail").Value)%></td>
          </tr>
        </table>
<%End If%>

<%If Session("MM_Username") = (rsUsers.Fields.Item("userInternalEmail")
➥ .Value) Then
'this is the user whose details are displayed
%>
<input type="hidden" name="formuser" value="true" />
    <table width="60%"  border="0">
      <tr>
        <td><label for="userJobTitle">Job Title:</label>
          </td>
        <td><input name="userJobTitle" type="text" id="userJobTitle"
value="<%=
➥ (rsUsers.Fields.Item("userJobTitle").Value)%>" /></td>
        </tr>
        <tr>
          <td><label for="userInternalPhone">Internal Phone:</label>
            </td>
          <td><input name="userInternalPhone" type="text"
id="userInternalPhone"
➥ value="<%=(rsUsers.Fields.Item("userInternalPhone").Value)%>"
/></td>
        </tr>
        <tr>
          <td><label for="userInternalEmail">Internal Email</label>
           </td>
          <td> <input name="userInternalEmail" type="text"
id="userInternalEmail"
➥ value="<%=(rsUsers.Fields.Item("userInternalEmail").Value)%>"
/></td>
        </tr>
```

```
    <tr>
      <td><label for="userPassword">Password:</label>
        </td>
      <td> <input name="userPassword" type="text" id="userPassword"
value=
➡ "<%=(rsUsers.Fields.Item("userPassword").Value)%>" /></td>
    </tr>
    <tr>
      <td> </td>
      <td> </td>
    </tr>
    <tr>
      <td><label for="userHomeAddress">Home Address:</label>
        </td>
      <td> <input name="userHomeAddress" type="text"
id="userHomeAddress"
➡ value="<%=(rsUsers.Fields.Item("userHomeAddress").Value)%>" /></td>
    </tr>
    <tr>
      <td><label for="userHomePhone">Home Phone:</label>
        </td>
      <td><input name="userHomePhone" type="text" id="userHomePhone"
value=
➡ "<%=(rsUsers.Fields.Item("userHomePhone").Value)%>" /></td>
    </tr>
    <tr>
      <td><label for="userHomeEmail">Home Email:</label>
        </td>
      <td><input name="userHomeEmail" type="text" id="userHomeEmail"
➡ value="<%=(rsUsers.Fields.Item("userHomeEmail").Value)%>" /></td>
    </tr>
  </table>

  <p>
    <input type="submit" name="Submit" value="Update Details" />
  </p>
  <%End If
If isSiteAdmin = true And Session("MM_Username") <>
(rsUsers.Fields.Item
➡ ("userInternalEmail").Value) Then
'site admin
%>
  <table width="60%"  border="0">
    <tr>
      <td><label for="userJobTitle">Job Title:</label>
        </td>
      <td><input name="userJobTitle" type="text" id="userJobTitle"
➡ value="<%=(rsUsers.Fields.Item("userJobTitle").Value)%>" /></td>
    </tr>
    <tr>
```

```
            <td><label for="userInternalPhone">Internal Phone:</label>
            </td>
            <td><input name="userInternalPhone" type="text"
id="userInternalPhone"
➡ value="<%=(rsUsers.Fields.Item("userInternalPhone").Value)%>"
/></td>
        </tr>
        <tr>
            <td><label for="userInternalEmail">Internal Email</label>
            </td>
            <td> <input name="userInternalEmail" type="text"
id="userInternalEmail"
➡ value="<%=(rsUsers.Fields.Item("userInternalEmail").Value)%>"
/></td>
        </tr>
        <tr>
            <td><label for="userPassword">Password:</label>
            </td>
            <td> <input name="userPassword" type="text" id="userPassword"
➡ value="<%=(rsUsers.Fields.Item("userPassword").Value)%>" /></td>
        </tr>
        <tr>
            <td>Department:</td>
            <td><select name="select">
            <%
While (NOT rsDepts.EOF)
%>
            <option value="<%=(rsDepts.Fields.Item("deptID").Value)%>"
➡ <%If (rsDepts.Fields.Item("deptID").Value) = (rsUsers.Fields.Item
➡ ("userDept").value) Then%> selected="selected"<%end if%>>
            <%
   rsDepts.MoveNext()
Wend
If (rsDepts.CursorType > 0) Then
   rsDepts.MoveFirst
Else
   rsDepts.Requery
End If
%>
            </select></td>
        </tr>
        <tr>
            <td>User level: </td>
            <td>
            <%
While ((Repeat1__numRows <> 0) AND (NOT rsLevels.EOF))
%>
            <input name="levelID" type="checkbox"" id="levelID" value="<%=
➡ (rsLevels.Fields.Item("levelID").Value)%>" <%If
(rsLevels.Fields.Item
```

```
➡ ("levelID").Value) = (rsUserLevels.Fields.Item("levelID").Value)
➡ Then %> checked="checked"<%End If%> />
          <%=(rsLevels.Fields.Item("levelName").Value)%><br />
          <%
  Repeat1__index=Repeat1__index+1
  Repeat1__numRows=Repeat1__numRows-1
  rsLevels.MoveNext()
Wend
%></td>
     </tr>
     <tr>
     </table>
     <p><input type="submit" value="Update Details" /></p>
     <%End If
If isSiteAdmin = false And isManager = false And Session("MM_Username")
➡ <> (rsUsers.Fields.Item("userInternalEmail").Value) Then
' just a regular user
%>
<p><strong><%=(rsUsers.Fields.Item("userJobTitle").Value)%></strong></p
>
     <p>Internal Phone:
<%=(rsUsers.Fields.Item("userInternalPhone").Value)%>
➡ <br />
     Internal Email:
<%=(rsUsers.Fields.Item("userInternalEmail").Value)%></p>
<%End If%>


     </form>
```

## Editing employee information

The final step for this section is to insert the data into the database. As with the original insert form, the Dreamweaver Server Behaviors are not flexible enough to cope with this form, so we'll write our own script.

The logic for this script is as follows:

- Check which type of form has been submitted—a user updating their own details or a site administrator updating basic details.
- Based on the preceding get the data from the form.
- Update the user's record with the relevant details.
- If this is a site administrator, we need to update the levels. The easiest way to do so is to delete the existing levels information and then reinsert it based on the checkboxes from this form.
- Redirect back to the users list.

The complete script follows; some of it will look familiar from the insert script that we created earlier:

```
<%@LANGUAGE="VBSCRIPT"%>
<%Option Explicit%>
<!--#include virtual="/Connections/dsnGNN.asp" -->

<%
'dimension variables
Dim userFirstName, userLastName, userJobTitle, userInternalPhone,
➥ userInternalEmail, userPassword, userDept, levelID, rsAddUser,
➥ aLevelID, i, strSQL, userID, adoCon, isUser, userHomeAddress,
➥ userHomePhone, userHomeEmail

'function to remove single quotes from input
Function stripQuotes(strQuotes)
Dim strOutput
strOutput = Replace(strQuotes, "'","''")
stripQuotes = strOutput
End Function

'which form are we updating user or admin
isUser = false
If Request.Form("formUser") > "" Then
  isUser = true
End If

'put the values from our form into variables, using the function
'stripQuotes to remove quotes
'these are common to both forms
userFirstName = stripQuotes(Request.Form("userFirstName"))
userLastName = stripQuotes(Request.Form("userLastName"))
userJobTitle = stripQuotes(Request.Form("userJobTitle"))
userInternalPhone = stripQuotes(Request.Form("userInternalPhone"))
userInternalEmail = stripQuotes(Request.Form("userInternalEmail"))
userID = Request.Form("userID")

If isUser = true Then
  'form fields for user form
  userHomeAddress = stripQuotes(Request.Form("userHomeAddress"))
  userHomePhone = stripQuotes(Request.Form("userHomePhone"))
  userHomeEmail = stripQuotes(Request.Form("userHomeEmail"))
  strSQL = "UPDATE tblUsers SET userFirstName = '" &
➥ userFirstName & "',
➥ userLastName = '" & userLastName & "', userJobTitle = '" &
➥ userJobTitle
```

```
➥ & "', userInternalPhone = '" & userInternalPhone & "',
➥userInternalEmail
➥ = '" & userInternalEmail & "', userHomeAddress = '" &
➥userHomeAddress
➥ & "', userHomePhone = '" & userHomePhone & "', userHomeEmail =
➥ '" & userHomeEmail & "' WHERE userID = " & userID
Else
  levelID = stripQuotes(Request.Form("levelID"))
  userDept = stripQuotes(Request.Form("userDept"))
  strSQL = "UPDATE tblUsers SET userFirstName = '" & userFirstName &
"',
➥ userLastName = '" & userLastName & "', userJobTitle = '" &
➥userJobTitle
➥ & "', userInternalPhone = '" & userInternalPhone & "',
➥userInternalEmail =
➥ '" & userInternalEmail & "', userDept = " & userDept & " WHERE
➥userID = " & userID
End If

Set adoCon = Server.CreateObject("ADODB.Connection")
adoCon.Open MM_conn_STRING

'update the record
adoCon.execute(strSQL)
if isUser = false Then
  'delete the levels from the database
  strSQL = "DELETE FROM tblUser_levels WHERE userID = " & userID
  adoCon.execute(strSQL)
  'insert the levels
  'split the values sent for levelID into an array using the VBScript
➥ Split function
  alevelID = Split(levelID, ",")
  'loop through that array inserting the levelID and userID
  For Each i In alevelID
    strSQL = "INSERT INTO tblUser_levels (userID, levelID) VALUES
➥ (" & userID & ", " & i & ")"
    adoCon.execute(strSQL)
  Next
end if
adoCon.Close
Set adoCon = Nothing

Response.Redirect "/list.asp"
%>
```

You can now add Contact List to the menu options for all users.

# Events calendar

To create our events calendar for our intranet, we will use a free third-party extension. There are a variety of free and commercial calendar extensions available; the one we are going to use here is available from www.dreamlettes.net and is the ASP Events Calendar Pack. Download this extension and install it using the Extension Manager. You will then need to restart Dreamweaver for the calendar extension to be available for use.

## Create the calendar table

Open Access, and create a new table named tblEvents that contains the fields shown in Figure 4-55.

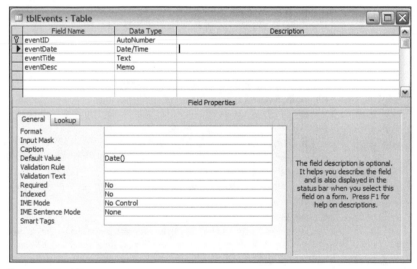

**Figure 4-55.** tblEvents

The field eventID is an AutoNumber and the primary key of the table; eventDate is a Date/Time field with a default value of Date(); eventTitle is text with a size of 100 and eventDesc is a memo field.

## Create the calendar page

In Dreamweaver create a new page within the site named calendar.asp. This page should be a new, blank XHTML document that we will put into our site styles later, as the calendar extension does not apply properly due to our includes.

Create a Recordset named rsEvents that selects the eventID, eventDate, and eventTitle from tblEvents (see Figure 4-56).

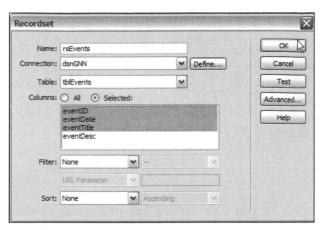

**Figure 4-56.** rsEvents

In the Server Behaviors panel select the +, then select Dreamlettes ➤ ASP Events Calendar.

In the dialog box that opens name your calendar and complete the fields appropriately. For Details File type events.asp as shown in Figure 4-57—we have not yet created this file, but it will be where we click through to from the calendar to display the event details.

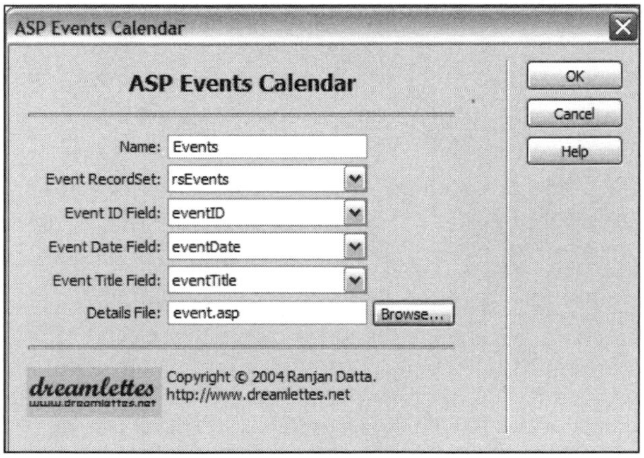

**Figure 4-57.** Events Calendar dialog box

Click OK and an alert will display telling you that a style sheet has been added to your site; the style sheet controls the look and feel of the calendar.

Click OK on this message and a placeholder calendar will display on your page (see Figure 4-58).

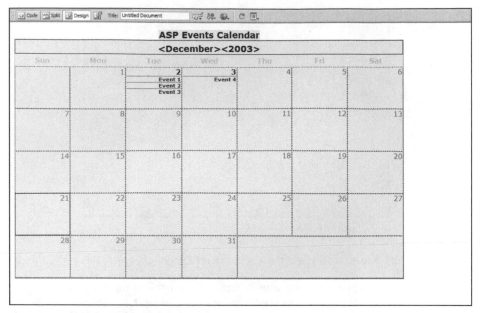

**Figure 4-58.** The placeholder calendar

To get your calendar into the rest of the page design, simply copy the includes around the basic calendar, taking care not to disturb the function or Recordset in the ASP code. You will see that the calendar is called by one line of code in the body of the document.

```
<% Call EventsCalendar %>
```

My complete document after pasting the includes back into the calendar page looks like the following code. If your calendar placeholder does not display after doing this, check that your document looks like mine.

```
<%@LANGUAGE="VBSCRIPT"%>
<!--#include file="Connections/dsnGNN.asp" -->
<%
Dim rsEvents
Dim rsEvents_numRows

Set rsEvents = Server.CreateObject("ADODB.Recordset")
rsEvents.ActiveConnection = MM_dsnGNN_STRING
rsEvents.Source = "SELECT eventID, eventDate, eventTitle FROM
tblEvents"
rsEvents.CursorType = 0
rsEvents.CursorLocation = 2
rsEvents.LockType = 1
rsEvents.Open()

rsEvents_numRows = 0
%>
```

```
<%
Function EventsCalendar
If Request("EventDate") <> "" Then
EventDate = DateValue(Request("EventDate"))
Else
EventDate = date()
End if
CurrentMonth = Month(EventDate)
CurrentMonthName = MonthName(CurrentMonth)
CurrentYear = Year(EventDate)
FirstDayDate = DateSerial(CurrentYear, CurrentMonth, 1)
FirstDay = WeekDay(FirstDayDate, 0)
CurrentDay = FirstDayDate
Dim tmpHTML
tmpHTML=""
tmpHTML = tmpHTML & "<table summary=""Events"" id=""calendar""
➥cellspacing =""0"">" & Chr(10)
tmpHTML = tmpHTML & "<caption>Events</caption>" & Chr(10)
tmpHTML = tmpHTML & "<tr id=""title"">" & Chr(10)
tmpHTML = tmpHTML & "<th colspan=""7"">" & Chr(10)
tmpHTML = tmpHTML & "<a href=""?EventDate=" & Server.URLEncode(DateAdd
➥ ("m",-1, EventDate)) & """>&lt;</a>" & CurrentMonthName & "<a
➥ href=""?
➥ EventDate=" & Server.URLEncode(DateAdd("m",1,EventDate)) &
➥"""">&gt;</a>"
tmpHTML = tmpHTML & "<a href=""?EventDate=" & Server.URLEncode(DateAdd
➥ ("yyyy",-1, EventDate)) & """>&lt;</a>" & CurrentYear & "<a href=""?
➥ EventDate=" & Server.URLEncode(DateAdd("yyyy",1,EventDate)) &
➥"""">&gt;</a>"
tmpHTML = tmpHTML & "</th>" & Chr(10) & "</tr>" & Chr(10) & "<tr
id=""days"">"
Response.Write(tmpHTML)
For DayLoop = 1 to 7
Response.Write("<th>" & WeekDayName(Dayloop, True, 0) & "</th>" &
➥Chr(10))
Next
Response.Write("</tr>" & Chr(10) & "<tr class=""firstweek"">")
If FirstDay <> 1 Then
Response.Write("<td colspan=""" & (FirstDay -1) & """
➥class=""blank"">  </td>" & Chr(10))
End if
DayCounter = FirstDay
CorrectMonth = True
Do While CorrectMonth = True
isEvent = FALSE
rsEvents.filter = 0
Dim iCheck
Dim chkStr
chkStr = (rsEvents.Fields.Item("eventDate").Name)
```

```
iCheck = CurrentDay
rsEvents.filter = chkStr & "=" & (iCheck)
If not(rsEvents.EOF) Then isEvent = TRUE
If CurrentDay = EventDate Then
Response.Write("<td class=""today"">")
Else
Response.Write("<td class=""day" & DayCounter & """>")
End if
If isEvent = TRUE Then
Response.Write("<a href=""event.asp?EventDate=" &
➥Server.URLEncode(CurrentDay)
➥ & """>" & Day(CurrentDay)& "</a>")
If Not rsEvents.BOF Then
rsEvents.MoveFirst
Do Until rsEvents.EOF
If (rsEvents.Fields.Item("eventDate").Value) = CurrentDay Then
Response.Write("<p><a href=""event.asp?id=" &
➥(rsEvents.Fields.Item("eventID")
➥ .Value)& """>" & (rsEvents.Fields.Item("eventTitle").Value) &
➥"</a></p>")
End If
rsEvents.MoveNext
Loop
End If
Response.Write("</td>" & Chr(10))
Else
Response.Write(Day(CurrentDay) & "</td>" & Chr(10))
End If
DayCounter = DayCounter + 1
If DayCounter > 7 Then
DayCounter = 1
Response.Write("</tr>" & Chr(10))
Response.Write("<tr")
If Month(CurrentDay+8) <> CurrentMonth Then
Response.Write(" class=""lastweek""")
End If
Response.Write(">" & Chr(10))
End if
CurrentDay = DateAdd("d", 1, CurrentDay)
If Month(CurrentDay) <> CurrentMonth then
CorrectMonth = False
End if
Loop
IF DayCounter <> 1 Then
Response.Write("<td colspan=""" & (8-DayCounter) & """
➥class=""blank"">  </td>")
Else
```

```
Response.Write("<td colspan=""7"" class=""blank""> </td>")
End if
Response.Write("</tr>" & Chr(10) & "</table>" & Chr(10))
End Function
%>
<!DOCTYPE html PUBLIC "-//W3C//DTD XHTML 1.0 Transitional//EN"
        "http://www.w3.org/TR/xhtml1/DTD/xhtml1-transitional.dtd">
<html xmlns="http://www.w3.org/1999/xhtml">

<head>
<title>GNN Intranet</title>
<link href="aspcalbasic.css" rel="stylesheet" type="text/css" />
<!--#include virtual="/inc/top.asp"-->
<h1>Calendar</h1>
<% Call EventsCalendar %>

<!--#include virtual="/inc/bottom.asp"-->
<%
rsEvents.Close()
Set rsEvents = Nothing
%>
```

## The events detail page

The calendar that we have created will have clickable dates—for dates that have events—and also event titles. We need to create a page that will display those items.

Create a new page named event.asp; you can create this page directly from your master page as it does not have any problem with the includes.

The calendar page passes EventDate to this page as a querystring parameter if the date is clicked; if the user clicks the title it will pass ID as a parameter (this is the eventID field from the database table).

We need to create two Recordsets on this page using the Advanced dialog box: one that looks for the eventID and one that looks for the eventDate.

### EventDate

Create a new Recordset and switch into Advanced. Name the Recordset rsDateDetails, select the connection, and in the SQL box type

SELECT * FROM tblEvents

WHERE eventDate = # MMParam #

ORDER BY eventID DESC

Click the + next to Variables and as shown in Figure 4-59, under Name type MMParam; under Default Value add a date; under Run-time Value type

CDate(Request.QueryString("EventDate"))

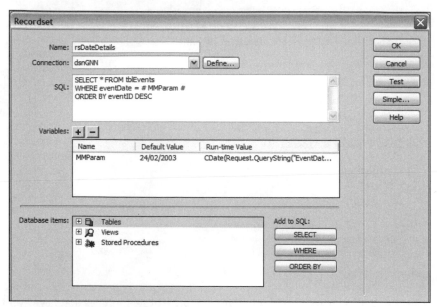

**Figure 4-59.** rsDateDetails

Click OK to create the Recordset.

Use the Recordset to add the eventTitle, eventDesc, and eventDate fields to the page. As there could be more than one event on a day, create a repeat region to show all records.

With the area selected, click the + in the Server Behaviors panel and select Show Region ➤ Show Region if Recordset is not Empty. The dialog box will ask you to confirm the Recordset that you are working with (see Figure 4-60).

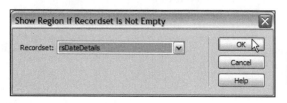

**Figure 4-60.**
Show Region If Recordset Is Not
Empty dialog box

## ID

We can now create the Recordset that shows the individual event selected if someone clicks an event title.

Create a new Recordset. Switch into Advanced once again and name this Recordset rsIDDetails.

Select the connection, then in the SQL box add

SELECT * FROM tblEvents

WHERE eventID = MMParam

As shown in Figure 4-61, under Variables set MMParam to have a default value of 0 and a runtime value of

Request.QueryString("id")

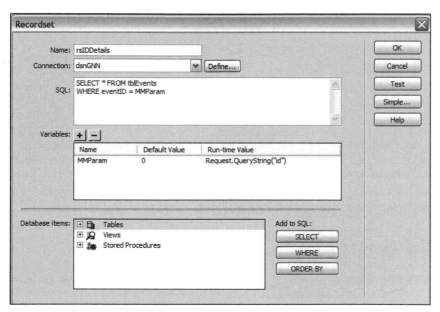

**Figure 4-61.** Recordset rsIDDetails

Click OK.

Making sure that you are outside of the repeat region for the first Recordset, add your fields to the page.

We don't need a repeat region this time as we are looking at an individual record. Once you have placed the fields on the page, select them and apply the Show Region ➤ Show Region If Recordset Is Not Empty Behavior once again, this time making sure to select the Recordset rsIDDetails.

Your layout in Dreamweaver should now look something like that in Figure 4-62.

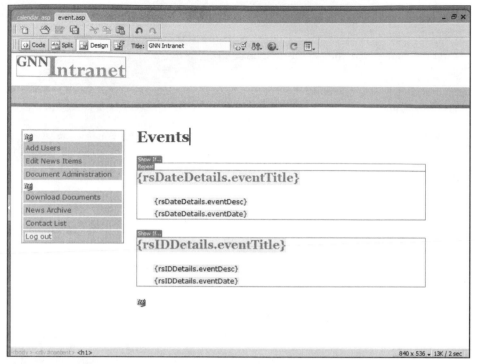

**Figure 4-62.** The layout

The calendar and event.asp pages should be accessible to all users of the Intranet.

## Adding events

We add events to the calendar by inserting them into the database. Create a new page in the admin section named addevent.asp.

On this page add a form that contains the fields from the table tblEvents.

```
<form name="form1" method="POST" action="">
<p><label for="eventTitle">Event Title:</label><br />
<input type="text" name="eventTitle" id="eventTitle"
➥ class="text" /></p>

<p><label for="eventDesc">Event Description:</label><br />
<textarea name="eventDesc" id="eventDesc"
class="textarealarge"></textarea></p>

<p><label for="eventDate">Event Date:</label><br />
<input type="text" name="eventDate" id="eventDate" class="text" /></p>

<p><input type="submit" value="Add Event" /></p>
</form>
```

Use the Insert Record Server Behavior to insert this record into the database.

If you only wish administrators to be able to add records, you will need to add this page into the section of the menu in top.asp that is only visible to those with authority and add a link to the main calendar page that is visible to everyone (see Figure 4-63).

```
<div id="nav">
<%If isSiteAdmin = true Then%>
<p><a href="/admin/useradd.asp">Add Users</a></p>
<p><a href="/admin/editnews.asp">Edit News Items</a></p>
<p><a href="/admin/adddocs.asp">Document Administration</a></p>
<p><a href="/admin/addevents.asp">Add Events</a></p>
<%End If%>
<p><a href="/documents.asp">Download Documents</a></p>
<p><a href="/newsarchive.asp">News Archive</a></p>
<p><a href="/list.asp">Contact List</a></p>
<p><a href="/calendar.asp">Events Calendar</a></p>
<p><a href="<%= MM_Logout %>">Log out</a></p>
</div>
```

**4**

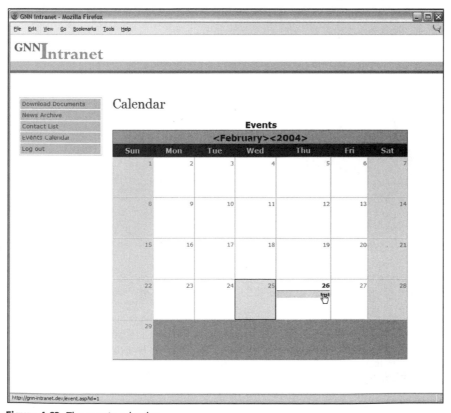

**Figure 4-63.** The events calendar

You can edit the CSS style sheet that is placed into your site when the calendar extension is used to make the calendar fit into your site design. All of the styles used in the calendar are in the style sheet.

# Tying up the loose ends

When we created the pages to add news (/admin/addnews.asp) and add new documents (/admin/adddocs.asp) we had an additional field in the database for both of these pieces of functionality—newsAddedBy and docsAddedBy. These fields allow us to insert the ID of the person who added the record into the database. At the time we created these tables we did not have our users functionality; however, now that we do, it is a simple job to add these to those pages.

Open the file /admin/addnews.asp. Insert a hidden field into that form with the name newsAddedBy. We will need to retrieve the value of this field by looking up the userID of the current, logged-in user. Create a new Recordset on the page; this Recordset will need to select the field userID, filtering on userInternalEmail found in the session variable MM_Username (see Figure 4-64).

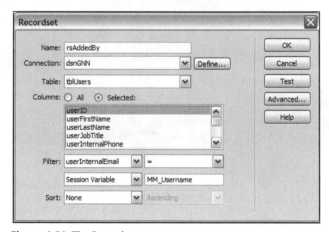

**Figure 4-64.** The Recordset

We can now select the hidden field newsAddedBy, and in the Properties inspector click the lightning bolt next to the value to set its value to that of userID from the Recordset rsAddedBy.

Then double-click the Insert Record Server Behavior in the panel and you will see your hidden field listed as Ignore in the form fields section. Select it and then select newsAddedBy and Numeric in the drop-down lists below so that when you do an insert it will insert the value of this field.

Repeat the same process on the page /admin/adddocs.asp, except instead of using newsAddedBy use docsAddedBy.

To display which user added a news item or document, we use this userID to look up the first and last name of the user in the database. Open the page news.asp. You will need to create a Recordset using the Advanced view because we need to use the value of the field newsAddedBy in the Recordset rsNews to select our userFirstName and userLastName from tblUsers. In the Advanced Recordset view add the following in the SQL box:

SELECT userFirstName, userLastName

FROM tblUsers

WHERE userID = MMColParam

Then add a variable called MMcolParam, with a default value of 1 and a runtime value of rsNews("newsAddedBy") as shown in Figure 4-65.

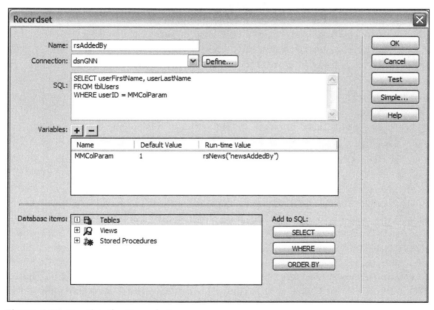

**Figure 4-65.** Creating the Recordset

Click OK. You should now be able to add the data from this Recordset to your page in the usual way to create a line that says

Added By: {rsAddedBy.userFirstName} {rsAddedBy.userLastName}

Again, you can repeat this process on the page documents.asp to add data about who uploaded a particular document.

You will need to make sure that you have either deleted older records from tblNews and tblDocs or manually added a userID to each of them; otherwise, you will get an error when the Recordset tries to look up the information in tblUser.

> You could equally create a query within the database for the main Recordset on *tblNews* or *tblDocs* which selects from both the main table and the *userFirstName* and *userlastName* from *tblUsers*. Then use that query to create the Recordset, as we did earlier.

## Validation for form fields

At this point it may also be a good idea to add some validation on your form fields to ensure that users do enter the correct data. Dreamweaver has JavaScript Form Validation Behaviors that you can use to do this. As an example open the page addnews.asp.

The Validate Form Behavior is in the Behaviors panel in the Design panel group. Select your form, then select Validate Form from the menu. In the dialog box that opens, you can select your form field and check the checkbox if it is required (see Figure 4-66). You also have some options to check for a number or an e-mail address, although for this form we just want to check for anything entered into the fields.

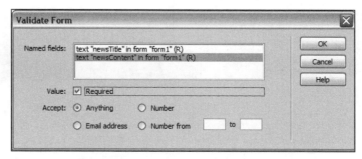

**Figure 4-66.** Validate Form dialog box

If you are using includes as I am, you will probably find that Dreamweaver adds the calls to the function on the form, but doesn't add the JavaScript—this is because it can't put it into our include. My way round this is to create a form on a blank page, add the behavior, and then copy the JavaScript from the head of the document into an include file called function.js. The content of this file looks like this:

```
function MM_findObj(n, d) { //v4.01
  var p,i,x;  if(!d) d=document;
⇒if((p=n.indexOf("?"))>0&&parent.frames.length) {
    d=parent.frames[n.substring(p+1)].document; n=n.substring(0,p);}
  if(!(x=d[n])&&d.all) x=d.all[n]; for (i=0;!x&&i<d.forms.length;i++)
⇒ x=d.forms[i][n];
  for(i=0;!x&&d.layers&&i<d.layers.length;i++)
⇒x=MM_findObj(n,d.layers[i]
⇒ .document);
  if(!x && d.getElementById) x=d.getElementById(n); return x;
}
```

```
function MM_validateForm() { //v4.0
  var
➥i,p,q,nm,test,num,min,max,errors='',args=MM_validateForm.arguments;
  for (i=0; i<(args.length-2); i+=3) { test=args[i+2];
➥val=MM_findObj(args[i]);
    if (val) { nm=val.name; if ((val=val.value)!="") {
      if (test.indexOf('isEmail')!=-1) { p=val.indexOf('@');
        if (p<1 || p==(val.length-1)) errors+='- '+nm+' must contain an
e-mail address.\n';
      } else if (test!='R') { num = parseFloat(val);
        if (isNaN(val)) errors+='- '+nm+' must contain a number.\n';
        if (test.indexOf('inRange') != -1) { p=test.indexOf(':');
          min=test.substring(8,p); max=test.substring(p+1);
          if (num<min || max<num) errors+='- '+nm+' must contain a
➥number between '+min+' and '+max+'.\n';
      } } } else if (test.charAt(0) == 'R') errors += '- '+nm+' is
➥required.\n'; }
  } if (errors) alert('The following error(s) occurred:\n'+errors);
  document.MM_returnValue = (errors == '');
}
```

Then, to include the ability to use this function on any page of the site, I simply reference the JavaScript in my include `top.asp`, adding the following line just below the links to the style sheets:

```
<script language="JavaScript" type="text/JavaScript"
➥src="/inc/functions.js"> </script>
```

You can now apply this behavior to any of the forms on the site. If you then go to the form and try and submit it without completing the required fields, an alert box will let you know that you need to fill them in before you can submit the form. There is a third-party behavior that offers more advanced validation than the default Dreamweaver Behavior. That behavior is called Check Form MX and is available from www.yaromat.com.

## Validation of markup and CSS

Validating your HTML/XHTML markup when the application is for logged-in users only or behind your firewall can prove tricky. The internal Dreamweaver validator cannot validate the page if it has server-side code on it and the W3C validator at http://validator.w3.org needs to be able to access your pages or have them uploaded to it and again won't be able to cope with the VBScript. My way around this situation is to validate my basic template right at the start of the process, so I know that the main page structure is valid. I then validate pages by viewing the source after they have been rendered by the browser and then saving the source as a separate file, which I can either validate using Dreamweaver or by uploading it to the W3C.

You can validate your CSS by pasting the CSS into the textbox at http://jigsaw.w3.org/css-validator/validator-text.html.

## Testing

With any application where you are expecting nontechnical users to add data to a site, testing is very important. Before launching your intranet on the full company, ask a selected group of users with a variety of skill levels to try and use the functionality. Sit with them as they complete the tasks and take notes on any problems they encounter. These notes can form the basis of help that you either add to the pages or maintain as a file (perhaps within the documents download area). If the users find the application easy to use, they are more likely to use it, and it is at the point where the users feel comfortable with the intranet and use it on a day-to-day basis that you can declare your project a success.

## Summary

In this project we have concentrated mainly on the core features of an intranet—user authentication and document sharing. The techniques that we have used can easily be applied to add new functionality to the intranet. For instance, the techniques used to create and display news articles could also be applied to longer articles, or to display a biography page linked to each user for instance. Document sharing could be expanded to include file upload as we discussed. You could easily add the ability to add new levels of management and access without needing to edit the database, by adding forms that would insert this data for us. The document sharing could be enhanced, as we have discussed, with the use of third-party file upload components or Dreamweaver Server Behaviors. Many of these techniques do not only apply in an intranet situation, and you could use them on any site that requires logins or an administration capability.

During the course of this project we have looked at two ways of working—using the built-in Dreamweaver Server Behaviors and by writing the code by hand. Even if you are new to server-side code, I hope you now have the confidence to work directly in the code. There are times when trying to use the Dreamweaver Behaviors for everything just isn't practical, although for simple functionality they can save you a lot of time.

# INDEX

updating site, 191
user authentication, 71, 245–246
User Authentication Server Behavior, 74, 245
user levels, checking, 248–250
users, adding new
    checkboxes for user levels, 241–242
    dynamic select menu, 239–241
    inserting user into database, 243–244
    overview, 239

## V

Validate Form Behavior, 85
validating
    code 20, 189
    form fields on intranets, 276–277
    markup and CSS on intranets, 277
value field (of meta tag), 147
vector-based design illustrations, 16–17
vertical navigation, 130
view options, 136
VirtualPC, 159

## W

WAI (Web Access Initiative), 2
W3 validating services, 189
W3C's validator, 20
warnings, 189
watermark, 128
Web Access Initiative (WAI), 2
web browsers. *See* browsers
Web folder, 132
Web standards, 18, 20
Windows operating system, 159
wireframe models, 17
Word application, 187–188
Word HTML cleaner, 187
World Wide Web Consortium, 18, 132

## X

XHTML, 20, 134